D0168921

Clifford S. Crawford

Biology
of Desert Invertebrates

With 181 Illustrations

Springer-Verlag
Berlin Heidelberg New York 1981

Clifford S. Crawford, Ph.D.
Professor, Department of Biology
University of New Mexico
Albuquerque, New Mexico 87131, U.S.A.

The figure on the front cover is a photograph of Coleoptera tracks on the Sonoran desert sand dunes. [Courtesy of F. G. Andrews (Andrews et al., 1979)]

Library of Congress Cataloging in Publication Data
Crawford, Clifford S.
  Biology of desert invertebrates.
  Bibliography: p.
  Includes index.
  1. Desert fauna. 2. Invertebrates. I. Title.
  QL116.C7   592.0909'54   81-9024

ISBN 3-540-10807-6 Springer-Verlag Berlin Heidelberg New York
ISBN 0-387-10807-6 Springer-Verlag New York Heidelberg Berlin

277649

Contents

Part 1
Deserts and Desert Invertebrates

Chapter 2
The Array of Desert Invertebrates   **19**

Part 2
Adaptations to Xeric Environments

Part 5
Invertebrates in Desert Ecosystems: Summary Remarks

Preface

What little we know of the biology of desert invertebrates stems largely from inferences based on intensive and repeated observations. Such information is not gained easily, since despite the actual abundance of these animals, relatively few of them are ever seen. In fact, except for species impacting on the well-being of human populations, historically most have been ignored by scholars in the western world. Indeed, it was ancient Egypt, with its reverence for the symbolism of the scarab, that probably provided us with the clearest early record of prominent desert types.

A more modest resurgence of the story had to wait until the arrival of the present century. To be sure, some of the more obvious species had by then been elevated by European collectors to the level of drawing-room curiosities, and expeditions had returned large numbers to museums. But by 1900 the task of describing desert species and relationships among them was still in its infancy; and as for careful natural history studies, they too were just coming into their own.

The expansion of biological endeavor in the early 1900's led to an enhanced awareness of deserts in general, and the biotas of these arid regions soon came under increased scrutiny by perceptive scientists. Among these individuals were P. A. Buxton, who emphasized Old World desert faunas, and W. M. Wheeler, who dramatized certain insect groups in the drier parts of North America. Meanwhile, H. Gauthier and G. E. Hutchinson were making distinct contributions to a special area of study, namely that of desert ephemeral waters and their inhabitants. Fortunately, each of these pioneers published in the context of desert habitats and environments, a practice also followed by most later writers in the field.

In the years that followed, increasing attention was given to the adaptations of desert species. This shift in emphasis is evident in the works of H. G. Andrewartha and L. C. Birch in Australia; F. S. Bodenheimer, J. L. Cloudsley-Thompson, and F. Pierre in North Africa and the Middle East; C. Koch and R. F. Lawrence in southern Africa; E. G. Linsley in North America; G. S. Medvedev in Central Asia; and S. Pradhan in the Indian subcontinent. Great progress was made simultaneously by students of desert locusts, in particular R. C. Rainey and B. P. Uvarov.

By the 1970's interest in the environment had grown to the point that another generation of biologists was now viewing desert invertebrates from the perspective of community and ecosystem biology. The impetus for this approach came partly from the intellectual and financial backing of the International Biological Program, and also from major advances taking place in ecological theory and physiological methodology. Inquiry of this kind is still gathering momentum and, fortunately for this author, has led to a number of comprehensive reviews. Among these I have found particularly helpful the treatments by J. L. Cloudsley-Thompson, E. B. Edney, E. G. Matthews, and R. R. Schmoller. Armed with such literature and bolstered by my own research interests, I sought to bring together much of the work of past and present investigations.

The resulting statement—this book—reflects my own conceptual and organizational bias in dealing with a topic not easily manipulated. As will be obvious to its readers, the book probes the ways in which invertebrate animals function in arid—and often stressful—environments. What these creatures do, how and when they do it, and how they manage to survive while doing it are questions I find fascinating. Moreover, since invertebrates represent the great bulk of animal life in deserts, the questions assume some importance.

As it stands, the book is a compromise of summary and synthesis. It introduces readers to the subject animals, and it also condenses information about these organisms into patterns that, it is hoped, reflect nature. It was written for no specific audience. At best, it will be enjoyed by serious naturalists, and used as a reference and source of ideas by students as well as active desert biologists. If nothing else, I trust it will stimulate others to question, explore, and ultimately respect the peculiar rhythms and pulses of desert life.

C. S. Crawford
Albuquerque, 1981

Acknowledgments

Many people contributed time, effort, and skill to the development of this book, and to them all I express my sincere thanks. I also thank the Biology Department of the University of New Mexico for its considerable and varied support. Much of the book was written while on leave as a Lady Davis Fellow at Technion-Israel Institute of Technology in Haifa, Israel, where M. R. Warburg kindly made available an extensive literature that I had not previously seen.

Because of the breadth of this book, it was helpful to have many reviewers. Of these, E. B. Edney read the entire manuscript and receives my special thanks. Others who read critically various portions of the work and to whom I am most grateful are: R. G. Cates, C. Dimentman, C. H. Eriksen, D. T. Gwynne, T. B. Keyse, K. E. Linsenmair, M. C. Molles, W. A. Riddle, M. Shachak, Y. Steinberger, E. C. Taylor, F. Taylor, E. C. Toolson, M. R. Warburg, W. G. Whitford, and J. R. Zimmerman.

Each of the above provided useful information or ideas as the manuscript progressed, as did the following: S. Andrews, W. Block, R. A. Bradley, N. C. Collins, G. N. Dodson, O. F. Francke, D. W. Freckman, U. Gerson, S. I. Ghabbour, R. Gordon, J. R. Gosz, N. F. Hadley, J. M. Hastings, A. R. Hardy, Y. Heller, R. Holland, Y. Kugler, G. Levi, D. C. Lowrie, E. Lubzens, J. Margalit, W. B. Miller, W. Paarmann, P. F. Santos, A. M. Shapiro, D. Simon, C. N. Slobodchikoff, R. Thornhill, S. Tucker, J. A. Wallwork, D. H. Wise, P. Wygodzinsky, and Y. Yom-Tov.

The following persons contributed photographs of desert specimens or scenes: F. G. Andrews, M. D. Boyers, R. G. Cates, E. B. Edney, T. D. Eichlin, H. E. Evans, J. M. Evans, D. W. Freckman, D. T. Gwynne,

A. R. Hardy, G. P. Minion, W. Paarmann, G. A. Polis, J. T. Rotenberry, M. K. Seely, D. Simon, S. J. Upton, and J. A. Wallwork.

Original drawings or diagrams, or copies thereof, were made available by S. Andrews, W. G. H. Coaton, D. W. Freckman, N. F. Hadley, W. T. Hinds, M. McKinnerney, J. E. Moeur, M.-L. Penrith, M. K. Seely, and R. L. Smith.

The often difficult task of identifying biological specimens in photographs was undertaken by G. N. Dodson, C. H. Eriksen, R. Gordon, D. T. Gwynne, R. Holland, P. D. Hurd, Jr., Y. Kugler, E. G. Linsley, Y. Steinberger, and J. R. Zimmerman.

Assistance with preparing or photographing drawings was given by M. D. Boyers and L. Hickey, while A. M. Crawford and J. M. Evans went to great effort to prepare photographs of specimens. S. L. Bourgeault typed the final draft and provided valuable editorial help, and the aid of R. M. Crawford and D. M. Andrews was vital to completion of the index.

Finally, I acknowledge the intellectual contribution of the many biologists, who, following J. L. Cloudsley-Thompson's initial stimulus, have helped to mold my thinking about deserts and desert organisms.

Part 1
Deserts and Desert Invertebrates

Introduction

Seemingly uninhabitated and sparsely vegetated to the inexperienced observer, vast desert landscapes extend over perhaps one-fifth of the earth's surface. Yet despite their monotonous façade, these stretches are the domain of a surprisingly diverse biota. Easily overlooked because of their small size and cryptic behavior, such organisms are the operational units of desert life, and they are energized and regulated by a meshwork of forces peculiar to arid zones.

The deserts of the world are indeed dynamic places. They encompass— for our purposes—a wide variety of environments ranging from arid extremes to semi-desert steppes, from subtropical sands to polar moraines. While they can be defined more precisely by using climatic and geographic criteria (see Logan, 1968, and McGinnies, 1968, for reviews), here we shall avoid formal definitions and instead emphasize characteristics of their physical and biological environments.

A large and highly diverse segment of the faunal biomass in deserts is composed of invertebrate animals. What these organisms are and how they function in their unique habitats form the basic subject matter of this book. But there is more to the story than mere description, because, like all other components of natural systems, these organisms influence both their living and nonliving surroundings. They perform, as it were, "roles" in the "play" of desert life, and collectively these roles can be seen as patterns—a view which is given considerable attention later on.

Expressed in space and over time, such patterns form the matrix through which the inexorable movement of matter and energy takes place in desert ecosystems. It is, in the final analysis, the contribution of invertebrates to the structure and function of these ecosystems that becomes the central issue of this book. And although the point shall remain largely untouched until the concluding remarks, the reader is advised to be aware of it throughout the text.

The central question will instead be approached obliquely, first by concentrating on patterns of adaptation (Part 2), then patterns of life history (Part 3), and finally those of community interaction (Part 4). Only at the end—in Part 5—is an attempt made to integrate conclusions derived from these separate treatments.

A very different purpose is assigned to this, the first part of the book. In Chapter 1, which follows, we will be concerned with *perspective*, which for our needs constitutes an overview of desert distribution, evolution, and abiotic as well as biotic elements. Then, in Chapter 2, we will review briefly the array and general distribution of invertebrate taxa inhabiting deserts. This overview is intended to prepare the reader for the subsequent, more intensive description and analysis of desert invertebrate biology comprising the main body of the text.

Chapter 1
Perspectives

A. Evolution and Present Distribution of Deserts

I. Physical Causes of Deserts

Deserts have been elements of our planet's topography throughout its evolution and convincing evidence of their selective effects is illustrated by the striking convergence in morphology and physiology of many arid-adapted plants and animals (Hadley, 1972). Whereas the relative importance of major selective forces in deserts is subject to debate, current theory suggests that abiotic factors have played a greater evolutionary role in stressful environments than have interactions among organisms (Connell, 1975). If we accept this idea, we then acknowledge a major contribution by climate to the organization of desert ecosystems. Of less importance in the past, but of increasing significance in recent times, has been the influence of human activity in creating and maintaining deserts.

1. The Role of Climate

Aridity is caused primarily by atmospheric subsidence, which builds up high-pressure belts or cells of initially dry, outward-moving air masses. Since atmospheric subsidence must have occurred regularly over land surfaces long before they were colonized by multicellular organisms, it can be argued that there have always been arid regions of some kind (Hare, 1961). If so, then aridity must have been experienced by many organisms evolving in terrestrial environments.

When the effects of appropriate global and hemispheric wind patterns are coupled either with edaphic phenomena that prevent water from entering the root zone or with situations that maintain water in the form of ice, the establishment of desert conditions is assured. It is obviously the *balance* of moisture in a region that results in a desert, and such places have in common an annual moisture loss by potential evapotranspiration exceeding that gained from precipitation (Goudie and Wilkinson 1977). Compounding the problem for desert organisms is the pattern of precipitation: In many deserts moisture from the atmosphere tends to arrive during one or more seasons, but within those seasons its arrival is quite variable. Moreover, mean annual variability of rainfall is highest in areas of extreme aridity or where tropical cyclones exert an effect (Bell, 1979). With these thoughts in mind we shall now consider a climatic classification of deserts (see Fig. 1) that relates to the spatial and temporal organization of their invertebrate communities. For more extensive information the reader may wish to consult Meigs (1953), Köppen (1954), McGinnies (1968), and appropriate chapters in Goodall and Perry (1979).

2. Classification of Present Deserts Based on Climate

a) Subtropical Deserts. Subtropical deserts are the most extensive of the world's deserts (Fig. 1), and are continuously maintained by the driving force of intense short-wave radiation striking the earth's equatorial region. Air heated directly and by long-wave reradiation from the land surface first rises and cools, and as its moisture condenses causes heavy tropical rains. The now drier air spills toward the poles, where at north-south latitudes in the vicinity of 30° it subsides to create bands of high pressure. Subsidence, accompanied by compression, warms the air and enhances its capacity to gain moisture.

High-pressure air flows toward regions of lower pressure. Most of the dry air at 30° latitude moves back toward the equator from the northeast or southeast, depending on the hemisphere, although some of it deflects poleward from the southwest or northwest at latitudes between 30° and 60°. Coriolis force accounts for the angular deflection. Air returning to the equatorial region replaces the continually rising warm masses that provided its origin. This returning air picks up available moisture from the earth's surface, thereby contributing significantly to the water imbalance of subtropical deserts like the Sahara. In the local winter the subsidence zone shifts toward the equator, allowing migratory frontal disturbances to bring in soaking rains. Such a winter rainfall pattern characterizes much of the southern Mediterranean coastline and other poleward margins of subtropical deserts often dominated by shrubs. In contrast, during local summer the winds tend to shift poleward, allowing warm moist tropical air to invade, rise convectively, and

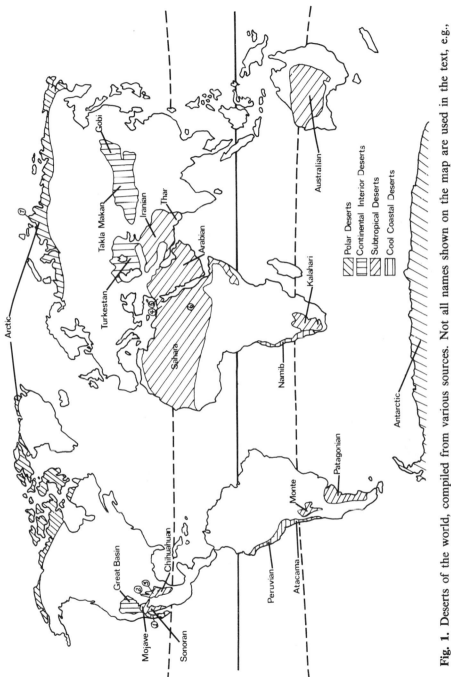

Fig. 1. Deserts of the world, compiled from various sources. Not all names shown on the map are used in the text, e.g., the term "Central Asia" covers deserts there, and "Indian desert" is used in place of "Thar." Approximate locations of sites mentioned frequently in the text are indicated by numbers as follows: *1* Baja California; *2* central New Mexico desert grassland; *3* Big Bend National Park; *4* coastal desert of northern Egypt; *5* Negev desert; *6* Sudan; *7* Taimyr Peninsula.

produce torrential rains. Equatorial margins of subtropical deserts experiencing these summer rainfall patterns are frequently covered by grasses.

b) Continental Interior Deserts. Continental interior deserts are also large expanses, but located at somewhat higher latitudes than subtropical deserts (see Fig. 1). Clear-cut examples are the deserts of Central Asia. During winter their daylengths are short and heat accumulation is minimal. Resulting atmospheric subsidence produces high-pressure cells of cold, dry air that effectively prevent influx of moist air.

The reverse occurs in summertime when long hot days cause heated air to rise and expand. Consequently, low-pressure cells beneath draw in moist "monsoon" air from great distances. As this air moves toward the interior it loses much of its moisture to mountain ranges and to convective storms; hence arriving air is generally quite dry. Continental interior deserts exhibit relatively light and unpredictable patterns of seasonal precipitation. They are often very cold in the winter and very hot in the summer.

c) Rain Shadow Deserts. Water vapor in air masses moving up and over mountain ranges condenses, causing cloudiness and precipitation as the rising air cools. Condensation itself releases heat, which, together with heat resulting from compression during the descent on the lee side, warms the now dry air. Rain shadow deserts are thus produced on the lee sides of some ranges. Sometimes, rain shadow deserts contribute to the aridity of continental interior deserts such as the Mojave. They are also found on islands and near mainland coastlines. Their seasonal patterns of temperature and precipitation are impossible to categorize neatly because each rain shadow desert is climatically and topographically unique.

d) Cool Coastal Deserts. To the west of certain long coastlines (Fig. 1), very high-pressure zones of warm dry air build up and flow east toward relatively low-pressure atmospheres existing over subtropical land masses. As this air blows above cold offshore ocean currents and upwellings it cools, losing its capacity to hold much moisture. Coastal strips like the Atacama and Namib deserts regularly experience such incoming air. What moisture it carries is frequently manifested as fog; actual precipitation seldom occurs until higher elevations are encountered inland. Near the coastline of these deserts there is little seasonal temperature change and the air remains cooler than that of the interior.

e) Polar Deserts. Examples of polar deserts are extensive portions of the Antarctic icecap, and much of the northern Palearctic land fringe together with its offshore archipelagoes. The landscapes of these places are dry because continuously cold air cannot hold much moisture. Such regions receive very little precipitation, and most of the moisture is in the form of ice, which is essentially useless to plants and animals.

3. Desertification

Current events reveal that interactions between unwise land-use practices and prolonged periods of natural drought promote the spread of deserts (Cloudsley-Thompson, 1974; Hare, 1977). Specific regions affected are usually grasslands, shrublands, and savannas adjacent to subtropical deserts. Because destruction of these regions has obvious effects on the structure of natural communities, it is appropriate to consider some of the mechanisms causing this change. Although the questions below focus on invertebrates, they apply equally well to other groups of organisms.

First we may ask: How does desertification affect invertebrate populations living in the original habitat? Presumably its effects are drastic, resulting in increased environmental heterogeneity (see Levin and Paine, 1974) and in local extinctions. Perhaps such massive disruptions also allow formerly subordinate groups to become dominant in the newly created desert. Second, to what extent do invertebrates in the originally adjacent desert colonize the newly desertified region? Topographical, climatic, and biotic barriers may be important screening agents affecting potential colonizers, which may also arrive from more distant regions. Successful colonization by invertebrates should depend on their adaptability to temperature and water stress, their intrinsic rates of increase and competitive abilities, and on the nature of the newly established vegetation together with newly associated microclimate regimes.

A brief review of the main causes and effects of desertification may provide insight as to how these questions can be investigated.

a) Effects of Vegetation Removal. Savannas lying to the south of the Sahara are frequently subjected to tree and shrub removal because of shifting cultivation, firewood and charcoal needs, and livestock provisioning (Cloudsley-Thompson, 1974). These activities, coupled with overgrazing, effectively denude the terrain and thereby increase run-off and erosion. Vegetation removal also causes the landscape to take on a lighter color generally and as a consequence to reflect more solar radiation than before. This increased albedo is thought to feed back on the system in such a way as to inhibit precipitation, although models attempting to explain the process differ considerably (Otterman, 1974; Charney et al., 1975).

From the standpoint of invertebrates experiencing the effects of desertification, we should recognize that surfaces of desertified landscapes, in addition to becoming lighter in color, also become cooler and less capable of storing heat. In addition, they receive more direct solar radiation and become much drier than before. Finally, if desertification models are correct, the new surfaces become subject to an altered pattern of annual or seasonal rainfall. Colonizing organisms must be able to cope with these modifications.

b) Effects of Withholding Fire. Fire tends to maintain grassland and to diminish the cover of desert shrubs, at least in western North America (Humphrey,

1958; Cable, 1967; White, 1969). This is due partly to the tendency of shrubs to mature for several years before setting seed, as opposed to grasses which reproduce annually via rhizomes or seeds. As a result, fire maintains many woody species in a juvenile, nonfruiting stage, unless of course it kills them outright.

Shrubs are often very susceptible to fire because their meristematic regions are often located well above ground, whereas meristems of grasses (in dormancy, as many are during prime fire season) are located at or beneath the ground surface. While there is good evidence that overgrazing completes the change to desert shrubland (York and Dick-Peddie, 1969), one should realize that fire promotes certain vegetation types as effectively as it destroys others. More to the point, in the aftermath of fire invertebrate components of a biotic community can also undergo considerable structural change (Kromarek, 1969; D. Gillon, 1971; Y. Gillon, 1971).

II. Continental Drift, Paleoclimates, and Desert Evolution

Having reviewed how deserts are caused and maintained we can now approach desert origin from an historical point of view. By reviewing past continental movements and corresponding paleoclimates, we can acquire a perspective for the forces that shaped the modern distribution of desert biotas.

1. Gondwanaland and Pangaea

During the Silurian and early Devonian, in fact about the time arthropods were beginning to evolve on land (Størmer, 1969), the arrangement of continental land masses was vastly different from that of today. The land masses that are now Europe and North America were united and situated near the equator, Asia was a separate continental unit (as may have been present-day China and southeastern Asia), and a large remaining continent called Gondwanaland existed separately and surrounded the South Pole. Drifting slowly, these continental plates apparently impacted by the late Permian to form a single supercontinent, Pangaea (Cracraft, 1974; Cox et al., 1976), which remained intact long enough to enable the broad dispersal of many plant and animal species. And, during the Permian some aridity evidently occurred in many parts of the world (Schwartzbach, 1963; T.B. Keyse, personal communication). Interestingly, traces of invertebrate burrows in eolian deposits from the Permian are similar to those of modern dune fields in arid regions (Ahlbrandt et al., 1978).

2. Mesozoic Events and Aridity

As Pangaea broke apart, the Atlantic Ocean was created, and shallow epicontinental seas began to penetrate continental interiors. Dry periods occurred in western North America and other continents during the Triassic and Jurassic. Before the Atlantic Ocean was large enough to significantly modify the climate, dry trade winds may have caused much of central and western South America to become relatively xeric (Solbrig, 1976). Later, in the Cretaceous dry conditions apparently occurred in North Africa (Cloudsley-Thompson, 1974).

3. Desert Formation in the Tertiary

Tertiary events further modified land and climatic patterns, and fossil floras from widely separated latitudes indicate a general trend to drier land climates during this Period. Thus, when Australia first split off from what is now Antarctica, it was covered by temperate rain forest. Eventually, open forest and grassland replaced the rain forest and persisted through the Miocene in Australia's interior (Axelrod, 1979). The Miocene junction of Africa with Eurasia (see Cox et al., 1976) resulted in a continuous land surface that may have enhanced the spread of aridity between North Africa and Arabia. Recent interpretations suggest a progression from tropical forest and savanna to Mediterranean sclerophyll forest in that region from the early Tertiary to about 10 000 years B.P. (Axelrod, 1979). Deserts in southern Africa were probably occupied by sclerophyll vegetation during the Miocene (Axelrod and Raven, 1978), while the core of the Namib has been very arid since the late Tertiary (van Zinderen Bakker, 1978). Rain shadows produced by orogenic events in the mid-Tertiary (Raven and Axelrod, 1974; Whyte, 1976) helped give rise to the deserts of western North America and Central Asia. As the raising of the Panama Isthmus joined North and South America in the Pliocene, xeric habitats began to spread on the two now-connected land masses (Solbrig, 1976). In the early Tertiary, however, some of South America's most arid regions must have been covered with tropical forests (Axelrod, 1979).

4. Quaternary Environments and Modern Deserts

Pleistocene events had a profound influence on the development of modern deserts. Glacial advances tied up enormous amounts of water, and cold phases may have resulted in aridity at low tropical latitudes (Raven and Axelrod, 1974). Whether glacial advances brought about only dry climates is debatable (Paramenter and Folger, 1974); however, dryness was at least temporally associated with a shifting of climatic belts. Periodic climatic change, therefore, characterized the Pleistocene and greatly influenced the boundaries of a number of deserts. The Sahara, for example, experienced at least two very arid periods between about 25 000 and 7000 years B.P. (Cloudsley-Thompson, 1974).

Current studies suggest that boundaries of some modern deserts were only recently defined. Thus, in the southwestern United States desert floras probably underwent rapid changes in dispersal and abundance in conjunction with climatic changes occurring 11 000 to 8000 years ago (Troughton et. al 1974; Wells 1974; Van Devender and Spaulding 1979). Postpleistocene oscillations in Saharan climates apparently continued between 7000 B.P. and the present. Hare (1977) cites reports of aridity in the Sahara for the next millennium, followed by a renewal of humid conditions until 4700 B.P. An eventual return of fairly continuous aridity then began in the Sahara, as it also did in what is now Pakistan and northwest India. Ramaswamy (1977) calculates an even more recent final development of central-Asian deserts, claiming that the process began around 25 000 B.P.

As for polar deserts, they too appear to be comparatively young, judging from the seral characteristics of their soil faunas (see references in Behan and Hill, 1980). Recent glacial retreat—a function of global warming and drying since the Pleistocene—has been important in establishing these depauperate polar landscapes.

B. Physical Environment of Deserts

I. Climate

1. Radiant Energy

Climatic patterns in arid regions result from combined meteorological events initiated by the incoming flux of solar energy. During most daytime hours sparse cloud cover typically allows this influx to approach its latitudinal and seasonal maximum. The absorbed radiation is mostly reradiated in the infrared portion of the spectrum; little is lost via evaporation because desert surfaces are so dry. At night, influx ceases in the absence of clouds, and the desert surface then cools rapidly (Gates, 1962; Fitzpatrick, 1979). It is the combination of high surface albedos and large nocturnal efflux that results in low values of net radiation in deserts (Graetz and Cowan, 1979).

One consequence of this set of conditions is an often tremendous variation in the excursion of diel (24-h) surface temperatures in deserts lying beneath dry air masses. Ranges of over 35°C (see Cloudsley-Thompson and Chadwick, 1964) are exceptional but illustrate the potential for selection of thermally adaptive traits in desert invertebrates and other organisms.

2. Wind

Heat and mass exchange between a desert surface and the air above is due primarily to turbulent convection generated by wind (Fuchs, 1979). Since deserts are often windy places this exchange can produce important physical and biological effects. One physical effect of biological significance is that of erosion caused by windblown particles. This action creates still more particles, which when moved by various agencies can modify habitats and redistribute soils.

Desert winds tend to be strongest in the local spring and early summer (Cloudsley-Thompson and Chadwick, 1964). Organisms which are active then must therefore cope with the consequences of wind-generated exchanges. Apart from the possibility of their being dispersed by wind, small desert invertebrates on or above the soil surface are exposed to potentially high, wind-facilitated evaporative stress. In addition, evaporation from adjacent soil surfaces can greatly reduce available moisture and steepen thermal gradients between air and soil. Both conditions can strongly influence invertebrate activity.

3. Water

As noted earlier, deserts are areas where evapotranspiration exceeds precipitation. As the deficit increases so does the importance of water as a dominant factor controlling biological processes (Noy-Meir, 1973). The importance of water is partly due to its impact on energy balance at the soil surface. For example, after rains, the flux of latent heat increases dramatically over that of sensible heat; in effect, evaporation increases and temperature variation is reduced (Graetz and Cowan, 1979). This temporary amelioration of usually severe daytime microclimates at the desert surface frequently coincides with arthropod activity while the soil is still wet and the ambient humidity still high.

Another way in which water controls life among desert biotas is through the physiological coupling of heat and water balance, which for most desert animals involves keeping body temperature below and hydration above critical levels (Noy-Meir, 1974).

Since desert-surface energy balance and biological homeostasis are so tightly linked to water availability, much of the "harshness" of desert environments can be attributed to the great variability of rainfall in space and time. Survival of endemic species depends, therefore, on their adaptive patterns being flexible enough to permit rapid responses when water is available. It should be noted, however, that the availability of water to such organisms is not necessarily a function of the absolute amount present, and may vary with the water-uptake abilities of different stages in a given species.

II. Surfaces and Soils: Their Properties and Microclimates

Directly or indirectly, desert surfaces are formed and shaped by radiant energy, wind, and water. On a large scale the action of these agencies brings about a variety of land forms, many of which have rocky, stony, or sandy surfaces. When surfaces are extensively flat or in the form of shallow basins, they often consist of fine-textured clays and silts. Cutting through these diverse landscapes, dry water courses of varying dimensions present characteristic relief patterns. These "arroyos" or "wadis" originate from the bases of mountains or elevated plateaus; following heavy rains they transport water, alluvial materials, and organic debris. Sometimes they end in undrained depressions that accumulate temporary bodies of water after runoffs. Oases, on the other hand, are places where water is permanently available, a condition that may have important implications for organisms needing a continuous supply of water.

Dispersal, feeding, and reproduction of many invertebrates take place in surface habitats. There is a subtle cost for the use of these places, since their microclimates can often be lethal. Therefore, their occupancy, particularly in the daytime, depends on the shelter they afford. Actually, what the human observer interprets as shelter may be quite deceptive. For example, large rocks provide better insulation than do smaller products of weathering, yet very rocky areas may have little or no soil for burrowing. Likewise, while many arthropods are well adapted to life in and on sand dunes, fine windblown sands sustain hotter daytime temperatures than do coarse sands and rock-gravel surfaces (Berry and Cloudsley-Thompson, 1960). At night, during warm seasons, shelter becomes a less important consideration because surface microclimates are temporarily moderated. Biotic constraints such as predation and competition may then gain in relative value as desert surfaces become increasingly populated by animals that avoid them by day.

Vegetation can exert a profound influence on the microclimate and properties of desert surfaces and their soils. As an example, the canopy of hopsage (Grayia spinosa) in parts of south-central Washington's desert steppe provides enough shade to keep about a tenth of the local soil surface 30% cooler than more exposed sites (Hinds and Rickard, 1966). However, as Fig. 2 illustrates, the quality of shade at any point beneath and within a shrub varies as the sun's position changes. Another example involves "nebkas," or mounds of accumulated soil at the base of shrubs. In North Africa, surface temperatures of nebkas have been shown to change dramatically during the course of a day (Heatwole and Muir, 1979).

Moisture beneath shrubs can also be strongly affected by these plants. Not only does shade inhibit evaporation, but the physical configuration of shrubs adds to moisture in the soil by allowing for stemflow during rains. Movement of water through the foliage and branches, down the stem, and into the soil produces infiltration that decreases with distance from the stem

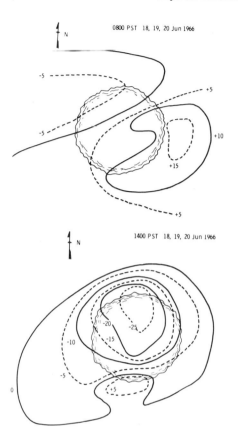

Fig. 2. Isotherm patterns around single *Grayia spinosa* shrub, desert steppe, south-central Washington. Data are averages at the indicated hour over three days. Temperatures (°F) are relative to unobstructed surface temperature. *PST* refers to Pacific Standard Time. (Hinds and Rickard, 1966; with permission)

(Pressland, 1976). The resulting horizontal and vertical distribution of soil moisture may well influence the organization of invertebrate communities in desert soils (see Chapter 14).

Plants modify desert surfaces by producing litter. Some of this dead organic material is blown, washed, or otherwise carried away from its original location, but much remains under shrubs in particular. Litter attracts water hygroscopically. It then becomes a source of water for invertebrate consumers (Tschinkel, 1972; Broza, 1979) and simultaneously presents a relatively cool, humid microclimate for microarthropods and microbial populations involved in its decomposition. Litter also acts as a vehicle for the return of organic carbon and nitrogen as well as minerals to the soil. In doing this, litter indirectly promotes the coagulation of colloids in the soil below plants (Kovda et al., 1979), thereby enhancing soil aeration and water-holding capacity.

Beneath their surfaces, desert soils generally have poorly developed profiles and are chemically similar to the parent materials from which they originated (Fuller, 1974; Kovda et al., 1979). The relatively low absolute amounts of nitrogen in these soils, together with their relatively high carbon : nitrogen ratios, are important limitations to both primary and secondary production.

Another quality of soil that particularly affects plant roots and soil-inhabiting invertebrates is its texture. Fine clay soils resist water penetration better than soils composed of larger particles, although clays retain moisture more effectively once water does penetrate. By the same token clays drain less well than do most other soils. Poor drainage can be inimical to soil-bound species when heavy rains cause flooding.

An additional feature shared by many desert soils is high alkalinity. This is caused by incomplete leaching as well as by groundwater that rises in response to evaporation. Characteristic deposits of calcium salts at or below the surface result from these processes and can produce deterioration of soil structure, elevated osmotic pressure, and toxicity (Goudie and Wilkinson, 1977). Depth of the calcium carbonate zone appears to increase predictably with mean annual rainfall, and since this layer is sometimes extremely hard, its vertical distribution should have a bearing on the depth to which many invertebrates can penetrate.

From this brief review it should be clear that microclimates of desert surfaces and soils may present formidable barriers to invertebrates. However, as we shall see in later chapters, many species have in fact adapted well to the comparatively severe stresses engendered by these conditions.

C. Desert Ecosystems: Producers

I. Introduction

Green plants, through their interaction with radiant energy, water, soils, and nitrogen, make available the nutrients and energy utilized in food webs. In deserts the limiting effects of water and nitrogen especially are translated through primary producers to higher trophic levels, where responses vary in quality and quantity. Thus the distribution and abundance of desert invertebrates is essentially a function of the variation in space and time by desert plants.

II. Role of Producers Relative to Arid-Climate Patterns

1. Production in Desert Plants

As with rainfall, net primary production (NPP) is low and extremely variable in deserts (see Hadley and Szarek, 1981, for a review of available data). Increases in shrub NPP of over 200% have been recorded between a dry and a wet year in the Mojave Desert, and show different species-specific patterns (Bamberg et al., 1976). More predictable, when major vegetation types are compared, are yearly changes in productivity per unit of plant biomass (i.e., turnover rates). A complete yearly turnover occurs in shoots and roots of "ephemeral" communities of annuals with their short growing seasons, while a 20%–40% rate characterizes "fluctuating perennial communities" and a 10%–20% rate applies to communities of "drought-persistent" shrubs, cacti, and trees (Noy-Meir, 1973). Consumers depending on these categories of primary producers for food and shelter must synchronize their life-cycle strategies accordingly if they are to utilize such resources successfully (Rhoades and Cates, 1976).

2. Production Relative to Major Physical and Climatic Factors

Rainfall is felt to "drive" production in deserts because of the close linkage of radiant and heat energy (which control photosynthesis) with atmospheric and soil water (which control transpiration), and because desert precipitation is far less predictable than levels of incoming radiant energy (Noy-Meir, 1973). This concept assumes that both inputs and responses occur in irregular "pulses." Since Noy-Meir (1973) estimates that 1–6 rain pulses occur each year over a span of 10–50 days per year in many deserts, the driving effects of rainfall should be decidedly erratic and discontinuous. It follows that flows of energy and nutrients between the production and reserve compartments of desert plants should also be somewhat unpredictable and that synchrony between consumer activity and producer turnover should take into account pulse effects.

III. Role of Producers Relative to Invertebrate Habitats and Feeding Patterns

Here it becomes practical to divide plants into three common categories: trees and shrubs, annuals, and cryptogams.

1. Trees and Shrubs

The "patchiness" of desert environments is accentuated by the spatial arrangements of these large and stable perennials, which on the whole are the most consistently prominent desert plants. As individuals they can be thought of as "islands" in terms of the ways in which they modify the immediate physical and nutritional environments of consumers.

Shrub-related microclimates were mentioned earlier, and specific interactions of invertebrates in the "perennial-shrub community" are described in

Chapter 16. It is sufficient at this point to recognize that "satellite faunas" of shrubs may be extensive (Seely et al., 1977), and that interactions within these assemblages reflect the temporal and spatial resources that shrubs provide.

2. Annuals

Just as many desert arthropods seem to have co-evolved with shrubs, the evolution of many such consumers appears closely associated with that of annuals. Among desert plants the "annual" category includes the largest number and variety of species. However, these ephemeral plants are less dependable as food and shelter than are perennial shrubs (Rhoades and Cates, 1976). Consequently, it has been predicted that when annuals are temporarily abundant, competition for their resources should be comparatively intense. Another prediction, recently confirmed, is that short-lived plants and plant tissues should have evolved patterns of resistance to consumer exploitation differing from those of perennial plants (Cates and Rhoades, 1977). This point is discussed in more detail in Chapters 15–16.

3. Cryptogams

It is surprising that so little is known about how algae and lichens interact with desert invertebrates, because in some deserts these cryptogams are important contributors to total NPP. In dry, antarctic valleys, for example, endolithic bluegreen algae are the only primary producers (Friedmann and Ocampo, 1976), while in other deserts surface crusts contain a considerable biomass of algae and lichens (Friedmann and Galun, 1974; Kovda et al., 1979).

D. Desert Ecosystems: Consumers

I. Introduction

In this section the effects of desert climates on secondary production are first examined in general terms; then the potential effects of consumers on primary production are considered. This approach provides a transition between the earlier general treatment of physical and biotic features of deserts, and the more specific appraisals of desert invertebrate biology found in forthcoming chapters.

II. Production, Life History, and Climate

Life-history parameters associated with production in populations and communities of desert consumers vary considerably in space and time. This is well documented for vertebrates (Chew and Chew, 1970; Raitt and Pimm, 1976; Turner et al., 1976; Whitford, 1976), invertebrates (Whitford and Creuscre, 1977), and fungi (Borut, 1960; Taylor, 1979). Secondary production in deserts appears limited primarily by lack of food (resulting directly or indirectly from rainfall deficiency), low moisture levels, extreme temperatures, or reduced shelter (Andrewartha and Birch, 1954; Low, 1979). Not unexpectedly, in such unstable environments many consumers can rapidly recolonize temporarily inhospitable regions. Herbivores especially should be able to do this, as should many consumers relying on herbivores for food. Probably most desert fungi (assumed to be decomposers) also have rapid growth responses to favorable conditions (Taylor, 1979).

A minority of desert consumers have less responsive life-history patterns. These relatively stable groups include mainly carnivores and detritivores, many of which live longer than a year. Characteristically, they depend only indirectly on rainfall for food, water, and shelter.

Certain fundamental life-history traits have a bearing on annual rates of production in deserts and elsewhere. In addition to such standard population parameters as reproduction, development, and mortality, attributes relating to foraging may also be mentioned. One of these is temperature control. Endotherms forage more independently of temperature than do ectotherms (Reichman et al., 1979), although the relative costs of growth and development for endotherms are far greater (see references in Petrusewicz and Macfadyen, 1970). Another attribute relating to foraging is phenology. Closely related species of many desert arthropods, for example, have distinct foraging and dormacy seasons, a matter taken up later in this book. Finally, trophic level is associated with secondary production since trophic levels tend to have specific ranges of ecological efficiencies (Kozlovsky, 1968).

Regardless of life history, taxon, or trophic level the problem of maximizing energy gain while minimizing water loss applies generally to desert animals (Noy-Meir, 1974). Its solution is achieved by a spectrum of behavioral and physiological traits. Thus, while one set of adaptations may work well for desert ectotherms, which on the whole have comparatively low metabolic rates and high surface-to-volume ratios, another set may function for desert endotherms, which have the opposite characteristics.

III. Influence of Consumers on Primary Production

Consumers can affect primary production by exploiting plants for food, by interacting in various ways with other consumers, and by feeding on materials destined for nutrient cycling. As regards plant exploitation, several kinds of desert herbivores are well known for their occasional population "explosions," but the effects of such outbreaks on host plants are poorly documented. An associated effect of heavy foraging by dense consumer populations may be to reduce competition among plant species (Chew and Chew, 1970). Likewise, by dispersing and burying their food, seed-gathering consumers may actually promote the fitness of the plants they "exploit."

Less can be said about how interactions among consumers affect plant production. Noy-Meir (1974) suggests that desert carnivores are more "opportunistic" than their more mesic-adapted counterparts, but whether dietary flexibility at any trophic level in deserts has much influence on primary production is an open question. Removal of either rodents or ants from experimental plots in a desert scrub causes an increase in the remaining population of these presumably competing consumers. The increase may in turn have a compensatory effect on seed resources and plant populations (Brown and Davidson, 1977).

In considering how consumers affect the recycling of nutrients used by desert and nondesert plants, we should distinguish between two broad classes: invertebrate detritivores and microbial decomposers. Detritivores translocate and transform dead organic matter (Kitchell et al., 1978). Some desert detritivores have extensive effects on the removal of detritus, while others may play more regulatory roles through their interactions with microbes (Crawford, 1979a). Microbial decomposers subsequently transform fragmented detritus to nutrients that can be utilized by plants. Whether ecological "bottlenecks" in deserts are created by periodic natural declines in detritivore–decomposer activity needs to be examined.

Chapter 2
The Array of Desert Invertebrates

The subjects of this book, except for inhabitants of ephemeral waters (see Chapter 17 for a treatment of those invertebrates), will now be introduced by way of an expanded outline. Initially, only a few comments about the broad geographic distribution of each major taxon are given. More comprehensive treatments are deferred until later chapters, which stress available information regardless of the distribution or size of a particular invertebrate group. Unfortunately, there is really little alternative to such an approach if a synthesis of current knowledge is to be presented. Hence "equal treatment" occurs only in this chapter.

Throughout the chapter and the book as a whole no attempt is made to follow a single classification system. In fact, names of major taxa are used according to the author's perception of the reader's general familiarity with them. Invertebrate zoology texts should be consulted for more precise classifications.

A. Protozoans

Undoubtedly these ubiquitous organisms populate the soils of all deserts; however, practically nothing is known of their distribution and biology in arid regions. In the Antarctic, testate amoebae and ciliates occur in moss peat, while ciliates and flagellates live in moraine soil (Wallwork, 1976). Russian studies report that protozoans are well established to depths of up to 30 cm in soils of continental interior deserts in Asia (Fuller, 1974). Encystment of protozoans in desert soils is referred to by Buxton (1923) and Bodenheimer (1953).

B. Nematodes

Judging from their known distribution in the Arctic desert (Chernov et al., 1977) and in deserts of the western U.S. (Freckman et al., 1974), nematodes must be very widespread in desert soils. Because recent studies (e.g., Freckman and Mankau, 1977) suggest that soil nematodes may have great influence in deserts, the distribution of desert species is sure to receive much attention in the near future. The ecology of these organisms is reviewed in later chapters.

C. Annelids

Enchytraeid oligochaetes (potworms) are common in the Arctic desert (Chernov et al., 1977). Introduced earthworms occur in riparian habitats in the Great Basin desert (Gates, 1967). Although earthworms do not seem to be indigenous to warm deserts, the South African *Microchaetus modestus,* at 7 m the world's longest earthworm, inhabits sandy grassland soils; it resists desiccation more effectively than other terrestrial species (Sims, 1978).

D. Gastropod Mollusks

Easily overlooked because most enter subterranean dormancy, desert snails are represented by many species and families in southwestern North America (Bequaert and Miller, 1973). Jaeckel (1969) discusses the distribution of "xerotherm" species from sparsely vegetated arid parts of South America. Land snails are perhaps most obvious on the desert surface in North Africa (Cloudsley-Thompson and Chadwick, 1964) and the Middle East (Yom-Tov, 1971a; Shachak et al., 1976a). Many groups are adapted to desert life in Australia (McMichael and Iredale, 1959), and many high-density populations inhabit deserts of southern Africa (van Bruggen, 1978). Apparently, land snails have not been well studied in continental interior deserts.

E. Isopods and Other Crustaceans

Terrestrial oniscoid isopods are widely distributed in warm deserts of Africa and Asia (Cloudsley-Thompson and Chadwick, 1964; Schneider, 1971; Linsenmair and Linsenmair, 1971; Warburg et al., 1978; Kheirallah, 1979), as well as Australia (Warburg, 1965a). Isopods are also present in North American deserts (Allred and Mulaik, 1965; Warburg, 1965b), but not abundantly so. Calanoid copepods and bosminid cladocerans have been reported from soils of xeric habitats in Australia (Wood, 1971). A species of potamonid crab, *Holothuisana transversa,* is also known from arid regions in Australia (Bishop, 1963).

F. Solifugid Arachnids

Most species of these highly active carnivores live in warm, arid environments (see references in Cloudsley-Thompson, 1977a) and are well represented in deserts of North Africa and the Middle East (Cloudsley-Thompson and Chadwick, 1964; Levy and Shulov, 1964); however, they are not found in Australia. About a quarter of the world's known species occur in southern Africa (Newlands, 1978) and contribute to distinct regional faunas (Lawrence, 1972); although they are common in deserts of North America (see references in Muma, 1974), species-richness there is lower. Solifugids appear well distributed in arid environments of South America (Deboutteville and Rapoport, 1968; Mares et al., 1977a).

G. Uropygid Arachnids

Whipscorpions are mainly nondesert arthropods of the tropics and subtropics (Cloudsley-Thompson, 1968). *Matigoproctus giganteus,* however, inhabits both humid (Muma, 1967a) and arid (Jaeger, 1957) regions of North America. Although this large-bodied species can be locally abundant, its physiological constraints (Ahearn, 1970a; Crawford and Cloudsley-Thompson, 1971) probably restrict it to moist microhabitats.

H. Pseudoscorpions

The order Pseudoscorpionida consists of relatively tiny carnivores also confined to moist microhabitats in a broad latitudinal range. Several families have been reported from arid parts of North America (Weygoldt, 1969), where they are best known from shrub and tree litter (Hoff, 1959). They are also found in arid parts of South America (Deboutteville and Rapoport,

1968), North Africa (Ghabbour et al., 1977), and southern Africa (Newlands, 1978).

I. Scorpions

Major desert carnivores, scorpions are essentially inhabitants of warm and tropical regions (Cloudsley-Thompson, 1965a). They are also known from continental interior deserts (Johnson and Allred, 1972; Byalynitskii-Birulya, 1965) and from cool coastal deserts (Newlands, 1978). While only about half a dozen families are actually found in deserts, their continental and local distributions are somewhat family-specific, except for the polar regions where none occur. Species populations in arid locations sometimes reach relatively high densities (Williams, 1970; Shorthouse, 1971; Polis and Farley, 1980). Faunal diversities may also be considerable in locations such as Baja California, where many kinds of habitats have resulted from a complex succession of geological events (Williams, 1980).

J. Opilionid Arachnids

Harvestmen are not at all well known in deserts but have been reported from the Mojave and Great Basin in North America (Allred, 1965) and from arid elevations in central Tunisia (Cloudsley-Thompson, 1956).

K. Spiders

At least 20 aranean families have xeric-adapted species (see examples in Fautin, 1946; Cloudsley-Thompson and Chadwick, 1964; Allred and Beck, 1967, Newlands, 1978). Spiders are probably common in all but polar deserts. The large-bodied orthognath suborder includes the trapdoor spiders (Ctenizidae) and tarantulas (Theraphosidae), both being well known in deserts of North America (Gertsch, 1949). The more diverse labidognath suborder is represented by a much larger array of families. These include dune-adapted araneomorphs such as the giant crab spiders (Sparassidae) in southern Africa (Newlands, 1978), as well as crab spiders (Thomisidae), jumping spiders (Salticidae), funnel-web spiders (Agelinidae), wolf spiders (Lycosidae), comb-footed spiders (Theriidae), and orb-weaver spiders (Araneidae) in many deserts (Cloudsley-Thompson and Chadwick, 1964).

L. Mites

Acarine arthropods are surely one of the largest and most diverse of all animal groups, yet they are poorly known from deserts, where they occur mainly in soil and litter. The most obvious desert forms are the spectacular prostigmatid giant velvet mites (Trombidiidae), which can have enormous local densities in Africa (Cloudsley-Thompson, 1962a) and North America (Tevis and Newell, 1962). There seems to be a general tendency for the prostigmatid : cryptostigmatid (oribatid) ratio to increase as soils become drier and more mineralized in Australia (Wood, 1971), South Africa (Loots and Ryke, 1967), South America (Deboutteville and Rapoport, 1968), and North America (Santos et al., 1978). Cryptostigmatid populations are also of low density in deserts of the U.S.S.R. (Krivolutskii, 1966, cited by Wood, 1970). More cryptostigmatid than prostigmatid families (but an equal number of species) are found in the south polar region; however, the most southern of all the soil arthropods is a prostigmatid *(Nanorchestes antarcticus)* from extremely barren soils (Wallwork, 1976). Interestingly, while gammasid mesostigmatids appear instead to be the common soil mites in Arctic deserts of extreme north Asia's Taimyr Peninsula (Chernov et al., 1977), polar deserts of North America reflect the shift in prostigmatid : cryptostigmatid ratios cited above, and do not appear to contain mesostigmatids in unexpected numbers (Behan and Hill, 1980).

M. Millipedes

Large spirostreptid diplopods are known from arid parts of Africa (Kraus, 1966; Lawrence, 1966), the Middle East (Verhoeff, 1935; Kaestner, 1968), and North America (Loomis, 1966; Causey, 1975). High densities of these Spirostreptida have been recorded in the Chihuahuan desert (Crawford, 1976). Smaller atopetholids (Spirobolida) are endemic to but usually obscure in the Chihuahuan desert (Hoffman and Orcutt, 1960). A few millipede species have been collected in the Great Basin desert (Allred, 1971).

N. Centipedes

Desert chilopods belong mainly to the Scolopendrida, which are also large-bodied. These mobile carnivores are found in arid regions of North Africa (Cloudsley-Thompson, 1956; Cloudsley-Thompson and Chadwick, 1964), southern Africa (Lawrence, 1975), and North America (Chamberlin, 1943; Crabill, 1960). A few geophilomorphs and lithobiomorphs are also known from these environments.

O. Entognath Hexapods and Apterygote Insects

These include the primitively wingless machilids (Archaeognatha) and lepismatids (Thysanura), as well as springtails (Collembola) which despite their small size are widespread desert insects. Among the Collembola the genus *Folsomides* is known from soils of semi-arid locations in Australia (Greenslade and Greenslade, 1973) and from the Mojave desert (Wallwork, 1976). Springtails also inhabit soils and cryptogamic vegetation of the Arctic (Chernov et al., 1977) and Antarctic (Wallwork, 1976) deserts. Desert archaeognaths and thysanurans are somewhat larger and more inclined to exploit the soil surface, although many are also found in soil, litter, and ant nests. They are known from deserts in the Sudan (Cloudsley-Thompson and Idris, 1964), southern Africa (Edney, 1971a), Central Asia (Kaplin, 1978), and North America (Wygodzinski, 1972).

P. Cockroaches and Lesser Orthopteroid Insects

Twenty-eight species of cockroaches are considered xerophyllic by Roth and Willis (1961). Many of these are polyphagids, which reach their maximum diversity in the Sahara and Asiatic deserts (Schmoller, 1970). In northern Egypt the polyphagid *Heterogamia syriaca* is the major contributor to soil mesofaunal biomass (Ghabbour et al., 1977), while in western North America (Hebard, 1943; Edney et al., 1974) and in central Asia (Guthrie and Tindall, 1968) the genus *Arenivaga* is well adapted to life in sandy deserts. Relatively large, flightless blattids appear to be the main cockroaches in arid Australia (Mackerras, 1970).

Among the "lesser orthopteroids," stenopelmatine gryllacridids ("sand crickets") are conspicuous in sandy and rocky parts of southern Africa (Rentz, 1978) and the southwestern deserts of North America (see references in Tinkham, 1968), as are the rhaphidophorines or "camel crickets" (Tinkham, 1948). True crickets (Gryllidae) are important elements of desert communities (Cloudsley-Thompson and Chadwick, 1964); Rehn (1958) discusses their presence and that of gryllacridids in North American deserts. Mantids and phasmatids in the Sahara (Chopard, 1938; Leouffre, 1953) and North America (Tinkham, 1948), dermapterans in North American arid environments (Helfner, 1953), and embiopterans in the Mojave desert (Beck and Allred, 1968), have been reported, but their ecology is poorly understood.

Q. Locusts and Grasshoppers

Locusts (migratory) and grasshoppers (nonmigratory) are the most conspicuous orthopterans in deserts. The former reach "plague" proportions in extensive arid regions of Asia and Africa (Uvarov, 1977), as well as in Australia (Matthews, 1976). A variety of chaeliferan and ensiferan grasshoppers are found in nonpolar deserts. In general densities tend to be low, and species abundance varies according to soils and topography (Uvarov, 1977), and historical biogeography (Otte, 1976). For example, significantly more species of grasshoppers are found in the Sonoran desert than in the floristically similar Monte desert of Argentina (Mares et al., 1977a), while in the ancient fauna of Australian deserts flightless eumasticid grasshoppers are especially species-rich (Key, 1970; Matthews, 1976).

R. Termites

Essentially confined to the tropics and subtropics, these social insects are very common in humid parts of Africa and South America. However, relatively few genera and species live in deserts (Lee and Wood, 1971) in proportion to their potentially tremendous influence on decomposition and nutrient flow in certain of these regions. *Amitermes,* on the other hand, is the largest Australian genus and is widely distributed in deserts elsewhere as well (Calaby and Gay, 1959). Termites are treated as a unit later in the book.

S. Hemipteroid Insects

Schmoller's (1970) assessment of desert Heteroptera, namely that "little specific ecological data is available for this order," still applies a decade later. Family numbers listed in Beck and Allred (1968) and Edney (1974) for given locations in the Mojave desert are relatively high, suggesting that plant-feeding bugs are common in continental interior deserts. This should be true for mirids in particular (Fautin, 1946; Putshkov, 1978). Other common hemipteran and homopteran families in deserts are the Tingidae, Pentatomidae,

Reduviidae, Lygaeidae, Coccidae, Cicadellidae, Fulgoridae, and Chermidac (Aphidoidea). Thysanoptera (thrips) can exist in exceedingly high densities in deserts and desert grassland (Andrewartha and Birch, 1954; Watts, 1965); nevertheless, relatively few species actually inhabit deserts, species richness being proportional to that of desert vegetation (T. Lewis, 1973). Psocopterans are known from the Mojave desert (Beck and Allred, 1968) and from arid South America (Deboutteville and Rapoport, 1968). Ectoparasitic groups of hemipteroid insects are of course present in deserts but will be considered only sparingly in this book.

T. Neuropterans

Ant-lions (Myrmeleontidae) are well known in deserts of North America (Wheeler, 1930; Stange, 1970), Africa (Cloudsley-Thompson and Idris, 1964; Ghabbour et al., 1977), and Australia (Riek, 1970). Owlflies (Ascalaphidae) resemble myrmeleontids and occur in deserts of the Middle East, North America and Australia. Chrysopid, hemerobiid, and berothid lacewings are also found in these regions, as are several other neuropteran families (Beck and Allred, 1968; Riek, 1970; Borror et al., 1976; J. Kugler, personal communication).

U. Beetles

It is difficult to dispute the claim that the Coleoptera are "the insects best adapted to desert life" (Cloudsley-Thompson and Chadwick, 1964). Certainly, as members of the world's largest animal order they are widespread and often abundant in all but the polar deserts. The best-represented family in deserts is probably the Tenebrionidae, but the Scarabaeidae, Curculionidae, Cerambycidae, Chrysomelidae, Meloidae, Cicindellidae, Carabidae, and many others are sometimes prominent members of desert faunas. Many references to desert beetles appear in later chapters.

V. Butterflies and Moths

Nearly as ubiquitous in deserts are the Lepidoptera, a major order of plant-associated insects. However, in deserts nearly devoid of plants, like the coastal strip of the Namib, there are few, if any, permanent species (Pinhey, 1978).

Also, relatively small numbers of butterfly species are endemic to Australian (Common and Waterhouse, 1972) and North American (Schmoller, 1970) deserts, but lycaenids can be common in the latter (Hurd and Linsley, 1975) and in Palearctic deserts (Buxton, 1923). Larsen (1979) reported only 15 species of butterflies from Saudi Arabia. Spectacular swarms of *Vanessa cardui* nymphalids periodically migrate through deserts of the Old and New Worlds (Tilden, 1962; Johnson, 1969). Another cosmopolitan migrant is the sphingid moth *Hyles* (= *Celerio*) *lineata* (Grant, 1937, cited by Casey, 1976). In contrast to butterflies, families of moths in nonpolar deserts are often plentiful (Cloudsley-Thompson and Chadwick 1964; Matthews, 1976).

W. Flies

The order Diptera is perhaps more widely dispersed in deserts than any other insect order, partly because of chironomid midges in the Arctic (Chernov et al., 1977) and Antarctic (Holdgate, 1977). Flies belonging to many families in deserts occupy a large number of feeding niches ranging from plant galls to carrion, yet specific associations with arid regions are difficult to summarize owing to the large numbers of species (see Edney, 1974; Table 1). Some groups, however, such as highly specialized genera of Mydaidae in southern Africa (Bowden, 1978) and a widespread mydaid genus in Australia (Paramonov, 1959), are particularly well represented. Others include the Asilidae and Bombiliidae (Paramonov, 1959; Cloudsley-Thompson and Chadwick, 1964; Schmoller, 1970; Orians and Solbrig, 1977a,b), and a number of muscoid families (Colless and McAlpine, 1970).

X. Bees and Wasps

Hymenopterans are prominent desert insects except in polar regions, where like most other insect orders they are rare or lacking. While some species in the suborder Symphyta are found in arid environments (Riek et al., 1970), it is the Apocrita that populate deserts. Desert bees and wasps are largely solitary, but social groups do exist. Solitary bees are major pollinators; their species richness in deserts seems proportional to the seasonal availability of blooming plants (Orians and Solbrig, 1977a). At least eight families of bees are known from deserts. Many wasps attack a variety of arthropod prey either by laying eggs directly on them (as in the ichneumonoid and chalcidoid superfamilies) or by paralyzing them with the sting. Immobilized, prey are then used in burrows as provisions for the new generations. Sphecid, pompilid, scoliid, mutillid, tiphiid, and chrysidid wasps are conspicuous provisioners in a variety of deserts (see Evans, 1966; et al., 1970; Borror et al., 1976; Prins, 1978). Desert Vespidae include both social (paper) wasps and several solitary subfamilies that provision nests with prey or with pollen and nectar (Borror et al., 1976). The Apidae contain all of the highly social bees (Michener, 1969); their distribution in deserts has probably been facilitated by man.

Y. Ants

Surely no other family is as abundant in deserts as the Formicidae. The influence of these social hymenopterans is directly or indirectly evident in all but the coldest deserts. Harvesting, predatory, and other feeding guilds seem to have their ecological equivalents in widely separated deserts. For instance, harvesting genera, which are found mostly in the warmer deserts and semideserts (Wilson, 1971), seem best represented by *Pogonomyrmex* in North America (Cole, 1968; Whitford, 1978a), *Messor* in the Middle East and North Africa (Cloudsley-Thompson, 1956; Délye, 1968), perhaps *Ocymermex* in southern Africa (Prins, 1978), and *Pheidole* in Australia (Briese and Macauley, 1977). While the genera of harvesters occurring in the Sonoran and Monte deserts are often the same in both regions (Mares et al., 1977a), the guild is less rich in species in the Monte (Orians et al., 1977).

Z. Fleas

While these insects are not uncommon in the burrows of desert mammals, they, like other ectoparasites, are mentioned only briefly in this text.

Summary Comments: Part 1

In review, we can conclude that at least five broad categories of deserts exist. These are maintained by regional climates, geographic and topographic influences, and the activities of man. The human influence on desertification is increasing, and the concomitant redistribution of organisms—including invertebrates—needs to be followed more closely.

Although atmospheric subsidence has probably produced arid areas for the duration of terrestrial metazoan life on our planet, the distribution of present-day deserts has been greatly influenced by tectonic, orographic, and climatic events. Climate in particular has repositioned the borders of many deserts since the late Pleistocene. Alternating advances and retreats of vast ice sheets during that epoch surely produced a series of faunal extinctions, refugia, and colonizations that profoundly affected distributions of desert invertebrates. Consequently, many populations of these animals have probably existed in their current habitats for relatively few millennia.

Deserts are regions of low primary production, and often of extreme physical environments. These forces must have exerted strong selection effects on the types of desert biotas now in evidence. As to the selective effects of biotic agents, shrubs and trees as well as annuals and cryptogamic plants provide food and shelter for consumer organisms, but the trophic-level interactions involved are just beginning to be understood. The possibility of coevolution involving invertebrates and plants in desert environments is examined in later chapters, as are inter- and intraspecific interactions.

We are now aware of a wide variety of invertebrate taxa in deserts. While their geographical distributions are often difficult to account for, it will become apparent in Part 2 that local distributions are strongly correlated with specific adaptations to aspects of xeric environments.

Part 2
Adaptations to Xeric Environments

Introduction

In Part 1 an evolutionary and ecological rationale was developed to account for the distribution of desert invertebrates, which were then introduced in terms of their broad taxonomic and geographic array. In Part 2, we begin to inquire as to how these organisms actually live in their arid environments, and we do so here by examining their adaptations to conditions of climate and energy that characterize their habitats.

The topic is approached by focusing on four interrelated features clearly associated with evolutionary fitness. The first of these is covered by a chapter dealing with light, discussed in relation to temporal activity. Next, the complex matter of water relations is taken up, and also presented—in two chapters—within the framework of time. A chapter on temperature relations follows, this matter being considered largely in the context of thermally extreme climates. Finally, in the last chapter of Part 2 the subject of energetics is addressed, with emphasis on the physiological basis of energy use.

While there is certainly much more to adaptation than the way an organism contends with the conditions listed above, the special attributes of climate and energy affecting desert habitats suggest that response patterns to these variables must have a strong bearing on survival. Hence, a unit treating these adaptations seems appropriate at this juncture.

Chapter 3

The Use of Light and Timing of Activity

A. Introduction

Unless they remain shielded from daylight, animals in all but the highest latitudes experience recurring diel (24-h) changes of photoperiod, light intensity, and wavelength. Responses to these changes in illumination can in a very general way be categorized as either simple or complex. In stationary or moving animals simple responses (often termed orientations) involve adjustments of the body axis to the intensity or direction of a stimulus; for example, light of a certain intensity. Complex responses often have a temporal aspect and include diel as well as seasonal periodicities. The purpose of the present section is to explore a broad range of responses to light among desert invertebrates and to determine if a set of aridity-associated response patterns applies to these animals. Since the timing of biological events can be especially critical to the survival of desert organisms, we shall scrutinize in particular the relationship between illumination and temporal activity.

In the discussion below I have slightly modified Corbet's (1966) definitions of certain key terms, which are now given as follows: (1) a *periodicity* is a recurrent temporal pattern, regardless of its control; (2) a *rhythm* is an endogenous, time-measuring component of a periodicity and is called *circadian* if diel and *circannual* if annual. Many diel periodicities seem to be entirely under the control of exogenous cues, while many others have a demonstrated circadian component. Circannual rhythms have seldom been demonstrated in invertebrates.

I. Photoperiod

This most predictable parameter of diel illumination is widely used by individual organisms and their populations as an environmental timer (Zeitgeber). One assumes that photoperiod also synchronizes community interactions over a wide range of latitudes, although in deserts, where the concept of community is itself questionable (Part 4, Introduction), responses to photoperiodic cues are more realistically examined at the population level. There, as elsewhere, we expect biotic responses to reflect present or previous photoperiod inputs and, in doing so, to be manifested as adaptations to seasons or to times of day. Because these adaptations are of ultimate evolutionary value, the photoperiods that trigger them serve as useful proximate signals.

Since growing seasons are relatively irregular in deserts, it would be a mistake to assume that photoperiod signals perceived by desert animals are necessarily more important to such organisms than they are to others living in more seasonally regular environments. Indeed, in the ensuing discussion it should become evident that the periodicities of a number of desert invertebrates are often much more closely tied to patterns of temperature and moisture than to expressions of photoperiod.

II. Light Intensity and Wavelength

The intensity and wavelength of light undergo continuous variation as the sun's arc changes relative to the horizon on a given day. Furthermore, subtle changes occur in their average values at the same time of day during the progression of seasons at temperate latitudes. The generally clear skies of deserts permit maximal expression of such daily and seasonal variations, thereby maximizing their potential capacity as transmitters of environmental information. Similarly, the clarity of night skies in deserts allows the full impact of moonlight to be felt by invertebrate populations on the surface.

Usually measured in units of lux, changes in naturally occurring light intensity during the daytime are best expressed on a log scale because of the proportionate sensitivity of animal visual systems (Nielsen, 1962). Wavelength, on the other hand, is measured more directly. About half of the incoming solar radiation when the sun is directly overhead in clear desert air is in wavelengths longer than 700 nm, while about 60% is contained in such wavelengths in the early morning or late afternoon (Henwood, 1975a). Here then are two sets of potential signals that may have great significance to desert invertebrates with appropriate receptors.

B. Simple Light Responses and Diel Periodicities of Desert Invertebrates

Intuitively, one might expect many desert invertebrates to have well defined responses to light. In the following review we shall first examine this assumption using a taxonomic rather than a conceptual approach. At the end of the review we shall attempt to generalize our findings and to judge whether the initial assumption has merit.

I. Mollusks

Very little can be said of the light responses of desert snails, a poorly studied group to begin with. Riddle (1977) showed that light-dark (LD) changes elevate metabolism in active *Rabdotus schiedeanus*. For the time being we can assume that other desert snails probably have similar responses, but a great deal of experimental work remains to be done.

II. Isopods

Some Middle Eastern and North American xeric species (e.g., *Armadillo albomarginatus, Venezillo arizonicus, Porcellio olivieri*) are photonegative; however, at high temperatures this reaction is reversed in the first two of these isopods. In contrast, the crepuscular *Hemilepistus reaumuri* is only photonegative at high temperatures (Warburg, 1968). In Central Asia *H. aphganicus* is a day-active forager, and its running activity is independent of light intensity at 19°C–20°C. Nevertheless, light-dark cycles at 23°C–24°C entrain the activity of this isopod (Schneider, 1975). Simple light-associated responses and diel periodicties are obviously not consistent among species of desert isopods.

III. Arachnids

Except for such arachnids as salticid and lycosid spiders (Fig. 3), which seize their prey after a quick run, most desert species in this order appear to have eyes that are more suited to detecting light-intensity changes than to perceiving objects. In some species not even light intensity seems to mean much. For example, the whipscorpion *Mastigoproctus giganteus* makes no

a

b

Fig. 3. Hunting spiders with well developed eyes. **a** Tiny salticid (about 3 mm in length) on small stone in New Mexico desert grassland. **b** A lycosid, *Geolycosa wrightii*, closely related to arid-land species in western North America. Dune area, Long Point, Ontario. [Photograph courtesy of D. T. Gwynne (Gwynne and Watkiss, 1975); with permission]

noticeable response to a light-dark change (Crawford and Cloudsley-Thompson, 1971), yet this roving hunter is nocturnal when it feeds aboveground. More typical desert orders such as the Solifugae and Scorpiones (Fig. 4) are also largely nocturnal, although some of the smaller and often brightly colored Solifugae are diurnal (Cloudsley-Thompson, 1977a). Night-active spe-

Fig. 4. Nocturnal hunting arachnids with eyes probably best suited to detecting light-intensity changes. a Eremobatid solifugid foraging at night, Mojave desert. b The diplocentrid scorpion, *Diplocentrus peloncillensis,* in burrow entrance following removal of covering rock, Peloncillo Mountains, between Chihuahuan and Sonoran deserts. (Photograph a, courtesy of G. A. Polis; b, by the author, with permission of John Wiley and Sons, Inc.)

a

b

cies in both orders usually show pronounced, light-entrained circadian rhythms under controlled conditions (Cloudsley-Thompson, 1978a).

Among scorpions there is at least one exception to the previous statement, and in a curious way the lack of a rhythmic response may allow a noncircadian species to coexist with a circadian species. *Diplocentrus peloncillensis* (= *spitzeri*) (Fig. 4b) is found in or near the mouth of its shallow burrow beneath rocks in southwestern New Mexico, while *Centruroides sculpturatus* is sometimes found clinging to the undersides of the same rocks (Crawford and Krehoff, 1975). However, *C. sculpturatus,* with its demonstrably nocturnal circadian rhythm, is not likely to hunt in such a habitat during daytime hours. In contrast, *D. peloncillensis* is not so constrained and is often seen feeding during the day on freshly captured beetles or centipedes. Habitat separation occurs at night when *C. sculpturatus* forages on the open surface, an environment in which *D. peloncillensis* is infrequently seen.

Extreme sensitivity to light in desert scorpions may account for observed population changes during periods of bright moonlight. Recently Fleissner (1977a,b,c) demonstrated that the lateral and medial eyes of *Androctonus australis* from the Sahara are highly sensitive organs for circadian entrainment of amazingly low levels of illumination. So low, in fact, is the threshold for response that *A. australis* is probably even able to orient to objects and shadows on clear, moonless nights. The full light of the moon may, on the other hand, be virtually blinding to the scorpion. This physiological dimension may explain why Hadley and Williams (1968) recorded decreased densities of scorpion species during the full moon in Baja California, and why Polis (1980a) noted that *Paruroctonus mesaensis* mates and feeds less frequently at such times in the Mojave desert than it does under less well lighted conditions.

Unlike scorpions, some desert spiders as well as giant velvet mites seem to be quite labile in responding to light-intensity changes. For example, while several species of Sonoran desert tarantulas were shown to be nocturnal in aktograph studies (Cloudsley-Thompson, 1967), *Aphonopelma chalcodes* can and does hunt in the daytime (Minch, 1978). Likewise, even though wolf spiders are well known as diurnal predators, *Lycosa carolinensis* is strictly nocturnal in the Sonoran desert (Shook, 1978). Moreover, *Dinothrombium* mites (Fig. 5) in the Sonoran and Mojave deserts sometimes emerge from the soil in spectacular numbers in broad daylight following heavy rains (Newell and Tevis, 1960; Tevis and Newell, 1962), but at least in the Sudan they become increasingly crepuscular as the soil begins to dry (Cloudsley-Thompson, 1962a).

IV. Myriapods

Desert myriapods display activity patterns that probably reflect both feeding behavior and body mass. For example, the scolopendromorph centipede *Scolo-*

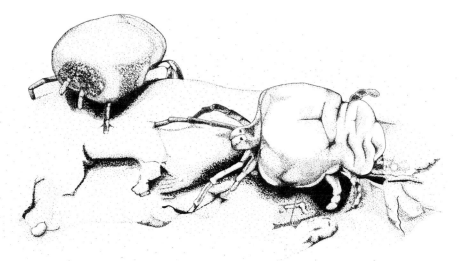

Fig. 5. *Dinothrombium* mites on soil surface after summer rain, Big Bend National Park, Texas. (From a photograph by the author)

pendra polymorpha (Fig. 6a) is decidedly nocturnal in its habitat and in controlled environments (Cloudsley-Thompson and Crawford, 1970), while the larger species, *S. heros,* can sometimes be seen moving freely in the open during daylight hours (personal observation). If the cuticle of *S. polymorph* is an impermeable as that of *S. heros,* the greater size of the latter may account for its unexpected diurnal behavior.

The desert millipede *Orthoporus ornatus* (Fig. 6b) is a large detritivore that feeds diurnally and nocturnally during the summer in deserts of North America (Wooten et al., 1975). Unlike large desert centipedes, its aboveground behavior seems to be a complex function of seasonal rainfall and temperature, with photoperiod having no demonstrable influence. The same may be true for smaller atopetholid millipedes with which *O. ornatus* is generally sympatric, although the atopetholids are usually more confined to dense patches of vegetation (personal observation).

V. Insects

Since the small body mass of thysanurans and other apterygotes (Fig. 7) increases their potential for water loss in dry air, we might expect them to be nocturnal when on the desert surface. Indeed, it is only when temperatures are unusually high that the strong photonegative response of *Machiloides*

a

b

delanyi and *Ctenolepisma longicaudata* in southern Africa is modified (Heeg, 1967a).

Among the orders of desert orthopteroids one encounters two broad categories of light-associated diel behavior. A diurnal pattern applies to many hebivores such as locusts, grasshoppers, and phasmatids, as well as to carnivores like mantids (Fig. 8). Many of these fly, hop, or wander actively in search of their hosts. Phasmatids, however, tend to be sedentary. Studies of migratory locusts suggest an intriguing explanation for the relatively weak diurnal circadian rhythms of *Locusta migratoria* (Edney, 1937) and of *Schistocerca gregaria* (Cloudsley-Thompson, 1977b). The plasticity of their responses may allow these species to take advantage of ephemerally favorable food supplies and oviposition substrates, whereas if their rhythms were well entrained by photoperiod this opportunistic behavior would not be possible (Cloudsley-Thompson, 1977b).

While the example of the desert locusts suggests that strongly stereotyped *diurnal* behavior may be detrimental to some highly mobile species, a number of orthopteroid taxa seem to be rigorously *nocturnal*. This category of light-associated behavior characterizes many fossorial and crevice-inhabiting detritivores including true crickets (gryllids), and/or camel crickets (gryllacridids), and cockroaches. Assured of a relatively constant food supply in perpetually moderate microhabitats, insects like these have less need to move long distances for purposes of nutrition and reproduction.

It becomes more of a problem to distinguish between nocturnal versus diurnal patterns among the remaining groups of desert insects. In most families such behavior is at best only anecdotally documented. Thus, while it is obvious to anyone sampling with a sweepnet that many hemipterans in deserts are present on vegetation during the day, the relative activity of these insects at night is not at all clear. Among the Homoptera, desert cicadas are characteristically diurnal in their acoustic behavior (Heath and Wilkin, 1970; Heath et al., 1972), yet a floodplain species in arid regions of North America has a well defined crepuscular onset of chorusing that is partly attributable to a decrease in light intensity (Crawford and Dadone, 1979). Leafhoppers (Cicadellidae), treehoppers (Membracidae), and planthoppers (Fulgoroidae) are active by day in deserts (personal observation), but their nocturnal behavior seems not to have been examined. When one recalls that the polymorphic and sexual development of nondesert leafhoppers is highly responsive to photoperiod (Danilevsky et al., 1970), it makes sense to suspect that LD changes

---

Fig. 6. Myriapods with different diel activity patterns. **a** *Scolopendra polymorpha,* a nocturnally active scolopendromorph centipede, after removal of covering rock, Peloncillo Mountains. **b** *Orthoporus ornatus,* a spirostreptid millipede with diurnal and nocturnal activity, feeding on plant debris, central New Mexico desert grassland. (Photographs by the author)

a

b

a

b

Fig. 8. Mantids from the Negev desert. **a** Unidentified species with no unusual features. **b** *Eremiaphila* sp. with body coloration closely matching that of the soil in its habitat. (Photographs by the author)

Fig. 7. Apterygote insects on the underside of rocks. **a** Lepismatid thysanuran, Negev desert. **b** Machilid archaeognath, Peloncillo Mountains. (Photographs by the author)

can significantly affect life histories in these and other homopterans living in deserts.

One should be cautious in stating that butterflies, bees and wasps, and many flies and beetles are strictly diurnal, not only in deserts but the world over, for this observation applies generally to *adults,* and not necessarily to *larvae.* In the same vein, one usually associates moth activity with evening and night (there are, however, plenty of day-active moths in deserts—see, for example Fig. 9—and elsewhere), and tends to ignore diel patterns of their larvae. Larvae of most ants are subterranean and would not be expected to have activity rhythms, yet in some nondesert species adult males have LD-phased mating flights (McCluskey, 1965). Desert ants themselves forage at various times in the diel cycle, depending on the species as well as the season (Whitford, 1978a).

An example involving myrmeleontid neuropterans shows why generalizing about periodic activity can be misleading, even in a single species. It is not unusual to see the adults of these ant lions flying during the day in arid regions, and simultaneously to observe the conical pits their larvae make in sandy soil. However, larvae of *Myrmeleon obscurus* in southern Africa possess

Fig. 9. Example of a day-flying moth, *Zygaena graslini* (Zygaenidae), on annual flower, Negev desert. (Photograph by the author)

a circadian rhythm of pit-building activity that actually peaks at dusk (Youthed and Moran, 1969a). This is clearly adaptive behavior, because high soil-surface temperatures during the day often exceed the upper limits of thermal tolerance of virtually all desert insects. It is only in the evening, then, that the ant-lion larvae, buried below the pit bases by day, begin to ready their pits for a bout of nocturnal foraging (Youthed and Moran, 1969b).

Evening is also a time for adult emergence and mating among certain dune-associated coleopterans, and patterns of such behavior are known for Scarabaeidae in the southwestern U.S. Thus Hardy (1971) reports *Pseudocotalpa andrewsi* burrowing to the surface, emerging as darkness begins (Fig. 10), and then flying close to the surface for 10–15 min prior to copulating. In the same region short evening flights are also known for at least two other scarabaeid species (Howden and Hardy, 1971; Hardy, 1973). Instead of flying after crepuscular emergence, the dune-inhabiting lucanid *Pseudolucanus mazama* wanders over the surface before copulating (Hardy and Andrews, 1974).

One coleopteran family in particular deserves separate mention because of its ubiquity in deserts and because of the distinctly cyclic diel, as well as seasonal activity, found among many of its species. I refer to the Tenebrionidae, whose adults are often very common on desert surfaces at certain times of day, depending on the species and the season. For example, in the Namib desert locomotion of tiny *Cardiosis* tenebrionids is unimodal on cool-windy

Fig. 10. The scarabaeid, *Pseudocotalpa andrewsi,* after recent emergence from dune at dusk, Algodones Sand Dune System, California. [Photograph courtesy of F. G. Andrews (Hardy, 1971); with permission]

days and bimodal on hot days (Hamilton, 1971). Other genera in the Namib also have temporally predictable periodicities under natural conditions (Louw and Hamilton, 1972; Holm and Edney, 1973). *Eleodes* species in the southwestern U.S. exhibit similar patterns (Krehoff, 1975). No detailed tests of the separate effects of photoperiod and other abiotic factors seem to have been made, although Krehoff's work was done at a constant 26°C for 24 h under natural (window) illumination.

In a thorough review of flower visitation by solitary bees in the southwestern U.S., Linsley (1978) notes that in overcast weather there may be departures from pattern norms. In general, however, visitations occur during morning, afternoon, or evening. The first of these visitation periods is often associated with oligolecty (i.e., visiting few host species). Polylectic species appearing at certain flowers in the early morning are frequently larger-bodied than those arriving later on. Some bee species visit before dawn and after sunset. Other species work in shifts that are essentially staggered—with some overlap—throughout the day. Still others forage in early morning and late afternoon. Linsley believes that each generation learns when to visit flowering species relative to a number of variables including opening and closing of flowers, secretion of nectar, timing of anthesis, competition by other bees, and several physical factors. Light signals as well as temperature conditions seem to be important in regulating the relationship between nest-leaving and anthesis in the host flower.

VI. Assessment of Diel Periodicities

The assumption raised at the beginning of this section was that desert invertebrates possess well defined responses to light. Subsequent examination of the known facts showed that some periodicities are indeed well defined (e.g., nocturnal behavior in many Solifugae), while others are more faculative in expression (as in migratory locusts). Some groups such as scorpions and fossorial or crevice-dwelling orthopteroids are almost exclusively nocturnal. Many adults and probably larvae of butterfly species seem correspondingly diurnal. *Orthoporus ornatus* is an arthropod with activity patterns probably unrelated to light, while ant lions exemplify stage-specific temporal activity. Obviously, an enormous variety of patterns exists.

Yet two general sorts of ecologically meaningful trends seem to emerge from this assortment of temporal repertoires. One encompasses a large number of related as well as unrelated taxa that are basically nocturnal. These organisms range considerably in terms of their longevities, trophic levels, sizes, colors, and abilities to resist water loss. Presumably, they use LD cues for activity timing. In the absence of a more plausible explanation, it is tempting to conclude that avoidance of predation has been a powerful unifying link in the selection of nocturnality among these species. (A logical counter to this view is that there are many nocturnal predators in deserts.) It would be interesting to compare the extent that nocturnality characterizes desert versus nondesert taxa having close phylogenetic affinities. One might predict that the latter are also nocturnal if predation has in fact been a strong selective force in their evolutionary history.

The other general trend is of course diurnal, and it also applies to a bewildering array of species. If they have a common response to light in deserts, it may be that their diurnality is only loosely coupled with LD signals. In that sense they may be classified as "environmental opportunists" in comparison to strictly night-active taxa and perhaps in comparison to their nondesert relatives as well. Members of this second category may in fact be exposed to at least as much predation, and to even more physical stress than members of the nocturnal fauna.

Adaptations to a diurnally active life in desert invertebrates surely include resistance to water loss (although many nocturnal scorpions are superbly adapted in this respect), ability to thermoregulate behaviorally, and in many instances considerable mobility (although night-flying insects are certainly mobile too). Many of the more mobile groups (millipedes, locusts, adults of many insects) utilize "fine-gained" food, shelter, and oviposition resources. Furthermore, unless these species possess suitable defense mechanisms they are prone to predation and abiotic stress as they move from one resource to another.

It is evident that evolutionarily meaningful generalizations regarding adaptation to light in desert invertebrates are difficult to make. Moreover, we cannot readily distinguish between such adaptations in desert inhabitants and those in animals from more mesic environments. There is still not enough evidence available to make a valid claim for any uniqueness of diel light-response patterns among invertebrates in arid regions.

C. Seasonal Periodicities of Desert Invertebrates

Since seasonal periodicities may be viewed as adaptations to habitat heterogeneity in time and space, an adaptive life-history strategy should anticipate significant changes in the environment. For many temperate-zone species anticipation of habitat deterioration involves reception of and response to changing daylengths (Danilevsky et al., 1970). This capacity enables many arthropods to avoid potentially unfavorable conditions by migrating or by entering the developmental state known as diapause (Dingle, 1972). Additional forms of metabolic and/or physical inactivity in terrestrial invertebrates range from the practically nonliving state of crypto- or anhydrobiosis (Crowe and Cooper, 1971) to simple quiescence (Mansingh, 1971). Increased resistance to extreme temperatures and to dryness is roughly proportional to the intensity of the dormant state.

How reliable photoperiod is as a predictor of rainfall in deserts does not seem to be known. Granted, some deserts have relatively well-defined rainfall seasons, but as we noted earlier, a great amount of annual variation characterizes precipitation patterns in regions of low rainfall. Therefore, we can hypothesize that rather than relying extensively on photoperiod to predict activity-synchronizing rainfall events, desert invertebrates should in general be more responsive to other cues enabling them to take advantage of pulses of moisture. One possibility is to be phenologically responsive to seasonal temperatures—which are not as erratic as rainfall—and thereby to be in a state of physiological readiness when a suitable amount of moisture arrives. Dormant and/or soil-bound species such as *Orthoporus* millipedes may be examples of this category. Annual cycles of development in soil-bound larvae of elaterid and scarabaeid beetles may be geared to yearly oscillations of temperature in the absence of light (Danilevsky et al., 1970). At the thermally "correct" time of year these and many other species may be particularly susceptible to a rainfall stimulus (see below).

A more direct option is to be completely dependent on ambient moisture conditions. Desert nematodes are probably good examples of this alternative; they respond to decreasing soil moisture by undergoing anhydrobiosis (Freckman, 1978) (Fig. 11). Also, regional rainfall differences in the Sahara seem to correlate with the seasonal activities of certain geographically separated

Fig. 11. Bacterial-feeding nematode, *Acrobeloides* sp. from the Mojave desert, in state of anhydrobiosis. (Photograph courtesy of D. W. Freckman)

populations of tenebrionid species. Evidence of generally earlier seasons of activity in northern populations experiencing winter rainfall than in southern populations experiencing summer rainfall was presented by Mateu and Pierre (1974).

Opportunistic use of photoperiod, moisture, and temperature by the Australian plague locust *Chortoicetes terminifera* is reviewed by Matthews (1976). This arid-zone species lays diapause as well as nondiapause eggs. The latter are inserted more deeply into the soil in summer than in winter, thereby avoiding an inappropriate hatching stimulus of light rains arriving during hot weather. Similar rains promote hatching of nondiapause eggs near the surface in winter, but diapause eggs hatch later. Thus an array of hatching possibilities, conditioned by a combination of genetic and environmental factors, is available to this species and helps to insure its survival in an unpredictable habitat. It is the direction rather than the absolute value of photoperiodic and temperature change that determines whether the plague locust lays diapause or nondiapause eggs. In contrast, the grasshopper *Austroicetes cruciata,* which inhabits a part of Australia with a Mediterranean climate, lays only obligate-diapause eggs (Andrewartha and Birch, 1954). These remain dormant during the dry, hot summer and hatch during the relatively predictable, moist winter when survival possibilities are comparatively great.

Added flexibility of response in arid regions is shown by a desert strain of chrysopid neuropterans. Tauber and Tauber (1978) review their own earlier work indicating that while the *mohave* and *carnea* strains of *Chrysopa carnea* both have a photoperiod-controlled diapause in fall and early winter, the former (desert) strain can reproduce in spring in response to abundant prey. [Winter rainfall characterizing the Mojave desert in North America is associated with a considerable production of annual plants (Mulroy and Rundel, 1977), which in turn are fed upon by herbivorous insects.] Moreover, the *mohave* strain can enter or terminate summer diapause if prey are scarce, the response being regulated by the prey.

A set of general relationships among arthropods links daylength to diapause and voltinism (Danilevsky et al., 1970). Hibernal diapause in multivoltine species (those with more than one generation a year) is facultative and induced by the shortening of daylength. These species may also enter an aestival diapause and avoid hot, dry summers. Diapause in univoltine species, on the other hand, seems always to be obligatory and is induced by a variety of photoperiods. In both groups of arthropods diapause is affected by temperature. Finally, there is diapause in species with "perennial cycles"; these arthropods develop in water or solid substrates like wood. In certain "perennial" insects (e.g., lasiocampid moths) synchronization of pupation and adult emergence is based on a diapause controlled by photoperiod and temperature.

Are the above patterns as applicable to desert species as they are to taxa from climatically more predictable regions? In the first instance (multivoltinism) data are insufficient to allow a meaningful answer, although in regard to diapause induction one might expect short-lived species like aphids and leafhoppers to respond to photoperiod in deserts much as they do elsewhere. In the case of univoltine species, we have already noted an example (desert chrysopids) indicating photoperiodic induction of an obligate diapause succeeded in time by the facility to respond opportunistically to other kinds of environmental signals. Another option of course is to have both diapausing and nondiapausing individuals in the same species simultaneously (as in the plague locust); this also assures flexibility of response.

Diapause is maintained by several kinds of responses to daylength and temperature (Tauber and Tauber, 1976). While few demonstrations of this function have been recorded from field populations, it might be expected of multi- and univoltine desert species that rigid diapause maintenance of any sort would occasionally conflict with the need to take rapid advantage of unpredictable resources. The same argument can be extended to long-lived species like desert snails (Shachak et al., 1976a) and millipedes (Wooten and Crawford, 1974) that in warm weather rapidly shift from inactivity to a feeding state when sufficient moisture becomes available. However, this shift occurs only if moisture arrives during the "correct" season—otherwise intrinsic (diapause-maintaining?) constraints seem to prevent the possibility of such a response.

It is in fact questionable whether photoperiod has anything to do with the inactive states of these long-lived animals. Instead, it may be that physical inactivity accompanied by reduced metabolism is a direct or phenological response to a decreased supply of moisture and/or food. Thus desert snails must be activated by moisture before they can commence feeding on higher plants and cryptogams (Yom-Tov and Galun, 1971). Scorpions, which are also long lived, are also faced with an unpredictable food supply in deserts. For these carnivores starvation, accompanied by reduced metabolism, is likewise a useful way of coping with reduced food abundance (Riddle, 1978). Similarly, in *Dinothrombium* mites the decline in termite prey, once swarm-promoting rains have ceased, coincides with a return to their subterranean burrows (Tevis and Newell, 1962). Increasing heat and decreasing moisture are the most likely inducers of the return, and renewed rainfall—again in the appropriate season for the species concerned—can promote a rapid re-emergence. This pattern also characterizes certain species of Mojave desert tenebrionids (Thomas, 1979).

In effect, lack of rainfall maintains what amounts to a state of starvation, which can be extremely long in some desert species. Examples are cicada wasps and boarmiid moth pupae in Australia (Matthews, 1976), and a swallowtail butterfly pupa in the southwestern deserts of North America (Emmel and Emmel, 1973). Prolonged inactivity followed by rapid emergence at rainfall onset is also known for a univoltine tephritid fly pupa in arid parts of Peru (Smythe, 1960, cited by Bateman, 1972).

An interesting case of opportunistic timing in regard to rainfall involves *Callophrys macfarlandi*. This lycaenid butterfly displays a single, staggered adult emergence from March through May in southern New Mexico. Its larva feeds exclusively on beargrass, *Nolina texena,* which blooms between March and June. During one unusually wet summer *Nolina* flowered again in August. Simultaneously, and most unexpectedly, the butterfly emerged from its pupal diapause and presumably began to oviposit on the new growth (R. Holland, personal communication).

It seems, therefore, that the diapause model proposed by Danilevsky et al. (1970) needs to be modified for desert species. Resource availability (expressed directly or via moisture) can induce, enforce, and terminate a dormant condition in a variety of "perennial" species, and can in the right seasons also induce and terminate diapause in univoltine species. The significance of rainfall as a driving force in desert ecosystems must again be recognized, while the role of photoperiod—although important in many cases—seems of less general importance to the seasonal organization of the lives of many invertebrate species.

Chapter 4
Water Relations: Short-Term Water Balance

A. Introduction

Because small animals have relatively high surface-area:volume ratios they risk rapid desiccation in dry air. Nevertheless, many invertebrates, expecially arthropods, have successfully colonized arid environments. This apparent paradox has for many years intrigued biologists, who continue to investigate its ecological and physicochemical basis.

Recent reviews of the extensive literature on water relations in arthropods (Cloudsley-Thompson, 1975; Edney, 1977; Arlian and Veselica, 1979) reveal indirectly that most moisture-related studies of desert species are performed in laboratories using specimens of widely varying taxonomic affinities and ages. Although this approach provides useful comparative information, it also has some drawbacks. One problem is that examining water relations over a matter of hours or even days may tell us rather little about how an animal maintains moisture levels over longer periods. Another difficulty is the inevitable artificiality of the laboratory itself, which while allowing for a reduction in experimental variables also makes extrapolation of results to more natural situations somewhat unrealistic. Needless to say, if one's eventual goal is to understand how a species uses water in its environment, then both short- and long-term studies should be undertaken. Moreover, where possible, data should be obtained from animals in or only recently removed from their habitats. This caution applies to deserts in particular because of their generally low and unpredictable water resources.

The term "water balance" describes the state of hydration relative to water uptake and loss. We shall now briefly cover these two components of hydration state as they apply to desert invertebrates. Following that, a more holistic approach will be used to compare the desiccation resistance of species belonging to certain ecological categories. While looking at water balance in these two ways, we should recall earlier discussions of the significance of water in deserts, and also note accordingly whether desert species seem unusually well adapted for maintaining water balance.

B. Water Loss

The main avenues of water loss in most animals are integumentary, respiratory, and excretory. Defensive secretions are also potentially quite important in some desert species.

The integument of nonarthropodan invertebrates consists generally of a single-layered epidermis (in land snails) or a thin, chitinous cuticle secreted by the epidermis (in nematodes and annelids). In neither case does the extent of conspicuous fine structure match that seen in arthropods. Nevertheless, hibernating and aestivating desert snails resist water loss very well, one probable reason being that, when dormant, land snails appear to have an ill-defined but most effective waterproofing barrier within the apical zone of the epidermis (Machin, 1974). Water loss does occur, however, across both the mucous epiphragm and shell of desert snails (Warburg, 1965a). Likewise, cuticular thickness in earthworms from moist soils in Egypt is not in itself an adequate explanation for their comparative resistance to drying (El-Duweini and Ghabbour, 1968).

Among arthropods, on the other hand, it is generally accepted that a well-structured cuticle is responsible for a substantial amount of desiccation resistance. Moreover, data from many sources (see for example Edney, 1977) strongly suggest that resistance increases in species inhabiting arid environments. This relationship also holds for tenebrionid beetles (Edney, 1971a) and scorpions (Crawford and Wooten, 1973) when size—and therefore surface area—is eliminated as a variable. Such reduced cuticular transpiration has long been associated with epicuticular properties. Work at the biochemical level with desert tenebrionids (Hadley, 1977, 1978) and scorpions (Hadley and Jackson, 1977; Toolson and Hadley, 1977, 1979) suggests that epicuticular permeability decreases in certain species as a function of high levels of long-chain branched hydrocarbons and/or long-chain fatty acids. Hydrocarbons were the most abundant lipids in the epicuticles of *Diceroprocta apache* desert cicadas (Hadley, 1980). Not surprisingly, the adults of these homopterans, which are the only active stage exposed to hot dry conditions, possessed about five times the quantity of hydrocarbons determined for nymphs.

Recent studies of cuticular ultrastructure in a desert scorpion (Hadley and Filshie, 1979) and a desert millipede (Walker and Crawford, 1980) also implicate considerable lipid involvement. Other modes of cuticular resistance have been invoked as well (see Edney, 1977, for a review of these), and now it seems clear that the arthropod integument is far more complex than once imagined.

In nematodes, annelids, some acarines, and small apterygote insects, gas exchange takes place directly across the moist integument. Among other terrestrial invertebrates various structures reduce the size of respiratory openings or the degree to which these apertures are exposed to outside air. Thus, the highly vascularized lung of pulmonate gastropods opens through a single small pneumostome that closes following each inspiration. Also, branchial chambers in the Australian desert crab *Holthuisana transversa* enclose gills which have undergone reduction in size and number, thereby serving as functional lungs (Greenaway and Taylor, 1976).

Many terrestrial isopods have brush-like respiratory invaginations, the pseudotracheae, located on pleopods on the undersurface of the abdomen. In mesic species respiratory surfaces are kept moist and gas exchange is facilitated by a capillary system that transfers substrate moisture to the pseudotracheae, but in xeric species the capillary system is lost (Warburg, 1968).

Book lungs and tracheal systems are clearly ideal for gas exchange in dry air because of their small spiracular openings and vast enclosed surface areas. Spiracular closing mechanisms are common in insects and involve neuromuscular control. More indirect means of control seem likely in myriapods, although the picture is still far from clear in that group (Stewart and Woodring, 1973; Curry, 1974). In desert tenebrionids the abdominal spiracles open into a subelytral cavity, but whether this arrangement reduces transpiratory water loss between body and ambient air has not been tested (Edney, 1977:69).

A peculiar form of behavior, namely conglobation or rolling up, is common to some terrestrial isopods and many millipedes. It should be a useful way to protect pleopods of desert armadillid isopods from drying (see Warburg, 1968), but in a desert millipede such coiling seems effective against water loss only at high temperatures (Crawford, 1972).

In ectotherms gas exchange and ventilation rates are generally proportional to metabolic rates. For this reason, no matter how well-protected surfaces may be, when desert species are exposed to warm dry air for any length of time they can lose significant amounts of water via respiratory transpiration. Indeed, it has been shown that desert tenebrionids (Ahearn, 1970b) and scorpions (Hadley, 1970a; Crawford and Wooten, 1973) appreciably increase the ratio of respiratory to integumental transpiration as temperatures approach upper lethal limits. Even more striking is the case of insects in flight, since that activity requires a comparatively enormous uptake of oxygen. Respiratory water loss in migratory locusts, for instance, can more than double during flight (Loveridge, 1968; Edney, 1977).

Metabolic rates can be lowered upon exposure to low relative humidities, a response that conserves body water. This is true for the bilimulid desert snail *Rabdotus schiedeanus* (Riddle, 1975). Dehydration can also reduce metabolism, as was shown indirectly by Loveridge (1968) for locusts (fasted specimens in dry air lowered their frequency of abdominal ventilation) and by MacMillen and Greenaway (1978) for the desert crab *Holthuisana*. Starvation, which is probably associated with dehydration in those desert invertebrates which acquire most of their water through feeding, also lowers metabolism in *Paruroctonus utahensis* scorpions. When starved, these arachnids display a reduced dependence of respiration rate on temperature (Riddle, 1978). In fact any invertebrate that reduces its respiratory rate in a range of habitat temperatures should conserve water accordingly. The significance of lowered respiratory temperature coefficients (Q_{10}'s) in desert species is discussed in Chapter 6 (D.II.2.).

Loss of water during excretion in many desert invertebrates is controlled by both highly regulated reabsorbing mechanisms and the chemical nature of nitrogenous products. Moreover, it is now well established that the capacity to regulate water and ion fluxes is inherent in the excretory structures and/or alimentary tracts of many arthropods. Those tissues and organs in turn respond to endocrine control, but the extent to which this happens appears to be partly a matter of phylogeny. Conventional methods of analysis and interpretation show that insects such as the desert cockroach *Arenivaga* (Edney, 1968) and the tenebrionid beetle *Eleodes hispilabris* (Riddle et al., 1976) from North America, as well as *Trachyderma philistina* tenebrionids from the Negev desert (Broza et al., 1976) and larvae of the Namib desert tenebrionid *Onymacris marginipennis* (Coutchié and Crowe, 1979), maintain relatively constant hemolymph osmotic pressures (OP's) as they are dehydrated or rehydrated. A similar condition was found in species of desert meloid beetles (Cohen and Pinto, 1977). Osmoregulatory capability appeared less well developed in the desert millipede *Orthoporus ornatus*, females regulating better than males in summer (Riddle et al., 1976) but not in winter (Crawford, 1978). Comparatively poor osmoregulation was thought to occur in the desert grassland scorpion *Paruroctonus utahensis* (Riddle et al., 1976); however, a reevaluation of the *E. hispilabris–P. utahensis* relationship, using a different index of osmoregulation, suggests that the scorpion may actually be a better osmoregulator (W. A. Riddle, personal communication). More studies are needed to verify the phylogenetic associations of osmoregulation in desert arthropods.

In land snails the blood osmolality of some species (including *Otala lactea*, a semidesert snail) is inversely related to body water content (Burton, 1966). Blood osmotic pressure (OP) also seems to be highest in species inhabiting dry places and can become diluted by 30% following water uptake during rain (studies cited in Warburg, 1965a).

The hemolymph OP of desert invertebrates is sometimes associated with changes in fluid volume within hemolymph, tissue, and gut "compartments." This aspect of water balance is best known from insects, where blood volume varies with age, sex, molting cycle, and dehydration (see references in Edney, 1977). Amounts of water in the diet and ambient air should also have a bearing on compartment volumes (Shaw and Stobbart, 1972). We shall refer to this matter again in the ensuing discussion.

Although blood in the hemocoel and fluid in the gut or malpighian tubules may often be isosmotic, concentrations of ions and other solutes vary a great deal between and within such compartments. As with hemolymph OP, ion ratios in hemolymph appear to be associated with phylogeny (Sutcliffe, 1963). Maintenance of stable ion concentrations in the blood depends on control of fluxes between compartments, which in turn influences the directional movement of water. Thus as hemolymph volume changes in larvae of the tenebrionid *Onymacris marginipennis,* concentrations of various ions, amino acids, and trehalose remain relatively constant (Coutchié and Crowe, 1979). In the scorpion *Hadrurus arizonensis,* dehydration and starvation result in concentrations of sodium and potassium in the ileum that favor the uptake of water (Ahearn and Hadley, 1977). And in the desert millipede *Orthoporus ornatus,* a hindgut sodium–potassium exchange mechanism appears to maintain hemolymph salt balance without transferring water from one compartment to the other (Moffett, 1975). Each of these examples may be viewed as an adaptation to the special needs of invertebrates that must frequently retain water otherwise lost during excretion.

The excretory product itself has an important role in water balance. It is common knowledge that discharge of the products of purine degradation (uric acid, allantoic acid, and related compounds in insects; guanine in arachnids) is an efficient way of conserving water, since these materials are relatively insoluble and nontoxic. Furthermore, storage of uric acid or urates, together with sodium, potassium, and ammonium, may provide an "ion sink" useful in osmoregulation (Mullins and Cochran, 1974, cited by Edney, 1977). A disadvantage of uric acid-type compounds and, to a lesser extent, of the more soluble product urea is their high investment in carbon, which is invariably lost as they are released.

In contrast ammonia, which is both toxic and soluble, would seem at first to be a poor nitrogenous material to excrete in xeric situations. Yet it may have certain advantages in species of isopods and snails, in which ammonia excretion is apparently an evolutionary holdover. Thus, in terrestrial species of both groups a high proportion of ammonia may be excreted as a water-free gas via the integument, within which it may also contribute to an alkaline environment favorable to the deposition of calcium carbonate (Wieser and Schweizer, 1972; Loest, 1979). In addition, ammonia molecules are carbon-free and thus their excretion has no effect on nutrient conservation. However, ammonia is not an exclusive product in these animals. The semidesert snail *Bulimulus dealbatus,* for example, accumulates high levels of urea (intermediate in toxicity and solubility between uric acid and ammonia) and some uric acid in its tissues (Horne, 1973), and when rehydrated following aestivation probably voids the accumulated urea (Horne, 1971a).

Finally, defensive secretions common to many desert invertebrates at times constitute an important avenue for water loss. The secretion of benzoquinones

(Eisner et al., 1965) from the repugnatorial glands of spirostreptid millipedes has never been quantified but might well be considerable when disturbance is continuous. Defensive secretions by the desert tenebrionid *Eleodes armata* accounted for nearly half of its total water loss in dry air between 25°C and 40°C under laboratory conditions (Ahearn, 1970b).

C. Water Uptake

In desert invertebrates water may be gained by ingestion, direct diffusion through the integument, active absorption of vapor from the air, and metabolic activity. The first and last of these are common to all species.

Ingestion by drinking would not at first seem to be a frequent practice in deserts, simply because of the usual lack of free-standing water. The presence of such moisture is more frequent than once thought, however, as the following examples will show. Aside from its temporary presence after rains, free water occurs as droplets when the dewpoint is reached. In Israel it was demonstrated that droplets can be imbibed directly by desert hemipterans, ants and beetles, while detritivorous tenebrionids and isopods have been seen ingesting damp hygroscopic plant material during and after heavy dews (Broza, 1979).

Most intriguing is the ability of the Namib desert tenebrionid *Onymacris unguicularis* to utilize water droplets formed on its body surface by advective fog. A forward-tilted posture, which is a typical defensive stance of many tenebrionids, is assumed by *Onymacris* on dunes as fog arrives. Droplets then slide toward the head and are easily consumed (Hamilton and Seely, 1976). Three species of *Lepidochora* tenebrionids in the same region trap fog by digging catchment trenches on sand dunes (Fig. 12a). The trenches concentrate moisture during fogs and allow the insects to extract significant amounts of body water. Presumably, they do this by drinking condensed water droplets (as Fig. 12b shows for *Cardiosis fairmairei*), although they may be able to remove water from wet sand by suction (Seely and Hamilton, 1976).

A number of arid-zone arthropods are in fact adept at procuring water from moist soil by exerting negative pressure. Among these are the whipscorpion, *Mastigoproctus giganteus*, which scoops damp sand toward the mouth with its massive pedipalps and then imbibes capillary water (Fig. 12c) (Crawford and Cloudsley-Thompson, 1971). Second instar *Diplocentrus peloncillensis* scorpions probably do the same (Crawford and Wooten, 1973) because, following desiccation and after being placed on moist soil, they gain nearly 10% of their original body weight. Older instars of desiccated *Paruroctonus utahensis* (Riddle et al., 1976), as well as *Urodacus yaschenkoi* scorpions (Shorthouse, 1971), also absorb water from moistened substrates. Rectal drinking by desiccated millipedes achieves the same effect and is accomplished in *Orthoporus ornatus* by spreading apart the two large plates comprising the anal segment and extruding rectal tissues (Crawford, 1972). Millipede larvae within moist fecal egg pellets probably also gain water by this method since they can take up over 9% of their body weight by rectal drinking from moist filter paper (Crawford and Matlack, 1979). On the other hand, water ingested by reproductives of *Hodotermes mossambicus* termites near the Kalahari desert is first absorbed into the hemolymph and then passed into specialized salivary reservoirs termed water sacs (Watson et al., 1971).

Use of mouthparts to puncture plant and animal tissues and thereby to obtain internal fluids is of course well known and will not be elaborated on here. However, rapid uptake of large amounts of fluids can lead to the reverse of the problem usually visualized for desert invertebrates. In other words many sucking insects and arachnids need to be able to concentrate nutrients from nutrient-poor sources like sap and blood and, simultaneously, to rid themselves of most of the water taken in.

Water also enters the desert invertebrate gut during ingestion of solid food. Eating fresh plant or animal tissue is a more efficient way of acquiring water than is consuming seeds (Reichman et al., 1979), so granivorous species like many harvester ants are at a relative disadvantage in this respect.

Direct diffusion of water across the integument as a form of uptake has not been unequivocally demonstrated in arthropods (Edney, 1977), but is of importance to nematodes (Marks et al., 1968) and earthworms (Edwards and Lofty, 1977: 110). Coiled desert nematodes arousing from anhydrobiosis usually rehydrate in water within minutes and resume activity within 24 h (Freckman et al., 1977).

Certain acarines, as well as some wingless insects, can absorb water from unsaturated air (Edney, 1977). Those doing so in deserts include the Namib thysanuran *Ctenolepisma terebrans,* which can absorb water vapor at 47.5% relative humidity (R.H.) (Edney, 1971a). Nymphs and adult females of the Mojave cockroach *Arenivaga investigata* can do this at an R.H. of 82.5% (Edney, 1966), which means that in their sand-dune habitat they need only to burrow downward a short distance to remain in water balance no matter how hot and dry the sand surface may be.

Active water-vapor uptake mechanisms have been reviewed by Edney (1977) and by Arlian and Veselica (1979). Uptake of water vapor across the rectal intima of thysanurans and *Tenebrio* beetles seems fairly certain, and acarines may absorb a hygroscopic fluid secreted near the mouth. Presently, the role of the cuticle seems questionable as a site for vapor uptake. In the Australian desert snail, *Sinumelon remissum,* the epiphragm takes up water from unsaturated air, although not in quantities considered to be physiologically useful (Warburg, 1965a). This property may be due to sphaerites composed mainly of calcium carbonate.

Lastly, metabolic water contributes continuously to the water balance of all aerobic organisms. As is suggested by examples in the next chapter, metabolic water may at times be a most important contribution to the survival of desert invertebrates, particularly when moist food or other external sources of water are scarce. For reasons discussed by Edney (1977), on an equal-weight basis oxidized fat is a better source of water than carbohydrate; however, on an equal-energy basis less water is made available by fat oxidation. Whatever the ecological advantages of using carbohydrates or fats may be, one would expect the evolutionary legacy and metabolic needs of the organism at the time to be major determinants of the kind of substrate most utilized.

D. Patterns Of Desiccation Resistance

While there is little evidence that desert arthropods tolerate lower water levels in their tissues than do species from mesic environments (Edney, 1974), many desert taxa are superior in terms of restricting body-water loss when stressed by prolonged exposure to dry air. It is in this sense that we now use the term "desiccation resistance." Even so, arthropods and other invertebrates are a heterogeneous assemblage in almost any habitat, and they do not restrict loss of body water equally well. In view of these observations we may wish to look for patterns of desiccation resistance in desert species. And if patterns are indeed evident, we may desire to explain them. Phylogenetic and/or ecological constraints would seem to be general causes of pattern diversity, but as the examples below illustrate, it is difficult to derive satisfactory generalizations even among taxonomically related or ecologically associated species.

Previously, we characterized soil- and crevice-inhabiting species as being generally surface-active at night and seldom encountering extremes of heat and aridity. In deserts these taxa include certain isopods, many Solifugae and scorpions, some centipedes and apterygote insects, and a number of orthopteroid insect species. Because of their nocturnal and often fossorial behavior there is little a priori reason to expect well-developed desiccation resistance in these arthropods. It turns out, however, that such an assumption is partly incorrect; in fact a review of the several parameters of arthropod transpiration listed by Edney (1977: Table 6) for representatives of these groups reveals a rather startling lack of uniformity. On the other hand, this apparent paradox may obscure trends amenable to analysis, a matter we now consider by looking at resistance patterns among major taxa.

At the outset we can recognize with some assurance that resistance is much greater in a number of warm-desert scorpions than in less xeric species (Edney, 1977: Table 6). It is less well developed in the Solifugae and in tarantulas and rather poorly developed in the whipscorpion *Mastigoproctus giganteus* (which is at best a marginal "desert species"). Are large-bodied desert arachnids as a group exceptionally well adapted to resist water loss?

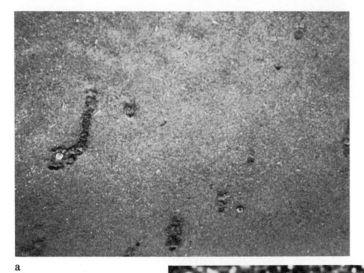

a

b

c

Perhaps, since body size is an important determinant of water-loss rates expressed in terms of original weight as well as surface area. However, we noted earlier that scorpion species living at different points along an ecological moisture gradient show a direct correlation between increasing habitat aridity and resistance to water loss. Since the same is true for nondesert spiders (Vollmer and MacMahon, 1974), one might expect such a relationship to hold for other arachnids as well. Thus, both phylogeny and habitat are probably strong determinants of resistance in this arthropod class.

Turning to nocturnal myriapods, it seems clear that large North American scolopendrid centipedes (Cloudsley-Thompson, 1956; Cloudsley-Thompson and Crawford, 1970) are not as resistant as many arachnids, being more like meloid beetles (Cohen and Pinto, 1977) and sphinx-moth larvae (Casey, 1977) in this respect. Still, these chilopods seem to have made some adjustment to desert conditions as they are definitely more resistant than congeneric and confamilial species from parts of eastern Africa (Cloudsley-Thompson, 1959), where pronounced dry seasons alternate with long rainy periods (J. G. E. Lewis, 1972). Therefore, both phylogeny and ecology seem also to have influenced the water relations of desert centipedes.

Certain apterygote insects are surprisingly abundant in deserts. That they are likely to be nocturnal is discussed by Wood (1971), and while the water relations of a series of desert species remains to be examined, it is apparent that collembolans in xeric habitats can be remarkably desiccation resistant (Poinsot-Balaguer, 1976; Vannier, 1978). Arid-adapted thysanurans are known to be most active on the soil surface just after sunset (Holm and Edney, 1973; P. Wygodzinsky, personal communication) and are also very resistant to water loss (Heeg, 1967b; Edney, 1971a). Thus nocturnal, primitive insects in deserts appear to have adapted in ways similar to arachnids and centipedes.

Judging from comparative transpiration studies of cockroaches (Edney and McFarlane, 1974; Edney, 1977) the well known North American desert polyphagid *Arenivaga investigata* (Fig. 13) is better equipped to resist water loss, particularly at high temperatures, than are several cosmopolitan species. During warm seasons *Arenivaga* species burrow upward in their sandy habitat at night (Hawke and Farley, 1973; Edney et al., 1974). Members of this fossorial genus have equilibrium receptors on their cerci that provide spatial-positioning information (Hartman et al., 1979). In addition, *A. investigata*

Fig. 12. Water uptake from moist substrates. a Use of catchment trenches in Namib desert sand dunes to trap fog; note *Lepidochora discoidalis* tenebrionids: one in a trench *(left center)*, the other in a shallow depression *(lower right)*. b Very small Namib tenebrionid (about 7 mm in length), *Cardiosis fairmairei*, tilting forward as it drinks condensed moisture from the sandy substrate. c The uropygid, *Mastigoproctus giganteus*, scooping moist sand toward its mouth; note extended chelicerae and use of pedipalps. (Photographs a and b courtesy of M. K. Seely; c by the author from a laboratory-maintained New Mexico specimen)

Fig. 13. The desert cockroach, *Arenivaga investigata,* from sand dunes near Palm Springs, California. Adult males (winged) and females. [Photograph courtesy of E. B. Edney (Edney, 1974); with permission]

follows vertical and horizontal moisture gradients, probably by using antennal sensilla (Edney et al., 1978). Likewise, the sand roach *Heterogamia syriaca* travels upward at dusk in its northern Egypt dune habitat, such behavior coinciding with temperature depression and dew formation (Ghabbour et al., 1977). Cockroaches therefore also conform to a general pattern of desiccation resistance explainable in phylogenetic as well as ecological terms.

What of diurnal desert species, most of which are insects? It can be inferred from a number of sources (see especially Edney, 1977) that their known resistance values not only vary within and among taxa but are also not as high as those of scorpions, which are mainly nocturnal. This suggests that maintenance of water balance in day-active species may depend less on highly developed desiccation resistance than on other attributes. Of these, the combined use of physiology and behavior on a scale somewhat different from that seen in nocturnal forms would seem likely.

Such reasoning gains support from a recent study of eupomphine meloid beetle adults by Cohen and Pinto (1977), who showed that all of the species they studied lost water with unexpected rapidity. Rapid water loss, however, is not always indicative of poor adaptation to xeric conditions. In fact, the osmoregulation of these beetles is comparatively strong. Even more significant, perhaps, is the observation that they eat plants containing all the water they need.

The premise that the hydration state of food may be a major determinant of desiccation resistance among diurnal desert invertebrates needs further examination. The issue was alluded to briefly in section C ("Water Uptake") and takes on added importance in the Coleoptera when one compares the high average resistance of largely detritivorous tenebrionids (Edney, 1977) to that of phytophagous meloids (Cohen and Pinto, 1977). Beyond that, there are simply not enough data to acquire a clear picture. Relatively poor resistance is seen in a locust (Loveridge, 1968) and a sphinx caterpillar (Casey, 1977), both of which feed on fresh plant material, but better resistance occurs in a carnivorous mantid (Délye, 1969). Data from desert ants (Délye, 1969; Whitford et al., 1975) tell us little because food gathered aboveground is not necessarily the same as that consumed (by adults) in the nest. Perhaps the relationship between desiccation resistance and food hydration would be most profitably approached by studying related taxa among which differences in food dryness are fairly pronounced and consistent, provided such species are available.

Timing of activity is another factor that may be generally related to water balance in diurnal species. For example, Krehoff (1975) showed that among five species of *Eleodes* tenebrionids in North American desert grasslands, two that are active in late afternoon or at night have relatively poor resistance to desiccation. Two others that are active when diel temperatures are higher are more resistant, while the species with the best ability to resist water loss is active during the hottest part of the day.

From these few examples we can see that to some extent physiology and, in particular, behavior must indeed be of great influence in the day-to-day regulation of water balance of diurnal desert species. Certainly phylogeny and habitat selection also contribute to the overall resistance to water loss, but the problem has different dimensions when diurnal and nocturnal groups are compared.

Chapter 5
Seasonal Water Relations: Long-Term Water Balance

A. Introduction

Surely the most informative periods for studying water balance in any organism are either over its lifetime or throughout the year if it is a perennial species. Periods of such magnitude allow the dynamics of water flux within the organism and between it and its microenvironment to be appreciated, and when enough is known about both fluxes it should be possible to predict from measurements of the physical environment the hydration state of a particular species. Unfortunately, achievement of such a comprehensive picture is technically difficult. Obviously, it would be most desirable to monitor water fluxes as they actually occur in nature. This has been attempted using isotopes for a few desert arthropods (Bohm and Hadley, 1977; King and Hadley, 1979), but such an approach is still in its pioneering stages in its application to invertebrates.

Patterns of long-term water balance are much less simple to describe in desert invertebrates than are rates of gain and loss recorded over short periods. Life-history considerations and changing habitat conditions introduce temporal complexity into any attempted description. For example, anhydrobiosis in desert nematodes (Freckman, 1978) and in Mediterranean scrub collembolans (Poinsot-Balaguer, 1976) enables those animals to survive long periods of extreme drought. Taking life history and habitat into account, we shall now review a number of cases dealing with water balance on a long-term basis. In doing this we shall concentrate first on species that spend most of their active lives associated with soil, and then look at an insect that begins life in the soil but develops, later, on and above the surface.

B. Soil-Associated Invertebrates

During the year or so that animals like desert cockroaches and isopods live, they must reach reproductive age and give birth to at least one new generation. This constraint sets them apart from other kinds of soil-associated invertebrates that have much longer prereproductive life spans. From studies in Egypt we can infer something about one of these short-lived arthropods, the polyphagid sand roach *Heterogamia syriaca.*

This common species of northern Egypt's coastal desert experiences two types of annual moisture pulse in its dune environment. Ghabbour et al. (1977) showed that the Mediterranean rainfall pattern effectively wets the habitat during winter, while between August and October condensation makes a lesser contribution. Feeding intensifies and reproduction occurs during these moist periods, and the density of *Heterogamia* at a depth of 50 cm correlates well with the percentage of soil moisture there.

Needless to say, climatic conditions in the hot summer are potentially more stressful to the water balance of *Heterogamia* than they are in winter. Moreover, since the species does not become truly dormant, a greater amount of respiratory transpiration should occur in summer. Of the avenues for compensatory moisture gain, ingestion of hydrated detritus near the surface would seem adaptive, as would uptake of water vapor. While the effects of neither of these sources have been analyzed to date, Ghabbour and Mikhail (1977) have examined aspects of the chemical composition of *Heterogamia* that relate to another way in which water (and energy for summer reproduction) may be made available.

These authors found that over the course of a year there is an inverse correlation between the animal's fat content (expressed as a percentage of body weight) and soil moisture at a depth of 50 cm. Actually, the correlation is better in summer than in winter ($r^2 = 0.42$ and 0.07, respectively). Ghabbour and Mikhail (1977) also took into account other meteorological factors and concluded that high fat contents are simultaneously associated with dry soil coupled with high temperatures and saturation deficits at the soil surface. If these conclusions are correct, then accumulated fat should contribute importantly to energy production in the hot, dry time of year. And, of course, it would remain an important source of metabolic water—along with carbohydrates—when acquisition of substantial moisture is otherwise improbable.

Another mechanism may also be responsible for maintaining water balance in summer. This entails a concomitant reduction of mineral ash content, which is felt by the authors to effect a release of bound water within cells at a time when metabolic activity most requires it.

Although desert cockroaches essentially "swim" through sand, the substrate collapses behind them as they move. In contrast, several kinds of long-lived soil invertebrates make extensive use of burrows they excavate. These include many scorpions, one of which is the Australian scorpionid *Urodacus yaschen-*

koi. Like *Heterogamia,* this fossorial arthropod seems not to undergo prolonged dormancy. In a study that encompassed a number of years, Shorthouse (1971) used computer simulation based on field and laboratory data to model various parameters of this carnivore's population and physiological ecology.

Urodacus forages nocturnally by remaining stationary at the mouth of its deep and rather elaborate burrow. However, individuals are not active every night, often staying instead inside the humid burrow. Thus whether the scorpion forages or remains deep within the burrow should have a distinct effect on its immediate water balance.

Shorthouse noted three important features of water loss in *Urodacus.* One of these is greater loss during summer, when ambient temperatures are high and humidities low, than in winter. Another is that scorpions coming to the surface at night lose markedly more water than do inactive scorpions in the burrow. A third feature is that large active scorpions lose a smaller proportion of their live weights per day than do second instar specimens. In summer this amounts to 1%–2% and 4%–5%, respectively, and means that without water gain adults should survive about 15 days while juveniles should live only half as long. During winter respective survival times should lengthen to 100 days and 20 days, depending again on size.

Predation itself does not provide enough ingested fluid to compensate for water loss by transpiration in *Urodacus.* Direct gain from wet soil is a potentially effective way of making up the difference, but the low frequency and quantity of moisture from local summer rains hardly insures this eventuality. Production of metabolic water is the final alternative for the active scorpion, although quantities of water provided this way were not estimated.

Clearly the best way of avoiding excessive water loss is to stay deep inside the burrow, but that tactic also precludes prey capture. Survival, under the circumstances, must therefore depend on the seasonal balance between frequency of nocturnal trips to the burrow entrance and time of arrival there with respect to ambient conditions. Shorthouse's study shows very effectively the close relationship that must exist between energy costs, potential water loss, and the probability of food capture by this burrowing scorpion.

Another long-lived burrower is the Australian desert crab *Holthuisana transversa.* Little is known about the life history of this unusual decapod. It spends the greater part of its life in burrows dug in heavy clay soils, which hold water effectively, and emerges only after heavy rains. Based on studies by Greenaway and MacMillan (1978) and MacMillan and Greenaway (1978), it seems that in response to progressively drier burrow air the crabs lower their oxygen consumption and enter a state of physiological dormancy. Naturally, this in turn reduces gas exchange and therefore total water loss as well.

During dehydration there is a corresponding rise in hemolymph OP and in concentrations of most major hemolymph cations. Changing rates of sodium concentration suggest that water in hemolymph and tissue compartments is lost proportionately. Apparently, burrow humidity does not remain constant because of diel fluctuations in soil temperatures; nevertheless, by ascending the burrows when burrow air temperature exceeds the dew point, the crabs should be in a position to have water condense on their surfaces. Droplets can then be absorbed across permeable surfaces like gills and the lung. On the other hand, when burrow R.H. is high, evaporative water loss is reduced, and metabolic water may then become a proportionately major source of water.

A less capable burrower, albeit a species that lives underground during most of its long life, is the North American desert millipede *Orthoporus ornatus*. Once ensconced in an overwintering hibernaculum, this large-bodied diplopod is usually unable to dig its way to the surface owing to the dryness of surrounding soil. Consequently, between the autumn months and early summer, when heavy rains wet the soil enough to permit emergence, *Orthoporus* can only adjust its water balance by physiological and metabolic means (Crawford, 1978).

The annual water balance cycle of a hypothetical animal 6 mm in diameter is shown in Fig. 14. Based on a gravimetric analysis of water in various compartments, it was shown that significant shifts take place within the animal while underground. The most striking of these is that water in cuticle and tissue increases progressively until the annual spring molt, which occurs in the hibernaculum and which causes some water loss. Since the amount of total body water between mid-winter and spring molt parallels that of the cuticle and tissue, it follows that water uptake must come from the immediate environment. Uptake by drinking is improbable because of the tightly coiled

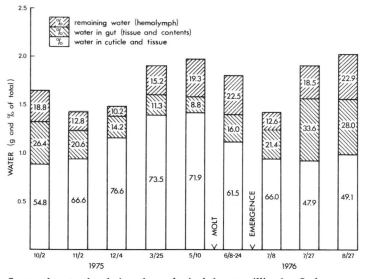

Fig. 14. Seasonal water levels in a hypothetical desert millipede, *Orthoporus ornatus,* having a midsegment width of 6 mm. Weights of water are based on regression analysis. (See Crawford, 1978, for details)

configuration of an overwintering millipede; also, calculated metabolic water production is insufficient to account for the entire influx. However, indirect evidence suggests that absorption from unsaturated air does occur, because regardless of the millipede's potential disadvantage with respect to measured concentrations of soil water activity, a net water gain takes place while *Orthoporus* is underground.

Behavioral regulation of water balance occurs once *Orthoporus* begins to feed on the surface. Uptake must then be mainly oral or anal. Although metabolism in summer provides more water than it does in winter, the contribution is relatively inconsequential. As reflected by the comparatively great amount of water in the gut of feeding specimens, uptake by oral or anal means must balance water lost mainly by cuticular transpiration. The latter is kept to appropriate levels by considerable cuticular resistance (Crawford, 1972) and by consistent behavioral thermoregulation (Wooten et al., 1975). Defecation and repugnatorial-gland secretions are water-loss routes in surface-active specimens.

Osmoregulation during the feeding and dormant seasons of the millipede appears to be an effective way of maintaining homeostasis, as is a certain amount of hemolymph ionoregulation (Pugach and Crawford, 1978). Early instars within their maternal fecal pellets are likewise capable of osmoregulation when surrounding soil begins to dry (Crawford and Matlack, 1979).

The food of *Orthoporus* and of the snail *Sphincterochila zonata* contains much detritus, although the snail is also a mud-feeding algavore. Both must ingest enough in the course of an active season to maintain energy and protein stores and, of course, to insure adequate internal water as well. Whereas *Orthoporus* has perhaps a quarter of the year in which to do this, only an average of 20 days a year is available to the mollusk, a common invertebrate in the Negev desert. The rest of the year it is inactive, but unlike *Orthoporus* its dormancy is most pronounced in the Mediterranean summer, which is hot and dry.

During the cool "rainy" season between December and April, most *S. zonata* are located under shrubs or are buried in the soil according to Shachak et al. (1976a). In a simulation model of water and energy flow through a snail population, these authors estimated that more water is lost during a day of winter hibernation (9–6 mg) than in a day of summer aestivation (0.5 mg). The same low summer loss value was also obtained Schmidt-Nielsen et al. (1971), who estimated that continuous drought conditions could therefore probably be tolerated for several years, even by animals on the surface.

Water balance in this desert snail is assured by the ability to switch quickly into and out of the active state in response to rainfall events. When the soil surface is adequately moistened, the activated snail can ingest about 45 times as much water in one day as it loses in a single day of hibernation. Reproduction as well as feeding is inhibited until sufficiently long wet periods occur, a fact that undoubtedly applies also to the other soil-associated species under discussion. In the case of *S. zonata,* the duration of habitat moisture must be on the order of a month, which means that new generations cannot be produced each year. Having a long life cycle is, in this instance, of fundamental importance to individual reproduction.

C. Desert Locusts

In the span of its annual lifetime, a desert locust experiences three kinds of environmental moisture regimes. The first is that of the soil, where independent life begins as an egg in a pod. Typically, the egg overwinters and the embryo inside is for some time in a state of diapause. The egg's chorion is so constructed that, unless the soil becomes exceedingly dry, water stress is probably seldom experienced by the embryo. So far as we know, liquid water, but not water vapor, is absorbed by eggs of locusts and other insects (Edney, 1977).

After hatching—which, depending on the locust species, may be delayed for over a year in severe drought (Andrewartha and Birch, 1954)—the growing insect is continually exposed to the ambient moisture of its second environment, the soil surface. Work by Loveridge (1974) with adult *Locusta migratoria* suggests that while young locusts are feeding in warm, dry air their main water loss should be fecal, provided food consists of fresh vegetation. However, if food is dry, then respiratory transpiration should become a major avenue of loss since internal water conservation results in increasingly dry feces. When very dry food is eaten for a prolonged period, water uptake in adults is reduced and metabolic water increases in relative importance (Loveridge and Bursell, 1975). An indirectly related effect of suboptimal food was made evident by Ellis and Carlisle (1965), who demonstrated that when adult *Schistocerca gregaria* feed on senescent vegetation their reproductive maturity is delayed. This response is important to the hydration of the next generation since it initiates events that bring about egg hatching when rains arrive.

As *Locusta* develops, a reciprocal relationship exists between its body water and body fat (Loveridge, 1973). (It would be interesting to know if this is a widespread condition. For example, does it occur in *Heterogamia* sand roaches?) Following the last molt, blood volume lowers, although blood OP remains steady and an internal redistribution of water and ions is effected (Lee, 1961).

The third milieu in which a desert locust spends much time is encountered during migration. Adults then travel considerable distances between feedings, often flying at altitudes of several kilometers above the desert floor. Here, daytime temperatures are cooler and relative humidities higher than at the soil surface. Internally, too, there is a major difference since the migrating locust has now become a functional endotherm. Not only does it generate considerable heat as it flies for hours at a time, but as a result of this effort it produces a much greater amount of metabolic water than before. Moreover, its ventilation increases by an order of magnitude (Weis-Fogh, 1967). However, because of the relatively cool air at a high altitude, diffusion gradients of water between spiracles and air are less steep than they would be simultaneously on the ground. Regardless of this, the energetics of flight dictate that respiratory transpiration must be a major form of water loss during migration and that, unless frequent stops are made to insure that more water is taken in via the gut, the obvious source of replenishment must come from water formed by oxidation.

D. Summary Comments

Taken as a whole, desert invertebrates are so diverse that their patterns of long-term water balance are not easily conceptualized. This becomes increasingly clear if the somewhat limited array of examples just cited is expanded by the addition of species capable of undergoing seasonal anhydrobiosis (e.g., desert nematodes and collembolans, taxa that have not been well studied in terms of seasonal water balance). Notwithstanding the attendant problems of exposing patterns, it is still possible to outline some general trends from the coverage given above.

One trend has to do with burrows and burrowing ability. Species able to construct well-defined burrows (e.g., certain isopods, crabs, and scorpions) or that are capable of moving freely about in the sandy substrate (e.g., sand roaches) seem to be active for most of the year, depending on temperature. They use behavioral means to gain access to ingestible water, condensation water, and regions of favorable humidity. In contrast, poor burrowers (e.g., certain millipedes and snails) tend to be inactive in or on the soil for long periods. In such a state behavior is not a determinant of water balance, which must instead be regulated by physiological means entirely.

Another trend is illustrated when desert invertebrates are active on or near the surface. There, the principal ways by which water is gained and lost are ingestion and defecation, respectively. Depending on surface conditions, cuticular and respiratory transpiration also contribute greatly to loss, as can occasional defensive secretions. Then, too, uptake can be augmented by water-vapor absorption and by metabolism. Whether principal or secondary, however, each of these avenues depends on behavior, for it is the combination of locomotion, body orientation, and use of shelter that controls exposure to factors that add or remove water.

Finally, in flying insects, and probably in heat-stressed nonflying forms as well, respiratory transpiration can markedly influence water loss. To some extent loss is compensated for by an automatic increase in the production of metabolic water. Paradoxically, metabolic water can also be a fairly significant moisture source for soil-bound species that are inactive.

Chapter 6
Temperature Relations

A. Introduction

Were it not for an integrated suite of adaptations, temperature extremes in desert habitats would allow few invertebrate species to survive. To be of value, especially in hot weather, these adaptations must result in a balance between incoming and outgoing radiant energy; in effect, they must insure that components of thermal flux sum nearly to zero on a diel basis.

In the present section we shall first discuss the major components of heat transfer that pertain to organisms like desert invertebrates, and then examine morphological properties that modify the thermal effects of such components. After that we shall turn to the more energetically expensive means of maintaining thermal balance, namely the involvement of behavior and physiology (including metabolism). Since seasonal changes and thermally stressful environments are typical of many deserts, special consideration is given to metabolic adaptations to these conditions.

B. Thermal Budgets Describing Thermal Balance

Knowing the conditions under which ectotherms achieve thermal equilibrium with their immediate environments tells us something about the ecological and physiological requirements of these organisms. A note of caution is in order, however, because ecologically and physiologically optimal thermal environments are not necessarily the same. Huey and Slatkin (1976) made that point for lizards, but it applies equally well to other ectotherms. Yet, while it is important to be aware of this caution, the development of a thermal budget is still a useful step toward predicting how an ectotherm should behave in a given habitat.

Thermal budgets are essentially models of heat fluxes existing between organisms and their ambient environments. Once fluxes measured under controlled conditions are related to field situations, one should be able to estimate parameters—such as rates of ingestion or metabolism—that affect reproductive fitness in natural populations. While complex models of this sort have not yet been generated for desert invertebrates, we can get an idea of the information they require by examining several simpler situations involving the thermal budgets of tenebrionid beetles.

Equations describing thermal budgets must be reduced to common terms, such as energy arriving or leaving per surface-area unit per time. Measurements of net energy input (gain) should include respiratory metabolism (M) and net radiation load (R), while those representing net energy output (loss) should include evaporation (E), conduction (K), and convection (C). Negative values can apply to R, and positive values to K and C.

Our first budget was developed for *Eleodes armata* by Hadley (1970b), who constructed a model based on laboratory conditions selected to simulate mid-morning conditions on the desert floor in June near Tempe, Arizona. All values in the following equation are in cal $\cdot$ cm^{-2} $\cdot$ min^{-1}:

$$\begin{array}{ccccccc} M & + & R & = & E & + & K & + & C \\ 0.003 & & 0.170 & & 0.005 & & 0 & & 0.134 \end{array}$$

By slightly altering the values for assumed reflectance (part of R) and actual wind velocity (which would affect C), Hadley came very close to balancing the equation. Even without perfect balance, however, this instantaneous picture of a desert beetle in equilibrium with its thermal habitat really only has two flux components of significance, namely R and C. It can be readily appreciated that the budget is appropriate for large, well-waterproofed black beetles whose long legs make minimal contact with the substrate.

A more comprehensive study of thermal budgets was made by Henwood (1975b) for two tenebrionid species from the Namib desert. Relatively hot, early May conditions were approximated and applied to interspecific differences in morphology, diel surface activity, and habitat. Of the two beetles, *Onymacris plana* is large, black, shiny, and pancake-shaped. It has a bimodal morning and afternoon periodicity, and inhabits a variable interdune environment where shrubs provide food in the form of blossoms and fruits. In contrast, *Stenocara phalangium* is much smaller. It is also black after its white emergence coat wears off. Pear-shaped with extremely long legs, this species is most active at midday and inhabits less variable interdunes where ephemeral grasses provide food in the form of dried crowns.

While Henwood's original report should be consulted for details of the model, body temperatures (T_B) of both species were recorded from a series of experimental conditions and were used to generate the following predictions: (1) if *O. plana* is placed in the habitat of *S. phalangium* its T_B will rise to lethal levels; and (2) each species will use the warmest sublethal environments available for as long as possible each day, a strategy called "maxithermy." Henwood concluded that since high temperatures result in high metabolic rates, which in turn necessitate high rates of food ingestion, maxithermy should work well when food is abundant. He also speculated that when food is limited because of environmental changes or competitive interactions, there should be subsequent selection for cooler thermal environments, which would bring about lower metabolic rates. For our purposes, the merit of these interpretations is of less importance than the fact that they were made from a thermal model in the first place. It will be interesting to see how far this type of research is pursued as increasing use is made of deserts.

C. Morphological Adaptations

I. Dead Air Spaces

By retarding heat transfer in rapidly changing thermal environments, insulation inherent in an ectotherm's morphology should allow time for behavioral adjustments to be made before T_B reaches dangerous levels. An example of this capacity is illustrated by the desert snail, *Sphincterochila zonata*. When aestivating in the Negev desert, its body is positioned in the shell directly above a large dead-air space between the bottom whorl and the ground (Fig. 15). When the ground surface is hot, nonmoving air in the space keeps the snail above about 5°C cooler than if the space were filled with water or tissue. Clearly, such a space can have great survival value to an immobile snail in hot weather (Schmidt-Nielsen et al., 1972).

Certain flightless beetles with subelytral cavities are examples of more mobile invertebrates with large dead-air spaces. While early studies suggested an insulating capacity for subelytral cavities (see references in Cloudsley-Thompson, 1964a, 1970), no difference between temperatures inside and directly outside the cavity was found by Cloudsley-Thompson (1964b) for *Pimelia grandis* in the Sudan. On the other hand, Hadley (1970b) determined that the subelytral cavity of *Eleodes armata* could be up to 7°C warmer than outside air when beetles were exposed to direct sunlight, and concluded that the space may function both in convective cooling and in buffering heat conducted inward. Since the configuration of the space itself is highly variable among flightless tenebrionids (Koch, 1961), its insulative effects are probably quite different in different species.

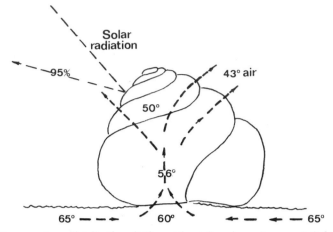

Fig. 15. Temperature distribution (°C) and heat flow in and around *Sphincterochila zonata* exposed to sun on the desert surface. Maximal recorded temperatures are shown, as are heat flows *(broken arrows)* and solar radiation *(long dashes).* (Schmidt-Nielsen et al., 1971; with permission)

II. Limb Length

Long legs that raise the body of an animal well above the ground increase its distance from the heat boundary layer next to the surface. In certain arthropods this combination of posture and morphology is augmented by minimal tarsal contact with—and therefore heat conduction from—the substrate. Desert species to which this description applies include ants, wasps, and beetles. Some anthicid beetles, for example, "stilt" on a warm surface by elevating their bodies as much as possible (Peterman, 1973). Stilting is also characteristic of the southern African scorpion *Opisthothalamus latimanus,* which, by remaining at the mouth of its burrow in the daytime, is exposed to high surface temperatures (Alexander and Ewer, 1958).

III. Color

The significance of dark coloration in desert animals holds much biological interest, because so many melanistic species live in xeric regions. The matter is also quite controversial. One school of thought considers dark coloration important because of a presumed association with maxithermy (Hamilton, 1973). Evidence for the maxithermy hypothesis was alluded to above, and some support for it can also be gained from experiments showing that both natural (Edney, 1971b) and artificial (Hadley, 1970b) white elytra of desert tenebrionids can lower T_B in direct sunlight.

A plausible argument can also be made that most ectotherms are in effect maxitherms regardless of their coloration (Cloudsley-Thompson, 1977c). Moreover, color itself appears generally to have only a minor effect on the T_B of insects exposed to sunlight, since a high proportion of energy is transmitted at infrared wavelengths (Bursell, 1974).

Those skeptical of an evolutionary association between maxithermy and melanism in desert invertebrates emphasize instead the importance of mimicking black coloration in order to escape predation. Such an emphasis implies that black is an aposematic or warning color, and seems mainly based on the fact that many black tenebrionid and carabid beetles (in deserts but also in other environments) secrete noxious chemicals when disturbed. Since these secretions are generally considered defensive (Eisner and Meinwald, 1966; Doyen and Somerby, 1974; Tschinkel, 1975), it follows that black coloration, which stands out vividly against most desert soils, may indeed be aposematic. While not all black desert tenebrionids secrete noxious chemicals, some other desert animals look and act remarkably like these and other black beetles. Mimics include the cerambycid beetle *Moneilema* (Raske, 1967) and even a juvenile lizard (Huey and Pianka, 1977). It should be mentioned, however, that experiments designed to test the effectiveness of tenebrionid secretions against vertebrate predators have not demonstrated conclusively a protective value (Slobodchikoff, 1978).

While more and careful research on the subject is called for, the indirect evidence is fairly convincing that among desert animals black is of aposematic significance and is frequently mimicked. Even melanic patches contrasting with red and orange are apparently mimicked among scarabaeid beetles in the Namib desert. According to Holm and Kirsten (1979), these patches are probably of little importance in temperature regulation.

Less controversy is attached to the thermal adaptiveness of pale (not white) coloration among desert animals. Since so many pale species are nocturnal, and since to human eyes at least they blend in well with most desert substrates, the idea that pale coloration has mainly a cryptic value (Cloudsley-Thompson, 1979) seems reasonable. Moreover, it has been widely accepted for more than a century that animals in arid regions are relatively depigmented compared to species in humid environments. This concept is usually called "Golger's Rule" (see discussions in Balsbaugh and Tucker, 1976; Holm and Kirsten, 1979). Still, the whole question of light and dark coloration relative to climatic variables is not subject to simple resolution. Too many variables are involved for that, a point made obvious by the seemingly contradictory associations of dark-colored insects with cool and dry, as well as humid climates (Balsbaugh and Tucker, 1976).

White pigment, on the other hand, is sufficiently reflective to be of demonstrable benefit in reducing T_B. Reference has already been made to the temperature-reducing effects of white elytra, and these effects are even more pronounced in desert snails having white shells. *Helicella seetzeni* and *Sphincterochila zonata* in the Negev desert, for example, reflect 80%–90% of incoming light at 500 nm, compared with 29% reflected by surrounding loess soil at the same wavelength. This finding may explain most of the difference between *S. zonata* shell temperatures and those of adjacent soil (Yom-Tov, 1971b). Schmidt-Nielsen et al. (1971) elaborated on these observations and demonstrated a life-enabling thermal gradient existing between the hot desert surface and the tissue of the snail (see Fig. 15). In actuality, high shell reflectance is augmented in this system by slow thermal conductance from the substrate, which, as mentioned earlier, is a function of insulation by a dead-air space.

IV. Integumental Properties Other Than Color

When the surface of an organism absorbs incoming radiant energy, a proportion of that energy can be transmitted internally, thus heating the inside of the organism. [Transmissivity is defined as the fraction of incident radiation at a given wavelength that is transmitted by a material (Campbell, 1977).] An example involves the Namib tenebrionid *Onymacris plana* (Henwood, 1975a). Transmittance in this animal is especially interesting because its rate varies with the position of the sun in the sky.

Specifically, when the sun is overhead in the Namib, the energy of solar radiation (R_{in}) is twice that of early morning or late afternoon. At midday, wavelengths are about equally divided between those in the visible range (V) and those is the near infrared range (NIR). Early morning and late afternoon ratios, however, are more like 60 NIR:40 V. Table 1 addresses the fate of the components of R_{in} on the surface of *O. plana* relative to the two kinds of solar positions.

Obviously, during the heat of midday when wavelengths are comparatively short, there must be some cuticular property that diminishes the proportion of R_{in} transmitted to deeper tissues. This effect is certainly desirable at a time when the elytral surface may reach 60°C, well above lethal T_B. (We

Table 1. Relationships between radiant energy and cuticle of *Onymacris plana* [a]

Time	R_{in} reflected by cuticle surface (%)	R_{in} absorbed by cuticle (%)	R_{in} transmitted internally (%)
Midday	8	78	14
A.M./P.M.	6	74	20

[a] Data from Henwood (1975a).

can further assume that convective heat loss and subelytral-cavity buffering are simultaneously taking place.) Earlier or later in the day when wavelengths are longer, a greater proportion (but a lesser absolute amount) of energy from R_{in} is transmitted internally. Henwood (1975a) argues that this effect prolongs heating and, therefore, accords with Hamilton's maxithermy hypothesis.

The example above suggests that certain physical properties of integumental surfaces in day-active desert invertebrates may have been greatly overlooked as biologists sought to elucidate mechanisms of thermoregulation. The recent report by Hadley (1979) on wax secretion and color phases in the Sonoran desert tenebrionid *Cryptoglossa verrucosa* bears out this point, since transpiration-reducing filamentous cuticular secretions may also increase reflectance.

D. Behavioral and Physiological Adaptations

While morphological properties alone can modify thermal balance, thermoregulation usually involves behavioral and physiological modes as well. When these are used in conjunction with the fixed features of morphology, a much broader spectrum of adaptive mechanisms becomes available for an animal selecting an optimal thermal environment. We now examine ways in which desert invertebrates thermoregulate behaviorally, and then turn to mechanisms that operate at the cell and molecular level to insure adaptive responses to changes in ambient temperatures. Reviews of the general topic as it applies to terrestrial invertebrates are found in Cloudsley-Thompson (1964a, 1970).

I. Behavioral Thermoregulation

1. Evaporative Cooling by Behavioral Means

This form of thermoregulation is neither common nor much expected for small ectotherms in hot deserts. Species with highly impermeable integuments (e.g., many scorpions) do not lose water rapidly enough to bring about significant evaporative cooling, while others with high rates of cuticular or spiracular transpiration run the risk of losing body water too fast. If, however, internal water can be replaced routinely, then evaporative cooling can be useful.

A case in point concerns the use of regurgitated alimentary-tract fluids to cool the body. Lowered T_B caused by the evaporation of regurgitated droplets was strongly implied for a sphinx moth (Adams and Heath, 1964) and convincingly demonstrated in the honeybee (Heinrich, 1979). Furthermore, the potential of regurgitated droplets for cooling bees flying at high temperatures and low humidities is considerable, as Heinrich points out, and would serve the added function of concentrating nectar pumped anteriorly from the honey crop. Perhaps the many solitary bees and sphingid moths found in warm deserts—and possibly less obvious insects as well—make common use of such a mechanism, or even of droplets of secretion taken up from plants (Fig. 16). Careful observations will contribute greatly to this interesting possibility.

Other species inhabiting arid regions regulate evaporative cooling by controlling their respiratory transpiration. An example is that of the tsetse fly *Glossina morsitans,* in which "fluttering" of the spiracles is an efficient cooling activity (Edney and Barrass, 1962), provided moisture can be replenished periodically by this small, blood-feeding species. Another cooling mechanism is the behaviorally regulated use of cuticular transpiration. Assuming this is under some degree of voluntary control in the desert isopod *Hemilepistus reaumuri,* it seems to be effective when the animal leaves its cool, moist burrow and ventures briefly into warm, dry air (Edney, 1960). However, the consequent lowering of T_B by nearly 3°C incurs the simultaneous loss of 6% of the isopod's total body water. Surface evaporation in dry air at about 40°C also depresses the T_B of *Schistocerca gregaria,* the desert locust, by 3°C–4°C below T_B in moist air (Bodenheimer, 1929, cited in Cloudsley-Thompson, 1970).

2. Microhabitat Selection

Orientations resulting in an altered T_B have been reported on a number of occasions (see reviews by Edney, 1974; Cloudsley-Thompson, 1970, 1975). Simply by observing a basking grasshopper or butterfly a patient investigator can infer a great deal about that animal's thermal needs, even if actual body and ambient temperatures are not known at the time. Stilting in scorpions and beetles, for example, is really a form of orientation. Likewise, it is typical of many cryptic species to hide beneath stones, bark, and debris, or to burrow in the presence of sunlight. Such behavior always involves some from of body displacement.

Burrowing usually insures a thermally stable environment, and the occupation of burrows made by other animals is additionally efficient because of its low energy demands. Many beetles, crickets, and opilionids use premade burrows; however, the fitness cost of this use of the underground ecosystem may be high because burrows are also used by predators.

Species including desert millipedes (personal observation) and whip scorpions (Crawford and Cloudsley-Thompson, 1971) are partly fossorial in that they often dig when the substrate is sufficiently moist. However, when soil entry is not possible they must instead use other means to regulate heat balance. In contrast to these moisture-limited burrowers, many isopods, scorpions, spiders, velvet mites, orthopterans, cockroaches, and provisioning

Fig. 16. Potential thermoregulation by insects in a herbaceous shrub. **a** Tiny sepsid fly on surface of *Curcubita foetidissima* leaf; note fluid droplet which may be used in evaporative cooling. **b** Chrysopid neuropteran exhibiting similar behavior on another such leaf. **c** The plant itself, which has many large leaves and therefore provides a shaded habitat to insect visitors attracted by its odor and/or secretions. (Photographs in central New Mexico desert grassland by the author)

wasps and bees are exceedingly good soil excavators, as shown in Fig. 17 and implied by references to a rather broad literature (Cloudsley-Thompson and Chadwick, 1964; Cloudsley-Thompson, 1975; Schmoller, 1970). Of course, the energy used in burrow construction and subsurface locomotion

a

b

Fig. 17. Soil excavation by gryllacridid orthopterans. **a** *Stenopelmatus fuscus* (Steno-pelmatinae) initiating burrowing in sandy loam, central New Mexico dry coniferous woodland-desert grassland ecotone. **b** Same species tunneling. **c** Burrow entrance being made by *Ammobaenetes* sp. (Rhaphidophorinae) in dune sand, Sevilleta National Wildlife Refuge, central New Mexico. **d** Another rhaphidophorine, *Daihinibaenetes giganteus* in its burrow, Great Sand Dunes National Monument, Colorado (scale is 15 cm long). (Photographs **a, b, c** by the author, **d** courtesy of H. E. Evans; **a** with permission of John Wiley and Sons, Inc.)

c

d

Fig. 17. c and d.

may be considerable, but the ultimate benefits—including those of thermoregulation—must made the effort worthwhile.

Thermoregulation underground is achieved by vertical movements in response to temperature gradients. This has been shown for the Sonoran desert
scorpion *Hadrurus arizonensis* by Hadley (1970b) and for *Dinothrombium
pandorae* mites by Tevis and Newell (1962). Juveniles of certain other soil

mites in the Mojave desert appear to migrate upward to warmer litter where development rates are enhanced (Wallwork, 1972). Also, vertical movements by desert cockroaches (Hawke and Farley, 1973; Edney et al., 1974; Ghabbour et al., 1977) are certain to affect body temperature. These few illustrations suggest that subtle behaviors influenced by substrate temperatures are most likely widespread among desert invertebrates. Here, too, is a fertile area for careful investigation.

Aboveground microhabitat selection offers a comparatively great range of thermal environments to an invertebrate seeking optimal T_B. In the Negev, the desert snail *Helicella seetzeni* avoids the lethal effects of a heated soil surface by climbing into shrubs (Fig. 18a) where it aestivates (Schmidt-Nielsen et al., 1972). The same is accomplished by another pulmonate, *Theba pisana,* in semi-arid coastal areas of South Africa. Aestivating individuals of this species orient the shell mouth upward while attached vertically to objects and, by so doing, allow air in the whorl between body and substrate to cool convectively (McQuaid et al., 1979). The North American desert milli-pede *Orthoporus ornatus* also uses vegetation (Fig. 18b) in such a way that it remains at a T_B of 35°C or less even on very hot days (Wooten et al., 1975). The diel locomotion activities of a number of xeric tenebrionids were referred to earlier and illustrate as well the close association of activity and temperature.

Desert cicadas (Fig. 19) in particular give evidence of fine-tuned, ther-moregulatory relocation behavior. One of these insects, *Diceroprocta apache,* feeds nocturnally in mesquite shrubs, then moves to leaves and twigs in the early morning. There it choruses, retreating later to cooler shade (Heath and Wilkin, 1970. Another species, *Cacama valvata,* feeds at the base of *Opuntia* cactus by night; by day it climbs to the upper pads where it sings when its T_B reaches 38°C. In its new location it uses a combination of shade and its own highly reflective ventral surface in order to thermoregulate (Heath et al., 1972).

II. Physiological Aspects of Thermal Relations

1. Acclimation to High Temperatures

Rates of thermal adaptation in ectotherms seem to be associated with habitat temperatures, acclimation being rapid in species experiencing varied thermal surroundings and slow in species occupying thermally stable habitats (Ander-son and Muchmore, 1971). Rapid acclimation might therefore be expected of many desert invertebrates and, as illustrated by examples given below, some of these animals can acclimate to high temperatures following rather brief periods of preconditioning.

Moreover, the level at which acclimation takes place should to some extent

Fig. 18. Examples of behavioral thermoregulation by remaining for varying periods in shrubs. **a** *Helicella seetzeni* aestivating in *Zygophyllum dumosum*, Negev desert. **b** *Orthoporus ornatus* basking and grazing on superficial tissues of *Larrea tridentata*, Chihuahuan desert. (Photographs by the author)

a

b

Fig. 19. Presumed thermo-regulation in cicadas. **a** Un-identified species on *Quercus* branch, base of San Mateo Mountains, New Mexico. **b** *Cicadetta musiva* on *Tamarix*, Negev desert. (Photographs by the author)

a

b

be controlled by upper lethal temperature, which varies greatly among desert species (Cloudsley-Thompson, 1962b). In cases of cryptobiosis and anhydro-biosis, however, the concept of temperature acclimation becomes relatively meaningless because temperatures tolerated are far higher than those at which active forms function. Examples of invertebrates with reduced metabolic states include eggs and larvae of a number of crustaceans and insects inhabiting ephemeral desert ponds (see reviews by Cloudsley-Thompson, 1975; Belk and Cole, 1975). This unusual system is dealt with in Chapter 17.

2. Metabolic Homeostasis in Changing Thermal Environments

Besides employing behavioral mechanisms to select for thermal constancy, ectotherms can achieve metabolic homeostasis by compensating for changes in habitat temperature and by maintaining low rates of respiratory change under a variety of thermal conditions. Thus Moeur and Eriksen (1972) found that *Lycosa carolinensis* wolf spiders from the Sonoran desert stabilized their oxygen consumption (QO_2) within 3 days of exposure to a temperature increase of 22°C to 39°C. A compensatory reduction of the respiratory temperature coefficient (Q_{10}) at temperatures below 39°C also occurred, implying that as days became warmer with the coming of summer, this long-lived arachnid becomes increasingly efficient in its use of energy for metabolic maintenance. As shown in Fig. 20, its metabolic-rate:temperature (R:T) curve also shifts to the right during this period, and rises more gradually in June than in January.

Interestingly, seasonal changes do not seem to affect the R:T curves of the desert grassland scorpion *Paruroctonus utahensis* (Riddle, 1978), a very different sort of predator. However, the same scorpion undergoes a compensatory reduction in QO_2 after 7 days following temperature increases from

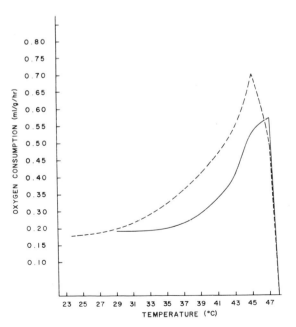

Fig. 20. Metabolic rate–temperature curves for January-collected *(dashed line)* and June-collected *(solid line) Lycosa carolinensis,* Sonoran desert. (Moeur and Eriksen, 1972; with permission)

Table 2. Respiratory temperature coefficients (Q_{10}) for selected adult desert arthropods

Order and species	Temperature range (°C)[a]	Q_{10}	Reference
Diplopoda			
Orthoporus ornatus	25–35	1.5	Wooten and Crawford (1974)
Uropygi			
Mastigoproctus giganteus	30–35	1.6	Ahearn (1970a)
Scorpiones			
Centruroides sculpturatus	20–30[b]	2.0	Hadley and Nill (1969)
Hadrurus arizonensis	30–35[b]	1.5	Hadley (1970a)
Paruroctonus utahensis	14–19	<1.7	Riddle (1976)
Araneae			
Lycosa carolinensis	23–39	1.3	Moeur and Eriksen (1972)
Aphonopelma sp.	30–40	1.1	Seymour and Vinegar (1973)

[a] Ranges given correspond to the lowest Q_{10} values recorded from more extensive temperature ranges in each case.

[b] Q_{10} values estimated from R:T curves (after Riddle, 1976).

14°C to 34°C, a pattern that again suggests conservation of metabolic reserves at high temperatures (Riddle, 1979).

Low respiratory Q_{10}'s are known for the apparently preferred temperature ranges of a number of large desert arthropods. Data from adults are given in Table 2, which shows only the lowest Q_{10} values available from a broad range of temperatures reported for each species. Original references should be consulted for more complete information, and the reader should not be mislead into assuming that values given in Table 2 necessarily also apply to immature stages. In fact they sometimes do not, as was shown by Wooten and Crawford (1974) for millipedes and by Riddle (1976) for scorpions. Moreover, the trend suggested for large, active desert arthropods seems not to apply to dormant desert snails, since under simulated field temperatures the Q_{10} of *Sphincterochila zonata* has a value of 2.4 (Schmidt-Nielsen et al., 1971). The extremely low QO_2 value of this species in hot weather aestivation, however, probably rules out the need for finely controlled Q_{10} adjustment. Studies of Q_{10} differences between dormant and active desert invertebrates would illuminate the adaptiveness of Q_{10} regulation in different seasons. This matter is given additional attention in section E of this chapter.

3. Flying Insects: A Special Case

Insects in flight become temporary endotherms. This can pose severe overheating problems, and if efficient contraction of thoracic flight muscles is to be maintained, heat generated by muscle contraction and accumulated from incoming radiant energy must somehow be dissipated. Furthermore, in hot, dry environments, where T_B's of these small organisms can rise more than 30°C above ambient temperature (Heinrich, 1975), rapid rates of respiratory transpiration are bound to occur. Clearly, there are limits to the performance of insects flying in warm desert habitats. Well-adapted species would be expected both to prevent excessive buildup of T_B and to regulate spiracular water loss.

Desert locusts seem to conform to this description (Heinrich, 1975). Their metabolic rates during long-distance flight are comparatively low, and they consequently lose less than 1% of their total thoracic heat production via evaporation. In addition, they exhibit effective control of spiracular transpiration while flying (Miller, 1960; Loveridge, 1968). Sphinx moths living in deserts appear to be less well adapted, and while they possess an effective means of unloading excessive thoracic heat (namely via convective and radiative loss after its transfer to the less well-insulated abdomen), 8%–13% of this heat is lost evaporatively.

Of course, significant respiratory water loss is not a drawback if water sufficient to compensate is taken up during nectar feeding. The fact that sphinx moths and bees use regurgitated moisture droplets for evaporative cooling (see above) suggests that in many cases foraging serves to rehydrate these insects to the point where evaporative cooling is not a liability. A combination, therefore, of behavioral traits and physiological controls appears to determine the thermal balance permitting flight in a number of desert insects.

E. Adaptations to Cold

I. General Responses to Freezing Temperatures

Exposure of many invertebrates to subfreezing conditions is a distinct possibility in warm deserts, particularly at night during the colder seasons. Many more species probably experience very low temperatures in deserts located at high latitudes and altitudes. Yet the responses of arid-adapted invertebrates to cold have received little attention, perhaps because of the misconception that deserts are essentially warm places.

Ectotherms respond physiologically to subfreezing temperatures in two ways. One is to become "freezing tolerant" and thereby to endure considerable T_B reduction without undergoing tissue damage. The alternative is to rely on tissue supercooling, which involves extending the temperature range over which the body fluids remain liquid below their freezing point (Baust and Miller, 1970). "Freezing-susceptible" species, which suffer tissue damage or die upon freezing, typically supercool. They can occasionally lower their supercooling points well below $-15°C$ and, in so doing, appear to use various polyhydric alcohols and glycoproteins. In theory any substance with polar properties can bond with the hydrogen atoms of water and consequently inhibit ice formation, so the variety of supercooling agents may be great indeed. Ice nucleation in the gut, a prelude to more massive freezing, is thought to be a function of the presence of food particles there (Salt, 1968).

II. Comparative Responses to Freezing Temperatures in Desert Invertebrates

Both types of responses to cold are known among desert species, but most organisms so far studied from polar regions appear to be freezing susceptible. Thus, mites and collembolans from the sub-Antarctic (Block et al., 1978) and from Alaskan taiga (Block, 1979) give strong evidence of supercooling.

The same is true for *Drosophila nigrospiracula* adults, which supercool at night whenever ambient temperatures in their Sonoran desert habitat drop well below freezing (Lowe et al., 1967). Desert locusts also supercool, and Cloudsley-Thompson (1973) found that while the supercooling point of *Schistocerca gregaria* was elevated upon hydration, it was lowered significantly after preconditioning for 18 h at $5°C$. The mean supercooling point in *Locusta migratoria,* but not in *S. gregaria,* was shown to be significantly lower in the dark phase of the circadian activity rhythm than in the light phase (Cloudsley-Thompson, 1978b).

Related taxa in arid environments may be either susceptible or tolerant to freezing. This was demonstrated recently by Zachariassen and Hammel (1976a) with tenebrionid beetles in the genera *Coelocnemis* and *Eleodes* from mountains in southern California. Hemolymph from freezing-tolerant, but not from freezing-susceptible, adults contained a substance that induced freezing at the unexpectedly high level of about $-6.5°C$. This effect was felt probably to cause extracellular freezing to occur close enough to the melting point of tissue fluids to prevent significant osmotic flux of water out of the cells (Zachariassen and Hammel, 1976b).

As with tenebrionids, scorpions may fall into either of the freezing-response categories. Figure 21 illustrates this point by showing the cold-adaptation patterns of two scorpion species. One, *Diplocentrus peloncillensis,* inhabits shallow burrows beneath rocks (see Fig. 4b) in low, arid mountains of southern New Mexico (Crawford and Riddle, 1974, 1975). The other, *Paruroctonus utahensis,* occurs in desert grasslands of central New Mexico and digs shelters a short distance into sandy-loam soil (Riddle and Pugach, 1976). The former scorpion can survive several supercooling episodes to temperatures as low as $-7°C$, but it displays no obvious seasonal pattern of supercooling. Temperatures reaching $-7°C$ in actual overwintering sites were predicted to account for mortalities of half the scorpions (and adult *Scolopendra polymorpha* centi-

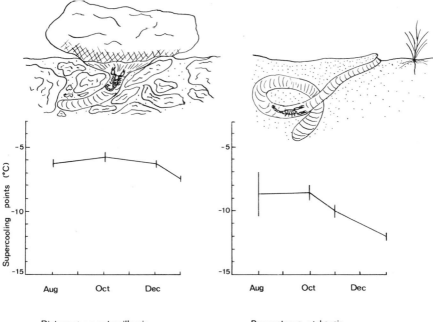

Fig. 21. Diagram of overwintering positions and seasonal supercooling points in two arid-land scorpions. *Left, Diplocentrus peloncillensis,* Peloncillo Mts. *Right, Paruroctonus utahensis,* central New Mexico desert grassland. (From data given by Crawford and Riddle, 1975; Riddle and Pugach, 1976)

pedes—see Fig. 6a) occurring at or just below the subrock surface, on an average of about 1 day a year (Crawford and Riddle, 1974).

Unlike the freezing-tolerant *D. peloncillensis, P. utahensis* is decidedly freezing susceptible and begins to lower its supercooling point in autumn until a level of about −12°C is reached. Except for highly unusual years in the habitat where it was studied, such a physiologic change ought to prevent death due to freezing. Whatever substance depresses the supercooling point is not known; hemolymph polyhydric alcohols were not found by Riddle and Pugach (1976).

III. Other Metabolic Responses to Cold

Energy utilization by ectotherms in the cold, low-production environments of temperate deserts in winter and polar deserts during much longer periods is subject to obvious limitation. Unless metabolism is reduced to the low levels typical of anhydrobiosis or diapause, it may be advantageous for species experiencing long periods of steady cold to undergo "metabolic elevation" (i.e., appropriate acclimatory increases in low-temperature metabolic rates). This should allow maintenance to occur at rates comparable to those of similar taxa in more temperate regions. Such a hypothesis was proposed by Block and Young (1978), who based the idea on comparative data from Antarctic and temperate-zone mites. Since habitat temperatures and activation energies for certain enzyme systems are correlated (Hochachka and Somero, 1973; Hazel and Prosser, 1974), the demonstrably lower activation energies of polar species may help to explain their characteristic metabolic elevation, according to Young (1979a).

It may also be useful for small ectotherms inhabiting these cold environments to compensate for occasional rapid temperature changes by decreasing their metabolic rates at high temperatures (as previously noted above for certain large desert arachnids) and by increasing them at low temperatures. Here, however, the matter of available metabolic reserves may be significant, since energy for metabolic homeostasis in a cold, energy-limited situation may have to be used at the expense of future growth and reproduction. The question of trade-offs in the context of cold adaptation and metabolic compensation of polar mites is reviewed by Young (1979b), who points out the potential importance of habitat temperatures in governing compensation responses.

F. Summary Comments

Adaptations to thermal stress in desert invertebrates are functions of morphological, behavioral, and physiological attributes, and as such do not fall into easily defined patterns. In fact, based on the evidence at hand, regulation of thermal balance is such a complex matter among ectotherms in thermally variable habitats that, if anything, special adaptations are more a matter of degree than of kind. Only thorough comparative studies will verify this assumption, however.

The simultaneous involvement of several thermoregulatory modes is probably common among desert invertebrates and is undoubtedly orchestrated by a highly evolved set of neural and endocrine controls.

Chapter 7
Energetics

A. Introduction

As a resource central to life itself, energy is of unquestioned importance. Less clear is the question of how limiting energy is to the evolution and maintenance of natural populations; the answer probably depends on the time scale used. On an evolutionary scale it has been suggested that natural selection maximizes energy consumed in growth and reproduction and that the proportion of such energy utilized in population regulation is the best measure of fitness (Van Valen, 1976). The amount of energy available to an organism at any given time is also felt by some to be finite (Congdon et al., 1978), even though on an ecological scale it is apparent to others that not all food energy available to an animal population is normally consumed (Andrewartha and Birch, 1954). In the latter instance, energy in the form of food may be only relatively unavailable—and therefore limiting—if the cost of its acquisition exceeds the benefit of its nutritional and caloric yield (Emlen, 1973). Acquisition cost itself may be subject to both evolutionary and ecological constraints: High cost may result from density-dependent factors operating in relatively nonstressful physical environments. In deserts, where density-independent factors are considered to predominate (Andrewartha and Birch, 1954), high cost of energy acquisition may reflect a combination of conditions including low food availability and high mortality due to predation or abiotic stress.

In earlier chapters we examined a number of interacting ways in which desert invertebrates adapt to seasonal stress. Clearly there are times when relatively unavailable environmental food energy makes some form of escape necessary. Escape in space, the well-known strategy of desert locusts, entails movement to regions where energy resources are once more available. Of course the migration itself takes energy and involves time during which mortality may rise. The alternative of escaping in time (i.e., some form of dormancy) may involve even longer durations; it also implies use of stored food reserves as the sole source of metabolic energy. Whether such sequestered energy actually decreases to the point of increasing mortality in nature has not been adequately tested. The remarkable desert snail *Sphincterochila zonata* can reduce its metabolic demands sufficiently to enable survival for several years without food (Schmidt-Nielsen et al., 1971).

In the present chapter we shall consider concepts of energetics as they relate to adaptation by desert invertebrates. The discussion will be based on one of a number of equations that describe energy flux in natural populations, namely $A = R + P$, where A is assimilation, R is respiration, and P is production. (Actual energy flux under field and simulated conditions will be dealt with in Part 4, and other parameters of flux such as rates of food consumption and feces production will also be referred to there.) The following treatment is based in part on a review by Crawford (1979b) and is used here as an introduction to the physiological and ecological energetics of desert invertebrates.

B. Assimilation

Ingested material assimilated by animals can be used for tissue synthesis or for direct energy needs. The remainder is excreted and therefore lost to the consumer unless reingested. Typically, carnivores assimilate most of what they eat, whereas animals consuming living plant material have a wide but lower range of efficiencies. Detritivores, which we shall define as saprophagous invertebrate consumers of organic debris, microflora, and fungi, tend to assimilate relatively poorly, but, as we shall see, there are some interesting exceptions in the desert.

Basically, assimilation efficiency is measured by comparing food ingested with feces produced in a given unit of time (see Petrusewicz and Macfadyen, 1970, for methodology). Ash-free, dry-weight values are conventionally employed, although some studies of desert invertebrates do not consider ash contents and use the term "approximate digestibility" instead (see Waldbauer, 1968). Table 3 presents both kinds of efficiency values (while not strictly comparable, they are probably rather close when expressed as percentages) for different trophic levels of mainly desert invertebrates. The list represents a fairly complete coverage of assimilation research to date; the large number of detritivore examples may reflect the ease of maintaining such animals in a laboratory. All values fall into predictable ranges except those of certain isopods. Of the animals listed, the termites—and perhaps the only arid-adapted (but not true desert) snail that has been examined for assimilation efficiency—should have higher than usual efficiencies for detritivores because of their gut symbionts and powerful digestive enzymes, respectively.

In a review of nondesert consumer strategies among terrestrial gastropods and isopods, Wieser (1978) concludes that the former are efficient assimilators but that the latter are not. This view may need to be qualified in desert situations, where assimilation in several *Hemilepistus* isopods is unexpectedly efficient (see Table 3). An explanation for the high efficiency of *H. cristatus,* found in Central Asia, is that microbial symbionts in the gut enhance assimilation (Kozlovskaja and Striganova, 1977). In both this species and in *Armadillidium pallasii,* a nondesert but xeric-adapted isopod with assimilation efficiencies ranging between 45% and 61% (Striganova and Valiachmedov, 1976), similar microbial dynamics were found within litter eaten, as well as in gut and excrement. In the more detailed study of *H. cristatus,* cellulose breakdown was caused mainly by myxobacteria, actinomycetes, and pectin decomposers. Another explanation for this animal's efficiency, which will be discussed below, has to do with the absence of soil in the diet.

Of the factors that can affect assimilation efficiency in a given species, three have been recognized for some time as being particularly important. These are: (1) the nature and amount of available food, (2) the physiological condition of the animal, and (3) the existing environmental conditions (Petrusewicz and Macfadyen, 1970). Considering food first, one aspect of its quality that may be quite relevant to some desert invertebrates is its percentage of dry matter, since low approximate digestibility in Lepidoptera, at least, partly reflects high dry-matter content in leaf food (Soo Hoo and Fraenkel, 1966). A case in point concerns a gelechiid moth *(Aroga websteri),* the larvae of which are primary defoliators of sagebrush *(Artemisia tridentata)* in the Great Basin desert. This insect has a low approximate digestibility when compared with nondesert Lepidoptera (Hsiao and Kirkland, 1973).

Another quality of food pertaining especially to detritivores is its soil content, because soil is consumed routinely by many of these invertebrates. In the Negev desert the isopod *Hemilepistus reaumuri* ingests soil as part of its natural diet, and Shachak et al. (1976b) showed that when soil was added to a food mixture of leaves from desert shrubs, assimilation efficiency was maintained between 25% and 35%. Leaves ingested without soil resulted in efficiencies between 51% and 82%, but simultaneous survival rates dropped appreciably. Perhaps the high value of 79% given for *H. cristata* by Kozlovskaja and Striganova (1977) is a partial consequence of a diet also containing no soil (see Table 3).

Another detritivore ingesting soil regularly is the North American desert millipede *Orthoporus ornatus.* In assimilation studies Wooten and Crawford (1975) noted that without the addition of a separate amount of moist soil, millipedes would not consume enough bark from dried shrub stems to enable data collection for calculations. Efficiencies in this desert millipede ranged from 20% to 37%, thus resembling the situation in which *H. reaumuri* was given soil with its diet of leaves.

Table 3. Trophic levels and assimilation parameters in mainly desert invertebrates

Taxon	Trophic level	Temperature (°C)	Experimental diet	Assimilation efficiency (%)	Reference
Gastropoda[a]					
Cepaea nemoralis	Detritivore	8–10	*Onionis repens, Taraxicum officinale*	30–44	Richardson (1975)
Isopoda					
Hemilepistus cristatus		20–22	Dead stems of *Zollikoferia* sp.	79	Kozlovskaja and Striganova (1977)
Hemilepistus fedtschenkoi		20–22	Pistachio litter	46	Striganova and Valiachmedov (1976)
Hemilepistus reaumuri	Detritivore	15–25[b]	Dead branches of *Hammada scoparia* and *H. alba*	51–82	Shachak et al. (1976b)
Hemilepistus reaumuri		15–25[b]	Above plus soil crust	25–35	Shachak et al. (1976b)
Desertillio sp.		20–22	Dead stems of *Zollikoferia* sp.	42	Kozlovskaja and Striganova (1977)
Protracheoniscus orientalis		20–22	Pistachio litter	32	Kozlovskaja and Striganova (1977)
Diplopoda					
Orthoporus ornatus	Detritivore	20–30	Bark of *Ephedra* sp. plus soil	20–38	Wooten and Crawford (1975)
Orthoporus ornatus		20–25	Bark of *Prosopis* sp. plus soil	22–34	Wooten and Crawford (1975)

Table 3. (*Continued*)

Taxon	Trophic level	Temperature (°C)	Experimental diet	Assimilation efficiency (%)	Reference
Isoptera Various spp.	Detritivore	—	Foods high in cellulose	54–61	LaFage and Nutting (1977)
Orthoptera					
Locusta migratoria	Herbivore	32	Grass	39[c]	Dadd (1960)
Schistocerca gregaria	Herbivore	32	Grass	39[c]	Dadd (1960)
Anconia integra		20	*Suaeda Torreyana, Atriplex canescens*	27–39	Burkhart (1978)
Lepidoptera *Aroga websteri*	Herbivore	30	Leaves of *Artemesia tridentata*	35[c]	Hsiao and Kirkland (1973)
Coleoptera *Paropsis automaria*	Herbivore	21–24	Leaves of many *Eucalyptus* spp.	15–46[c]	Fox and Macauley (1977)
Scorpionida *Urodacus yaschenkoi*	Carnivore	20	Cockroaches	92	Shorthouse (1971)

[a] From a sand dune system in southwest England.
[b] Programmed with photoperiod of L2:D22.
[c] Approximate digestibilities (%). See text.

Physiological condition also seems to have an effect on the ability of certain desert detritivores to assimilate. Assuming that physiology is somewhat age-specific, the example of *H. reaumuri* may be considered. Individuals aged 4 months assimilated 25% of what they consumed, while animals 2 months older assimilated 35% (Shachak et al., 1976b). In another example Norris (1961) found that approximate digestibility is also higher in *S. gregaria* during somatic growth than during ovarian growth (Mordue and Hill, 1970).

Finally, in regard to the effect of environmental conditions on assimilation efficiency, the importance of temperature is indicated by the temperature-dependent range of efficiencies found between 20°C and 30°C in *O. ornatus* (Wooten and Crawford, 1975). Obviously, this kind of response is expressed on a physiological or ecological time scale, but there is also some evidence that relatively high efficiencies in desert detritivores may be due to selection on an evolutionary scale. Data on isopods supporting this view were given or referred to by Kozlovskaja and Striganova (1977), while Wooten and Crawford (1975) made a similar point for millipedes. Although comparative assimilation studies tend to suffer because of methodology differences and absence of associated time-based feeding budgets, the evolutionary hypothesis should be strengthened if relatively short periods of feeding are found to characterize invertebrate feeding in stressful environments like deserts. In fact enhanced assimilation efficiency may be a compensatory adaptation among desert detritivores for the relative unavailability of food energy, caused in part by stressful temporal restrictions on feeding.

C. Respiration

The energy commitment to biomass production (expressed as the ratio of respiration to growth) in ectotherms is significantly less than that of endotherms, which must expend energy to maintain constant body temperatures. This means that even though ectotherms generally assimilate what they eat with less efficiency than do endotherms, their actual production of biomass from assimilated material is far more efficient (Engelmann, 1966). With this basic rule in mind, we can now ask if special adaptations or life-history patterns among desert invertebrates are associated with their relatively efficient production of tissue.

To begin with, we should recognize that certain inherent morphological and metabolic characteristics cut across the array of invertebrates inhabiting any ecosystem and that these features ought to have similar effects on energy expenditure whenever they occur. Particular reference is made to the correlation of ventilatory-system structure with metabolic rate. There is now good evidence from a single large group of related invertebrates, the spiders, that those species endowed with tracheal systems have higher metabolic rates than those with book lungs (Anderson, 1970). One might, therefore, expect correlations between structure and rate in other terrestrial invertebrate groups, and a glance at the oxygen-consumption values listed in Table 4 suggests that tracheated desert insects do indeed have higher rates than many non- or weakly-tracheated desert invertebrates.

Another complication that may well affect any invertebrate assemblage has to do with longevity. McNeill and Lawton (1970) compared production and respiration values from many studies and concluded that because long-lived ectotherms have relatively unproductive older individuals in their populations compared with short-lived species, the former should have higher respiratory costs at any level of production. This conclusion has been disputed (Shorthouse, 1971), and the insect:noninsect comparison in Table 4 would seem to be superficially in conflict with such a model; however, a comprehensive cost–benefit analysis will have to be considered before a final critique can be made.

This discussion of morphology and life history applies to invertebrates in any ecosystem and does not therefore come to grips specifically with the original question, which concerned reduced metabolic rates in desert species. Turning to this matter, let us first make and then examine the following relevant hypothesis: "Because deserts are unstable in terms of food availability to many invertebrates and also because water and temperature stresses on such animals are frequently considerable, desert invertebrates should exhibit relatively low rates of oxygen consumption in comparison to nondesert invertebrates."

The part of our hypothesis dealing with food availability is not easily testable, given the paucity of information at hand. Generally low metabolic rates in such diverse groups as desert-inhabiting *Pogonomyrmex* ants (Ettershank and Whitford, 1973) and gastropod mollusks (Riddle, 1977), when compared with rates among related taxa under similar experimental conditions, suggest that the idea does have merit; however, additional, carefully controlled studies are necessary before it can be adequately validated. In particular, the diet of experimental animals should be monitored, since it is now clear that starvation tends to depress metabolism in an assortment of invertebrates (see references in Crawford, 1979b), including desert scorpions (Riddle, 1978).

All else equal, we might expect respiratory transpiration induced by the stress of experiencing dry air to correlate well with metabolic rate in desert invertebrates. Low metabolism reduces the need to acquire oxygen, which in turn means that ventilatory apertures can be partly or completely closed if suitable mechanisms exist. Perhaps the best example of how a desert invertebrate compares with a nondesert relative in this respect comes from Riddle's (1977) study of respiration in *Rabdotus schiedeanus* and *Helix aspersa*. The former is a desert snail that reduces metabolism much more effectively in nearly dry air over a wide temperature range than does the latter, a common garden snail. Other comparative studies of this sort are apparently not yet

Table 4. Oxygen consumption in desert invertebrates

Taxon	Longevity[a]	Temperature (°C)	(R.H.) (%)	Seasonal condition[b]	Metabolism (μ liter O_2 g^{-1} h^{-1})[c]	Reference
Gastropoda						
Rabdotus schiedeanus	L	25	60	A	140 ± 15 (4 h)	Riddle (1977)
Rabdotus schiedeanus	L	25	60	D	20 ± 3 (6 h)	Riddle (1977)
Rabdotus schiedeanus	L	25	10	D	7 ± 3 (6 h)	Riddle (1977)
Bulimulus dealbatus	L	22	—	A	120 ± 20 (2–3 h)	Horne (1973)
Bulimulus dealbatus	L	22	—	D	20 ± 5 (2–3 h)	Horne (1973)
Sphincterochila zonata	L	25	—	D	1.7 (continuous)	Schmidt-Nielsen et al. (1971)
Scorpiones						
Urodacus yaschenkoi	L	20	—	A	54 (derived)	Shorthouse (1971)
Diplocentrus peloncillensis	L	20	—	A	92 ± 19 (1 h, $\bar{x}$ of 3)	Crawford and Riddle (1975)
Paruroctonus utahensis	L	20	80	A	28–48 (3 h)	Riddle (1978)
Aranaea						
Aphonopelma sp.	L	20	—	A	30–50 (1 h)	Seymour and Vinegar (1973)
Lycosa carolinensis	L	23	—	A	180 (3–22 min, $\bar{x}$ of 3)	Moeur and Eriksen (1972)
Chilopoda						
Scolopendra polymorpha	L	20	—	A	69 ± 5 (1 h, $\bar{x}$ of 3)	Crawford et al. (1975)
Diplopoda						
Orthoporus ornatus	L	25	90	A	107 (1 h, $\bar{x}$ of 3)	Wooten and Crawford (1974)
Orthoporus ornatus	L	25	90	D	44 (1 h, $\bar{x}$ of 3)	Wooten and Crawford (1974)

Table 4. *(Continued)*

Taxon	Longevity[a]	Temperature (°C)	(R.H.) (%)	Seasonal condition[b]	Metabolism (μ liter O_2 g^{-1} h^{-1})[c]	Reference
Orthoptera						
Schistocerca gregaria	S	24–28	—	A	200–700 (at rest)	Keister and Buck (1964)[d]
Schistocerca gregaria	S	27–30	—	A	630 (few min to several h)	Krogh and Weis-Fogh (1951)
Schistocerca gregaria	S	24–28	—	A	15000 (in flight)	Weis-Fogh (1964)
Anconia integra	S	20	—	A	790 ± 100 (1.5 h)	Burkhart (1978)
Coleoptera						
Lepidochora argentogrisea	?	30	—	A	100–420 (ea 0.5 h for 36 h)	Louw and Hamilton (1972)
Eleodes armata	?	25	40–60	A	130 (6 h)	Ahearn (1970b)
Meloinae: Lyttinae (8 spp.)	?	25	—	A	477–1796 (0.5 h)	Cohen and Pinto (1977)
Hymenoptera						
Various ant spp. (workers)	S	25	Variable	A	800–2000 (0.5–1 h)	Ettershank and Whitford (1973), Kay and Whitford (1975)

[a] L: more than 1 yr; S: less than 1 yr.

[b] A: active; D: dormant.

[c] Mean values approximated from published figures or rounded off from published data, except where expressed as x ± SE.

[d] From range of values given by several authors. Note the tremendous increase in energy expenditure associated with flight in Weis-Fogh's (1964) study.

in the literature, but a number of published works have related water and temperature stress to metabolism in desert invertebrates. For example, Etter-shank and Whitford (1973) showed that some desert ants are like *R. schie-deanus* in their capacity to reduce metabolism in dry air, while a similar response occurs in the desert scorpion *Hadrurus arizonensis* (Hadley, 1970a). Perhaps this reveals an enhanced ability to store energy reserves during dry seasons; in other words, this may be an effective way of reducing respiratory cost during environmentally difficult periods. On the other hand, since some desert ants increase metabolic rate with decreased humidity (Kay and Whit-ford, 1975), the pattern cannot be universal. It may be that differing patterns reflect not only the effects of humidity but also those of body-water content. Low humidity could well lead to increased activity (and thus metabolism), while low body-water content could depress metabolism (E. B. Edney, per-sonal communication).

Maintenance of low respiratory Q_{10} values was discussed as being an adapta-tion to thermal stress. One way of regarding its adaptiveness is in the context of lowered respiratory cost. In the earlier examples of large desert species (Table 2), we noted that Q_{10} values increase above and below what is presumed to be a set of temperatures where most routine activity takes place. While the idea of generalizing from this information certainly seems attractive, such an exercise is premature in view of the conclusion by Cohen and Pinto (1977) that there is no conspicuous pattern relating Q_{10} to habitat temperature in the 8 species of desert meloid beetles they studied.

We are left in the somewhat uncomfortable position of having to conclude that the hypothesis of reduced metabolism remains conceptually compelling, but largely unsubstantiated. Desert invertebrates investigated do tend to lower their oxygen demands when starved, but so do other invertebrates. Dry air seems to promote reduced metabolism in some species, but not in all. And finally, Q_{10} values at habitat temperatures where most activity occurs are sometimes low, but not in all cases.

D. Production

A convenient way of defining production is to regard it as the net balance between assimilation and respiration over a given period. Used in this sense, it can be expressed as energy expended or biomass produced. In the previous section we alluded to ectotherms being more efficient at production than endotherms, a condition one can verify by comparing ratios of production to assimilation in each category. If we assume that various combinations of sparse resources, predation, and abiotic stresses make the cost of acquiring food relatively great for many desert animals, then it is obvious that being an ectotherm under such conditions has its advantages. Yet to argue that efficient biomass production makes desert invertebrates exceptionally well adapted to their environment makes sense in an evolutionary context only if one can demonstrate that as an animal increases its production, it also increases the proportion of assimilated energy allocated to its reproductive effort.

As yet, clear demonstrations of this kind are lacking in desert invertebrates; therefore, we can instead ask whether such animals differ from nondesert forms in the way that they use assimilated energy for production alone. Reichle (1977) summarizes net growth efficiency (P/A) from accumulated trophic-level data as follows: saprovore (= detritivore), 0.17–0.40; herbivore, 0.20–0.40; and carnivore, 0.10–0.37. Very few desert studies have adequate data for comparison. Of those available the detritivorous desert millipede *Orthoporus ornatus* has a feeding-season value of 0.44 (calculated from Crawford, 1976), while annual net growth efficiency in the Australian scorpion *Urodacus yaschenkoi* is 0.37 (Shorthouse, 1971) and that of the Mojave desert grasshopper *Bootetix punctatus* is 0.32–0.45 (Mispagel, 1978). However, since the value given for the Sonoran desert grasshopper *Anconia integra* is only 0.16 (Burkhart, 1978), it is obvious that more research has to be conducted on this subject before we can ascertain a real trend in the relative growth efficiency of desert groups—if indeed there is any real trend. It should be clear by now that energy studies of desert invertebrates are themselves in short supply.

Summary Comments: Part 2

Evolutionary success is determined in part by a complex suite of structural and functional adaptations, each having special relevance for certain periods during the lifetime of an organism. For a desert invertebrate the temporal expression of a functional adaptation (e.g., a behavioral or physiological trait) may be critical to survival because of frequent extremes and irregularities in the physical environment. Thus, a strong dependence of diel and seasonal activity on photoperiod, which is highly predictable, may be inimical to the survival of a species in a habitat containing unpredictable resources. Indeed, although circadian and diapausing responses to changes in illumination are well known in some desert invertebrates, the presence or arrival of moisture may often have more profound effects on patterns of activity.

Morphological and physiological features associated with desiccation resistance are very well developed in some of these animals, e.g., many scorpions as well as some collembolans and apterygote insects. One wonders, however, how frequently these characteristics achieve real significance, since such animals are largely nocturnal. On the other hand, in diurnally active forms like some isopods, millipedes, and many insects, the ability to remain exposed to moderate microclimates becomes paramount. Moreover, the capacity to thermoregulate behaviorally may also be of great value in the daytime. While the radiant-energy fluxes involved in maintaining thermal equilibrium are now well understood, the fine-tuned adaptations to high temperatures of desert taxa such as tenebrionid beetles are far more subtle than formerly realized.

Two broad adaptive phases are presented by desert invertebrates over seasonal time. One—alluded to above—is manifested mainly by behavior and occurs on or near the desert surface. The other may be considered the "escape" phase, and is seen either as migration (which is also behavioral) or as some kind of dormancy. Dormancy is mediated by physiological and metabolic mechanisms, and in deserts—where energy, moisture, and surface shelter often prove to be ephemeral resources—these mechanisms take on considerable significance. Among other things, they can account for active water uptake (as in millipedes—but active uptake also occurs in thysanurans and cockroaches) and extremely low metabolic rates (as in aestivating snails and nonfeeding scorpions). In the few instances where cold-hardiness has been documented, mechanisms enabling either freezing-tolerant or freezing-susceptible patterns have been invoked.

The use of energy and the extent to which energy limits life in dormant and active desert invertebrates are both issues that will continue to intrigue physiologists and ecologists. For dormant stages the question revolves around how long inactivity can occur. Certainly, during anhydrobiosis or cryptobiosis (e.g., in nematodes and chironomid larvae), the duration seems indefinite, while during more conventional forms of dormancy (e.g., that occurring in snails, scorpions, and many immature insects) several years is not unexpected. In contrast, when desert species are active, the constraint of time seems causally associated with relative efficiency in the use of stored energy, as evidenced by R:T shifts and lowered Q_{10}'s of certain arachnids and in the assimilation of ingested food by some isopods and millipedes.

Part 3
Life-History Patterns

Introduction

The ecological and evolutionary success of desert animals depends in large measure on how well they time their reproduction relative to the conditions and resources needed by their progeny. Subsequent development of these offspring to a state of reproductive maturity depends in turn on their ability to cope with the temporal and spatial intensities of abiotic and biotic constraints. When levels of habitat moisture in particular are uneven—as they often are in deserts—we might expect well-adapted life histories to adjust readily to factors associated with low moisture levels; an alternative is to reduce the probability of experiencing them by behavioral and physiological means.

One way or another, desert species have by definition solved the general problem of survival, even though they show great life-history variation in patterns reflecting its solution. "Pattern" is used here to delimit one of several categories of biological activity applying broadly to all groups of organisms. Examples used in Part 3 are patterns of reproduction, development, and resource utilization.

Patterns so defined, however, say little about the evolutionary trends that produce them. It is, therefore, helpful to raise certain evolutionary explanations at this point so that we can approach our discussion of patterns with what might be called a "desert perspective." In an evolutionary context, a pattern becomes a "strategy" to some, a "tactic" to others. Both terms are teleological, which unfortunately makes it difficult to use them objectively. On the other hand, if we can ignore a connotation of purpose, the terms can be useful. At present we will stay mainly with "tactic" which is defined by Stearns (1976) as "A set of coadapted traits designed, by natural selection, to solve particular ecological problems. A complex adaptation."

Ways of explaining why certain "coadapted traits" are found together have been referred to as "r-selection" or "K-selection," or as a continuum of possibilities in between such extremes. Certainly these often-used terms can apply to desert organisms, but other concepts may be equally or more appropriate. Another explanation for observable patterns that may have intuitive appeal to desert biologists is called "bet hedging." A major distinction between r- and K-selection and bet hedging is that proponents of the former concepts are concerned with schedules of fecundity and juvenile mortality that remain constant, while advocates of the latter idea recognize that such schedules may fluctuate (Stearns, 1976). In a desert, where physical conditions are themselves subject to considerable flux, it seems reasonable to expect fluctuating schedules of this sort.

If so, then the effects of environmental variability should differ according to whether the variability impinges on juvenile or adult mortality. And complicating the matter even further are species-specific patterns of clutch size, longevity, and reproductive effort. In theory reproductive effort can refer to some measure of the ratio of reproduction to survival (Goodman, 1979). For our purposes we will regard it more in the context of fecundity—which is relatively easy to measure—and place less emphasis on survival, for which few data are available.

The validity of any explanation of observable life-history patterns in deserts must rest to a great extent on the proposition that well-adapted life histories in deserts take advantage of chance events. Put another way, this simply says that deserts are "risky" places in which to reproduce. Clearly, in order to survive and reproduce in such environments, it is useful to spread the risk over time (Cohen, 1966). One way to do this is to combine reduced breeding with an increase in longevity and reproductive life span (Murphy, 1968), although there are certainly plenty of short-lived desert species that must use a different approach.

Thus, evolutionary tactics underlying observable patterns of biological activity in highly stochastic systems like deserts should conform to the environmental peculiarities of those systems. However, while there is an ongoing effort to generate mathematical models of such tactics, it is difficult to quantify a "risky" environment in a generally acceptable way. Despite this problem, some general relationships between life history and environment can be delimited for desert invertebrates. These relationships are now formalized as *categories* and looked at fairly intensively in the chapters making up Part 3.

Chapter 8
Short Lives: Multivoltine Species

A. Introduction

Desert invertebrates with more than one annual generation should, assuming their life histories resemble those of similar species elsewhere, include many free-living and parasitic protozoans and nematodes, as well as rotifers and other pseudocoelomates. And using similar reasoning, it may be that many prostigmatid mites in deserts also have this kind of life cycle. The same may hold for some Collembola as well, although the recent discovery of an anhydrobiotic type of response to dehydration in this group (Poinsot-Balaguer, 1976) may imply longer-than-expected life spans in desert forms.

One would expect insects with comparatively high turnover rates in moderate climates also to be multivoltine in arid regions. Mirid bugs, aphids, and thrips come to mind in this regard. The multiple broods of some temperate-region Lepidoptera have not been well documented in deserts; although the possibility exists in lycaenid butterflies during unusually wet years and, one would think, in a number of microlepidopteran species as well. Wiltshire (1957, cited by Büttiker, 1979) mentioned the multivoltine habit of an anthropophilic geometrid that imbibes sweat and lachrymal secretions of humans and that feeds on *Acacia* spp. in deserts ranging from North Africa to India.

Parasitoid and provisioning Hymenoptera cannot, strictly speaking, be said to have discrete generations, since they tend to spread reproductive effort over periods when hosts are available; perhaps having "overlapping generations" would describe them more suitably. Notwithstanding this problem, we should be able to consider many of them in deserts candidates—in a loose sense—for the multivoltine category. Probably many groups of flies fit in here, too, especially species of higher flies that breed in soil, debris, dung, or carrion. A number of coprophagous and necrophagous beetles should be considered as well. Perhaps small predators in these habitats, e.g., staphylinid beetles, also belong. Again, ectoparasitic arthropods such as ticks, lice, biting flies, and fleas seem generally to have the potential to be multivoltine.

The array of multivoltine species is obviously considerable, yet for the most part these are among the most ignored of the desert invertebrates, probably because many are so small and seem superficially to be so unspectacular. Nevertheless, judicious placement of emergence traps and soil-litter extraction devices, together with careful field observations, can reveal what amounts to a virgin world insofar as general knowledge is concerned. Collectively, they may be the most abundant of the desert's animals, owing to their high turnover rates and to the association of many with soil.

B. Reproductive Patterns

Theory suggests that when regularly occurring periods of stress are interrupted by conditions favorable for rapid colonization, the following reproductive tactics should be favored: low age at first reproduction, large clutch size, and parthenogenesis during colonization (Stearns, 1976).

We might expect the capacity to reproduce early in life to occur whenever resources needed for development are uncertain in time and space. For reasons discussed earlier, this uncertainty should pertain to many species living on or above the desert surface. Prominent among these are larvae of insects that feed on carrion or dung. In fact a number of the higher flies fit this category well (James, 1947), some achieving reproductive maturity less than a week after hatching from the egg. The Australian bushfly, *Musca vetustissima*, normally averages about 120 h for its development (Hughes et al., 1972). Aphids are surely another good example, but our knowledge of their reproductive biology in deserts must at present be inferred from the literature of economic entomology. Other instances await investigation.

Clutch size needs to be compared carefully among related taxa from deserts and elsewhere. Better still would be a clutch size comparison within a single species having a broad geographical range that includes deserts. I know of no such work.

Parthenogenesis, particularly the form known as heterogony in which parthenogenetic and sexual generations alternate, allows for short life cycles and multiplication of efficient genotypes when favorable conditions occur in the habitat (Labeyrie, 1978). Among temperate-region (nondesert) aphids, genetic recombination tends to occur at the onset of a period of stress (e.g., winter) and should enable these insects to spread the chances for survival over this "risky" time. Doubtless other parthenogenetic invertebrates (e.g., many rotifers and cecidomyid midges) employ a similar tactic, although the extent to which the pattern in general occurs in deserts seems not to be known. In such places it would not seem unreasonable to expect stress of another sort to trigger the onset of sexual reproduction. Moisture—and perhaps temperature as well—comes to mind, because unlike the photoperiodic signals that control onset of sexual generations in aphids, moisture and temperature changes should be evident to subterranean invertebrates.

While yet another tactic may not be suggested by formal theory, it nevertheless occurs in this class of desert invertebrates. I refer to rapid but not necessarily early breeding. This is particularly well documented in the Australian bushfly, an annoying but opportunistic insect that oviposits on fresh cattle dung and sequesters protein from the blood and secretions of its defecating host. When the protein resource diminishes, there is a concomitant increase in flight mobility, which in turn enhances the opportunity for the bushfly to be blown by strong winds to presumably more favorable breeding areas (Hughes and Walker, 1970, cited by Matthews, 1976).

Another example of a fast-breeding insect is the mosquito *Anopheles gambiae* in the Sudan. During the dry season its ovaries develop very slowly; however, as soon as the rains arrive, females quickly become gravid and ready to oviposit (Omer and Cloudsley-Thompson, 1968).

C. Patterns of Development and Resource Utilization

Separating reproduction from development and resource use is obviously a procedure that stretches biological credibility. However, with the reader's indulgence it will be done here and in subsequent chapters as a matter of convenience.

Although a theoretical framework supporting optimal resource utilization by multivoltine desert invertebrates is only now being developed (see F. Taylor, 1980; and below), we can mention a number of empirical considerations that ought to apply. One of these is the option of developing rapidly, certainly a necessity whenever short life spans coincide with brief favorable periods.

The energetic commitment of short-lived, rapidly developing species to achieve rapidly either reproductive maturity or some intermediate stage where "escape" in time or space can take place should be comparatively intense. This is partly because of the absolute need for large amounts of energy in a short time and partly because these animals are usually small-bodied and, therefore, conform to the energetically "expensive" end of the size–metabolism relationship that characterizes ectotherms generally. On the other hand, the commitment by such animals to keeping reproductive individuals around for a long time should be relatively low, implying a relatively large allocation of energy directed toward growth and development.

Being able to switch to an escape tactic is another option that is at least theoretically attractive. Unfortunately, with a few exceptions we know little about it in multivoltine desert species. Temporal escape in the form of dormancy of some kind (including anhydrobiosis) is an option that probably occurs often. [It is not, however, an option of the Australian bushfly (Hughes et al., 1972).] It would be interesting to know if escape tactics are better developed in desert species than in their nondesert relatives. One might expect a spectrum of responses in desert populations as a way of "bet hedging" in habitats where resource collapse is imminent.

Spatial escape via migration or dispersal is commonly employed by multivoltine homopterans like aphids and leafhoppers to circumvent a rapidly deteriorating habitat and food supply. While these are sap-feeders, adults of *Drosophila nigrospiracula*—which during development consume bacteria and yeast in necrotic saguaro cactus—also respond by departing when this resource approaches exhaustion (Johnston and Heed, 1976).

The other side of the coin involves the ability of "escapees" to rapidly colonize a habitat when presented with the opportunity to do so. Thus, the reproductively immature adults of *D. nigrospiracula* have exceptionally high rates of dispersal. Likewise, *Folsomides* collembolans become active quickly after months in dry soil upon the arrival of rain (Wood, 1971). However, Santos (1979) showed that the colonization sequence of microarthropods in decomposing litter was independent of season in the Chihuahuan desert.

The Australian bushfly is well known for its ability to colonize grazing "paddocks" in the spring. Immigrants and their progeny are relatively large-bodied, but body size decreases progressively, as does fecundity and level of natality. Meanwhile, the level of mortality in the populations undergoes an increase (Hughes, 1977). While the causes of these population changes are not altogether clear, climate is considered to play a part. It was found that certain African scarabaeid beetles, imported originally to Australia to enhance burial and decomposition of cattle dung, also reduced bushfly breeding (Bornemissza, 1970). Apparently the mechanism involves the effect of dung disturbance on the survival of fly eggs (Hughes et al., 1978).

How best to adjust the multivoltine pattern to environments where conditions suitable for growth and reproduction have varying and limited durations is formally questioned by Taylor (1980). In his model, the process of population growth begins from an initial age distribution comprised either of individuals newly emerged from dormancy, or of immigrants. The model assumes that at the end of the period when the habitat can support growth and reproduction, only individuals in a limited spectrum of ages will survive— either by entering dormancy or by emigrating. The interval of ages doing so is called the "critical interval." Taylor then proposes that a potential optimization problem faced by such multivoltine organisms is to maximize the number of individuals in the critical interval at the end of the growing period. He shows the predictions from this model differ substantially from those derived from models based on simple exponential population growth— based in turn on the concept of a stable age distribution. The model applies well to the survival of multivoltine species in uncertain desert habitats, since all predictions stemming from it depend both on the length of time the environment remains compatible with growth and reproduction and on the life-history characteristics of the organisms colonizing those habitats.

Thus, the capacity to synchronize a short life span with ephemeral resources in an otherwise stressful environment should depend on some combination of rapid breeding, entry into a dormancy or dispersal mode, and rapid resumption of activity when appropriate conditions return. The effectiveness of this set of tactics should, moreover, be modified by climatic and biotic events associated with the duration of a usable habitat.

Chapter 9
Short Lives: Univoltine Species

A. Introduction

Many desert invertebrates have annual generations. Prominently represented are isopods, solifugids, and many spiders. A large number of orthopteroid insect species come under this category, too, as do many hemipterans, neuropterans, and beetles. As for Lepidoptera, Diptera, and Hymenoptera in deserts, the univoltine–multivoltine distinction is unclear for many and needs further study. Part of the problem of establishing well defined life-history categories is first how to define what a desert species is. For example, the sphinx moth *Hyles lineata* is found throughout the southwestern deserts of North America; unfortunately for definitions, this species also has a cosmopolitan distribution.

Despite these drawbacks it is appropriate as we begin this section to make two general comments about univoltine desert taxa. First, their abundance and diversity is overwhelming; and second, considerable information has been accumulated about the biology of a number of species, mainly locusts and coleopterans. Some of this body of knowledge is summarized in the following discussion, which again leads off with theoretical arguments that may or may not be supported by data.

B. Reproductive Patterns

When the annual period of an environmental cycle is about equal to the lifetime of an organism, but when conditions occurring in that cycle (e.g., drought, heavy runoff) are unpredictable and at times stressful, we have another "risky" situation (Stearns, 1976). A moment's reflection tells us that annual species in deserts must sometimes experience such cycles and that their survival should, therefore, be closely linked to the timing of their reproduction.

Two broad, though not mutually exclusive, temporal alternatives seem evident. First, if the timing of its reproduction is relatively rigid, a species should still be able to reproduce successfully providing conditions are appropriate in its habitat at the time. A tendency to migrate from deteriorating habitats should therefore be of value to a species with seasonally fixed reproductive habits. Second, if a species can postpone reproduction by entering prereproductive diapause in response to certain proximate signals, it may—depending on how long habitat deterioration lasts—be able to enhance its reproductive success regardless of its ability to migrate.

The matter is complicated by sometimes unaccountable variation in fecundity levels. Reference is made to Matthew's (1976) useful contrast of flightless, morabine eumasticid grasshoppers with plaque acridid locusts in Australia. The former have no diapause (Blackith and Blackith, 1969a), cannot migrate, and have low fecundities (Blackith and Blackith, 1969b). By comparison, the locusts have eggs that can enter diapause, are noted for their migrations, and are relatively fecund (see Uvarov 1957, for more extensive coverage of these traits). Both groups of orthopterans inhabit what can legitimately be termed "uncertain environments."

Paradoxically, fecundity patterns can be just the reverse in the gregarious and solitary phases of the African desert locust, *Schistocerca gregaria.* The former phase is migratory, and it is also less fecund (Roffey and Popov, 1968). A further complication results from the capacity of locusts to resorb eggs when nutritional conditions are inadequate (Phipps, 1966).

What this clearly signifies is that reproductive effort does not evolve independently of other life-history parameters, since the orthopterans mentioned above are all well established desert species. Other insects also illustrate this point. Arid-region tenebrionids, for example, show wide ranges in species-specific fecundities (see Chapter 10), although many of these species are univoltine. In a single population of the desert isopod, *Hemilepistis reaumuri,* the number of eggs per female ranges from 30–150, averaging 90 eggs per clutch, which Shachak (1981) considers higher than clutch size in mesic isopods. On the contrary, Warburg (1965c) points out that *Venezillo arizonicus* and *Armadillidium vulgare* in Arizona have smaller clutch sizes than does *A. vulgare* from mesic environments.

Variability in egg production is also seen in the diguetid spider, *Diguetia imperiosa,* inhabiting dunes and flats in an intermountain desert basin in Coahuila, Mexico. Bentzien (1973) determined the range of eggs laid by 30 mature females as 0–1657; the average being 734. A total of 89 female retreats contained 0–10 egg sacs, with an average of 3.6. Only 20% of the females produced more than 5 egg sacs.

While the fecundities given above seem moderate for univoltine arthropods, it is important to realize that there are conspicuous exceptions to such an apparent trend. Take, for instance, the case of *Abantiades magnificus,* a large hepialid moth. This insect flies in great numbers following rains in the arid interior of Australia, and it also lays enormous numbers of eggs—over 18 000 per female (Common, 1970). As might be expected, the mortality of its early stages is very high.

In passing we should take another brief look at parthenogenesis, but this time in its thelytokous form, which means that only parthenogenetic females are produced. It is a tactic—or pattern, if you wish—found in nondesert phasmids, curculionid beetles, and psychid moths, all very distantly related insects but all well represented in arid regions. Thelytoky does happen to be known, however, in the *Moraba virgo* group, a completely female species complex of Australian morabine eumasticid grasshoppers found in western New South Wales (White et al., 1963). A number of bisexual *Moraba* species also occur in arid Australia but are geographically well separated from the *M. virgo* group. White and Webb (1968) speculate that the wide gap in distribution may have been due to the inability of parthenogenetic populations to adapt by selection to pluvial Pleistocene or warm post-Pleistocene climates.

C. Developmental Patterns

Postembryonic development is sufficiently complex in univoltine species to warrant its separate treatment in this chapter. It pays to remember, though, that even when dealt with separately, development must continue to be viewed in the context of reproductive success ("fitness" broadly defined), as must all other life-history characteristics. Because one attribute of reproductive success involves the role of parental care, in this case expressed as brooding of early stages, we now review that role in the lives of certain invertebrates.

Brooding of young is tangential to development in the strict sense; nevertheless, since it helps to insure against high early-juvenile mortality and since it is common in some important annual desert invertebrates, we can justifiably cite it as a developmental tactic. Aside from brooding by social insects and solitary/subsocial bees, we find that the trait has evolved to a fairly high degree in certain arachnids and in *Hemilepistus* isopods.

Brooding is manifested in different ways. One is for the female parent to bear a portable chamber containing eggs or juveniles. Many spiders do this, but spiders have such diverse life histories that it is perhaps best to omit them from the present discussion. Another way of brooding is to retain early stages in some kind of shelter, where they can be fed and guarded. Use of both approaches has evolved in some Solifugae and in *Hemilepistus.*

Female solifugids produce eggs (Fig. 22), and these are deposited in burrows. Like the first instar scorpions discussed later in this chapter, the newly

Fig. 22. Gravid emerobatid solifugid entering burrow, Big Bend National Park, Chihuahuan desert. (Photograph by the author)

hatched young are nearly immobile and incapable of feeding until they molt, although unlike scorpions they apparently do not mount the female parent's back. *Hemilepistus* females, on the other hand, produce young viviparously. As with other offspring of terrestrial isopods, these are first housed in a marsupium on the ventral surface of the mother.

Cloudsley-Thompson's (1977a) review of solifugid biology refers to five North American genera shown by Muma (1967b) to abandon their eggs in nests at the ends of burrows, which are then plugged and concealed. Females of several old-world species, however, remain with their offspring and are said to guard them for a time, although the details of this behavior have not been clearly spelled out.

The situation is much more complex in *Hemilepistus,* several desert species of which are social. Their brooding behavior is but a part of a highly interactive family life, a story now briefly outlined.

Following a winter of hibernation in the family burrow, the surviving members begin to move about on the surface in early spring. This event is associated with a slight rise in surface temperatures. In the Negev desert, females are the first to be seen (M. Shachak, personal communication). Some of the isopods exit and move, sometimes for several days, in a more or less straight line using sun-compass and polarized-light orientation; until they are ready to form pair bonds, they stop only to feed (Linsenmair and Linsenmair, 1971). Prior to pairing, a shallow burrow is dug, usually by the female (Fig. 23a,b). Following pairing, both partners dig progressively deeper (Fig. 23c); this keeps temperature and humidity in the burrow within tolerable limits and raises the R.H. at the bottom (Shachak, 1981). Later, as the offspring commence to forage for themselves, this parental effort diminishes.

Fig. 23. Early burrowing activity in *Hemilepistus reaumuri,* Negev desert. **a** Initial digging by adult female. **b** Shallow burrow in loess soil; note fecal pellets of female (partly covered at bottom). **c** Continued digging by pair, rocky hillside. (Photographs by the author)

However, according to Linsenmair (1972), it is still some 6–8 weeks before the young isopods are capable of providing for themselves sufficiently to become nutritionally independent of their parents.

After that, the main role of the parents is to guard the burrow against intruders. Parents do this by plugging its entrance with their hunched bodies, which flick rapidly when disturbed. By late summer most females die; males live longer and serve as entrance guards for some time, occasionally preventing rain water from flooding the burrow (K. E. Linsenmair, personal communication).

Family cohesiveness is strong in at least two desert species of *Hemilepistus.* This has been shown for *H. aphganicus* by Schneider (1970), and for *H. reaurmuri* by Linsenmair and Linsenmair (1971) and Linsenmair (1972). It has been demonstrated experimentally that family-specific chemical "badges" enable individuals in such a unit to recognize each other (Linsenmair, 1972).

With the onset of winter the members of a family begin to hibernate. Apparently hibernation occurs independently of temperature (K. E. Linsenmair, personal communication), but our knowledge of factors controlling its duration is far from complete. It is during hibernation that the ovaries of female siblings mature. Therefore, one might expect all such individuals eventually to form pair bonds. Curiously, they do not (M. Shachak, personal communication), a situation having implications for population regulation.

Thus, from what we know of the life history of *Hemilepistus* isopods, their social existence appears to reduce the probability of having to face an unpredictable desert environment. Brooding and other forms of interactive behavior help to bring this about.

The theme of fitness as a partial function of developmental tactics can be continued by returning to the apparent paradox of low egg production in both nonmigratory eumasticid grasshoppers and migrating desert locusts. Superficially at least, the eumasticids seem to be conforming to what theory predicts should happen to species experiencing uncertain environments: They show reduced reproductive effort. But why should this also occur in locusts specialized to escape those conditions?

An answer is provided by Cheke (1978), who used Leslie matrices to generate responses in theoretical populations of both phases of *Schistocerca gregaria* to simulated conditions based on real data. Cheke showed that although the gregarious females do indeed produce fewer eggs per pod, they develop much faster and should be less exposed to predators than solitary females. Development, moreover, is synchronous in the gregarious phase and leads to rapid buildups of huge populations that eventually migrate. Migration in this case accomplishes two things: It resettles gregarious locusts in habitats of reduced risk to reproduction and, simultaneously, allows the solitary form, with its greater fecundity, to produce on the average at least some surviving progeny after a period of prolonged habitat deterioration.

The use of developmental options by single species populations has not been extensively documented in annual desert species other than orthopterans. Earlier, reference was made to diapause options in locusts and a Mojave desert neuropteran. Developmental flexibility seems to occur also in some desert meloid beetles, which, depending on circumstances, appear also to control their entry into a diapausing "pseudopupa" stage during complex hypermetamorphic development (Werner et al., 1966; Mathieu, 1980).

D. Patterns of Resource Utilization

Implicit in these discussions is the idea that each major life-history category includes species from different trophic levels and habitats. We should also assume that exploitation of food is often closely linked with that of shelter.

a

b

Fig. 24. Generalist lepidopteran feeders, central New Mexico desert grassland. **a** Larva of *Vanessa cardui* feeding on *Cryptantha* sp. **b** Larva of *Hyles lineata.* **c** Pupa of *V. cardui* on *Oryzopsis hymenoides.* **d** Adult of *V. cardui* feeding on nectar of annual flower. (Photographs by the author)

c

d

Fig. 24. c and d.

And, as in other ecosystems, we should expect to find more herbivores than carnivores in aboveground habitats, whereas beneath the surface detritivores, omnivores, and carnivores should prevail in varying proportions. Although systematic surveys of food and habitat use seem not to have been made for large assemblages of desert invertebrates, there is no a priori reason to expect a departure from the above patterns.

A more penetrating look at resource use by univoltine species in deserts shows not unexpectedly that shelter can indeed be used as food, in particular by leaf-feeding insects like chrysomelid beetles and mirid bugs, and that the same shelter may harbor predators like salticid and thomicid spiders and phymatid bugs which feed directly on these insects. Food plants themselves provide shelter of variable quality to generalist herbivores such as larvae of *Vanessa cardui* and *Hyles lineata,* while the pupal and adult stages of these lepidopterans experience still different conditions (Fig. 24). On the other hand, specialist feeders like the creosote bush walkingstick *Diaphero-mera covilleae* (Schultz et al., 1977) are necessarily associated with shelter of a more constant nature.

In the often uncertain environment of a desert, it is clear that the timing of resource use is most important to survival. And when the resource is another organism, the user–resource interaction may have coevolved, as is possible, for example, with the Mojave desert grasshopper *Bootettix punctatus* and its creosote bush host. Feeding by this insect may, under certain conditions, actually stimulate primary production and improve drought resistance (Mispagel, 1978), thereby benefiting both partners in the association. Coevolved relationships will be considered in greater detail in the Chapters 15 and 16.

A fundamental tenet of community ecology considers that competition for resources plays an important part in the structure of a community (see reviews in MacArthur, 1972; Schoener, 1974). Yet there are good reasons to employ the term "community" advisedly in referring to deserts (see Introduction, Part 4). Therefore, it would be useful from the standpoint of testing ecological theory to investigate the possibility of interspecific competition within these assemblages. Using sympatric species of tenebrionid beetles, Wise (1981) made such an attempt in central New Mexico. Despite careful use of enclosures and manipulation of populations, he was unable to demonstrate competition in these mostly annual detritus feeders. Earlier, Polk and Ueckert (1973) examined twig-girdling cerambycid beetles in mesquite and also could not prove competition, although they felt it was implied by their data.

There may also be competition for another "resource," namely mates, and a look at this phenomenon brings us back to tactics underlying reproductive effort. Reference is made here to several examples of competitive combat among males. In one instance Otte and Joern (1975) noted that male *Ligurotet-tix coquiletti* grasshoppers in the Chihuahuan desert establish territories in the creosote bushes they inhabit, thereby apparently insuring quotas of females for reproductive purposes. *Bootettix argentatus* also displays territorial behavior when its density is low on the same shrub (Schowalter and Whitford, 1980). More subtle but equally vicious competition for mates occurs in the phasmid *Diapheromera velii,* which lives mainly in *Dalea scorparia* shrubs in New Mexico. Large numbers of these well camouflaged insects copulate for long periods during most of the summer (Fig. 25), and battles among males for the opportunity to engage in prolonged mating sometimes result in wounds (Sivinski, 1978). A third example involves fast-running tenebrionid beetles living in Namib desert sand dunes (Hamilton et al., 1976). Many diurnal combats occur among these males of *Onymacris rugatipennis,* the

Fig. 25. Copulating pair of phasmids, *Diapheromera velii* on *Sphaeralcea.* Ordinarily this abundant insect is common, and highly cryptic, on nearby *Dalea scopiaria* shrubs. Central New Mexico desert grassland. (Photograph by the author)

"winner" being the individual managing to hold the space over a sand-buried female at the end of the day.

Finally, we refer to territory maintenance by sphecid wasps known as "cicada killers." In arid western North America, where *Sphecius grandis* nests in large aggregations, aggressive males with the best perches in high-density areas should best be able to copulate with newly emerging females. Strong attachment to—and continual defense of—such territories for several weeks is characteristic of the species (Alcock, 1975).

Univoltine carnivores like the desert spider *Agelinopsis aperta* also demonstrate how use of space relates to reproductive success (see Riechert, 1974, 1978; Riechert et al., 1973; Riechert and Tracy, 1975). In 1978, Riechert proposed that the largest territories established by this funnel web-builder should occur when the physical environment is "harsh" and the prey unpredictable. Thus, its territory size should be energy-based and should have evolved to optimize rate of maturation and to maximize reproductive success. Conversely, when an individual spider shares its territory with another, the accessibility to prey and the potential fitness of both should be reduced.

These few examples emphasize again how appropriate use of time and space is essential to the fitness of desert invertebrates. And although univoltine species were considered in the present chapter, the principle obviously has wider application.

Chapter 10
Long Lives: Herbivores and Detritivores

A. Introduction

Gastropod mollusks, several groups of millipedes, cryptostigmatid mites (see Mitchell, 1977), apterygote insects, cicadas, several prominent families of beetles, and certain root-feeding lepidopterans belong to this category. They have in common a diet consisting mainly of living or dead plant material, and a longevity of several to many years. These traits are associated with life-history options that, in the uncertain environments of deserts, are modifications of those already seen in multi- and univoltine species.

While most desert invertebrates are not perennial organisms, many that are appear to be exceedingly common and obviously well adapted. As such animals became established in arid regions, combinations of preadaptations and newly selected traits must have allowed them to persist; and in this chapter we note how some of these combinations, or tactics, are manifested in the context of their life-history patterns.

B. Reproductive Patterns

Both iteroparity and semelparity occur in these species. Iteroparity is well known in desert snails and conforms to the long life span of many land mollusks (Yom-Tov, 1971a). Most of the latter are pulmonate snails (Hunter, 1968) and, therefore, lay smaller clutches of eggs than do other gastropods (Morton, 1958, cited by Yom-Tov, 1971a). Although clutch size in desert and nondesert snails has not been thoroughly compared, we do know that in deserts it can be determined by both biotic and abiotic factors. Thus, Yom-Tov (1972) found that fecundity in *Helicella seetzeni* from the Negev desert is both density dependent and site specific.

The magnitude of fecundity in desert snails is hardly impressive. Yom-Tov (1971a) gave ranges of 14–141, and of 8–48 for *H. seetzeni* and *Sphinctero-chila zonata* (Fig. 26), respectively, and Shachak et al. (1975) recorded 4–62 eggs per clutch for *S. zonata* over a 5-year period. Likewise, *Levantina* spp. having desert populations lay clutches of 50–70 eggs (Heller, 1979). According to Stearns (1976), such small to moderate-sized broods should be expected from long-lived "bet hedgers" in uncertain environments when juvenile mortality is highly variable. Apparently, year-to-year fluctuations in juvenile mortality have not been assessed for desert snails; however, the suggestion by Herreid (1977) that juveniles of the North African *Otala lactea* are less able to use energy reserves over long periods than are adults implies that prolonged drought may induce differential mortality (see below). Large yearly changes in adult mortality due to exposure and/or predation are also

Fig. 26. *Sphincterochila zonata* digging a shallow hole in loess soil in order to lay eggs, Negev desert. (Photograph by the author)

strongly implied (Yom-Tov, 1970, 1972; Heller, 1975), and Shachak et al. (1975) give some indication of seasonal and yearly irregularities in the survival of *Sphincterochila zonata.*

Large spirostreptid millipedes inhabiting arid regions should also be iteroparous. This conclusion is supported by inferences from the literature (e.g., Blower, 1969), by the obvious longevity of one desert species (Crawford, 1976), and by the following information on its ovarian development. In North America the ovaries of *Orthoporous ornatus* begin to mature around the time summer rains arrive. Females with developing eggs range considerably in body diameter, and since this dimension changes only minimally at annual molt (Crawford, 1976), it would appear that a single female can breed for a number of summers. *Archispirostreptus syriacus* in the Judaean and Negev deserts is undoubtedly also iteroparous since reproductively competent females vary greatly in size. However, there the similarity between the two species ends, as some large eggs occur all year long in the ovaries of this winter-rainfall diplopod (M. R. Warburg, personal communication).

Clutch size in *O. ornatus* can exceed that known for desert snails. Estimates from dissections of large females in the Chihuahuan desert and from actual counts of egg pellets (eggs are individually covered by a layer of maternal feces) from underground clutches (Crawford and Matlack, 1979; Fig. 27) come to about 500 per clutch. Smaller-bodied females in New Mexico deposit smaller clutches of about 100 eggs. The comparatively large clutch size in *O. ornatus* may reflect a pattern of age-specific mortality that differs from patterns in desert snails, although there may certainly be other reasons for clutch-size differences. Cole (1954), for instance, has argued that there can be selection for iteroparity even when litter size is large. In the absence of a rigorous evaluation of mortality schedules, my own observations of *O. ornatus* clutches suggest that most are reproductive failures. The majority of pellets seem not to have emergence holes and contain only the fungus-ridden remains of eggs or early instars. By comparison later stages show no indication of the kind of heavy mortality one sees in desert snails (see below).

Some long-lived insects in deserts may also be iteroparous, if adult longevity is any indication of this trait. Among these, members of the thysanuran family Lepismatidae may live up to 5 years and apparently reach sexual maturity several years earlier (Kaplin, 1978). Some tenebrionid species can also live as adults for a number of years (Leouffre, 1953; Doyen, 1973; Hinds and Rickard, 1973). The remarkable diversity of life-history patterns in desert tenebrionids is reflected by life spans ranging from a few weeks to 5 years (C. N. Slobodchikoff, personal communication). Many species may be "K-selected" (Doyen and Tschinkel, 1974).

On the other hand, certain insect groups tend to have long immature and short adult lives. These species, therefore, are more likely to be semelparous. Known or suspected examples from deserts or regions having long dry seasons include taxa with developing stages that feed on roots or wood. Some cerambycid (Linsley, 1957; Gwynne and Hostetler, 1978), buprestid

Fig. 27. Egg pellets of the desert millipede, *Orthoporus ornatus,* in alluvial soil. Most have fallen below position of original clump about 20 cm (8 inches on the yardstick) beneath soil surface. Big Bend National Park, Chihuahuan desert. (Crawford and Matlack, 1979; with permission)

(Matthews, 1976), and scarabaeid (Moutia, 1940; Hardy and Andrews, 1974) beetles belong to this feeding category, as do some hepialid (Matthews, 1976) and sesiid (Duckworth and Eichlin, 1978) moths. Cicadas, which invariably have life spans of 4 years or more (Borror et al., 1976), are also candidates for semelparity. The slowly developing larvae of at least one nondesert species feeds on the xylem fluids of tree roots (White and Strehl, 1978). Large numbers of cicada species are known from North American arid lands [see many papers by W. T. Davis in the Journal of the New York Entomological Society (1915–1941)], but the biology of their immature forms has been ignored.

C. Developmental Patterns

I. Slow Growth and Its Consequences

Proximate signals of varying intensities inform long-lived desert snails, millipedes, and insects when to copulate, develop ovaries, and lay eggs. Environmental pulses also affect patterns of dormancy and growth in these invertebrates. It follows that their ability to colonize and to remain in a habitat reflects the successful timing of their reproductive and developmental responses. Yet when environmental change has a strong element of randomness, proper timing carries a certain amount of risk. Minimizing this risk is clearly the critical element underlying the life histories of long-lived desert invertebrates.

For a snail like *Sphincterochila zonata,* the rules of the game are very strict. This species will not lay eggs unless rains have fallen in the previous month, and unless habitat soil moisture and temperature are respectively 10% and 4°C or greater (Shachak et al., 1976a). Since this remarkable Negev desert snail undergoes virtually all of its growth and reproduction in a period averaging about 3 weeks each year, its adherence to such a rigid schedule is clearly adaptive.

Other desert snails seem comparatively labile developmentally, but all appear to have a strong arousal response from dormancy when significant rainfall (McMichael and Iredale, 1959; Heller, 1975, 1979; Shachak et al., 1976a), elevated humidity (Herreid and Rokitka, 1976; Riddle, 1977), and dew (Shalem, 1949, cited by Hunter, 1968) occur.

Brooding of eggs and young seems to be unknown in the long-lived invertebrates being considered; therefore, heavy early mortality may—as in desert millipedes—be typical of many, although appropriate life-table information is lacking. Moreover, length of life itself varies greatly among species. *Helicella seetzeni* lives for 2 to 3 years, *Sphincterochila zonata* and *S. prophetarum* for more than 10 years (Y. Steinberger, personal communication), and *Sonorella* spp. in the North American southwest for around 15–20 years (Walton, 1963). Since West African spirostreptids can also live for many years (implication from Demange and Mauriès, 1975), a decade or so is expected for desert *Orthoporus.* This is equaled by buprestid beetles whose larvae feed on dry eucalyptus wood in Australia and take a dozen years to mature (Matthews, 1976). While it is tempting to associate slow growth and long life with a diet of cellulose and other recalcitrant carbon compounds, or with xylem fluids, the reader will soon be reminded that a number of carnivorous desert species have long juvenile periods as well (Chapter 11).

Slow growth may also be correlated with seasonally restricted ingestion—although cause and effect are difficult to demonstrate and many short-lived species also have restricted feeding periods. Growth as estimated by biomass addition and energy accumulation seems to occur at rates dictated partly by the length of time available for foraging. Thus, *Sphincterochila zonata* gains all of its annual energy input during its brief period of yearly activity (Shachak et al., 1976a), while *Orthoporous ornatus* increases its dry weight 1.5 times during 3 or 4 months of summer feeding (Crawford, 1976).

The long, slow business of growing is punctuated by a series of events of critical importance to the species concerned. For all developing arthropods, one such occurrence is ecdysis. This occurs synchronously once a year (often within a week in a single population) in all but very young, and possibly some old, *O. ornatus* located in separate hibernacula (Fig. 28). And, while it permits external growth and some internal reorganization to occur, ecdysis also occasions the potential loss of water (Crawford, 1978), which may be a serious matter if soil is exceptionally dry.

Among holometabolous insects, eclosion from the pupa has unique ecological and evolutionary significance, because it presents the new adult with a habitat quite different from that experienced by the larva. As we noted earlier, this phenomenon may coincide with the onset of long-delayed rain; thus, a mass emergence followed by mating and oviposition was observed in the cerambycid *Prionus emarginatus* after a heavy night rain at Great Sand Dunes National Monument, Colorado (Gwynne and Hostetler, 1978). However, in some Australian buprestids (Matthews, 1976) and Mexican meloids (Mathieu, 1980), the appearance of adults is synchronous with the flowering of mallee scrub and mesquite trees, respectively.

During the development of most long-lived desert invertebrates, seasonal dormancy is a fairly predictable event. We discussed some aspects of dormancy in Part 2, but there is still another time-related feature that we should consider, namely metabolic shifts in the qualitative use of energy substrates. When dormancy is lengthy, there may be, in addition to internal change in temperature-related metabolism, a switch from carbohydrate use to that of lipid and/or protein. This is seen in the desert millipede *Orthoporus ornatus* (Wooten and Crawford, 1974) and in *Bulimulus dealbatus,* a snail from semiarid parts of Texas that undergoes enhanced tissue catabolism during aestivation (Horne, 1973). While a pronounced switch to protein use may signify an inherent inability to store much carbohydrate, it may also provide an adequate short-term solution to the problem of an energy shortage. However,

Fig. 28. Annual ecdysis in *Orthoporus ornatus.* Newly molted individual exposed in hibernaculum beneath volcanic rock following excavation of covering soil. Much of the exuvium will eventually be eaten. Central New Mexico desert grassland. (Photograph by the author)

a simultaneous accumulation of urea from detoxified ammonia produced by tissue catabolism (Horne, 1973) illustrates the long-term danger of such a switch.

Despite the ability of a number of snails to undergo prolonged dormancy, eventually their energy reserves must run out, as has been implied for *Helicella virgata* in Australia (Pomeroy, 1969) and for *Sphincterochila zonata* in Israel (Schmidt-Nielsen et al., 1971). Herreid (1977) makes the interesting observation that in *Otala lactea,* a Moroccan pulmonate, large individuals should survive starvation longer than small specimens, because the former have greater energy reserves. Since this species can remain dormant for 2 to 4 years (Machin, 1967) and since such a feat is approximately matched by other arid-land species (McMichael and Iredale, 1959; Schmidt-Neilsen et al., 1971), mortality of small juveniles in drought years—other things being equal—may be characteristic of desert snails. This point has a bearing on our previous observations about variable juvenile mortality in these animals (see section B, "Reproductive Patterns," above).

II. Interactions with Predators

A consideration of development in long-lived herbivores and detritivores would be incomplete without some mention of their interactions with predators. Since growth and predation are separate—albeit related—topics and since a fair amount of documentation of predation in this instance is available, we now turn briefly to a treatment of the subject.

Predation of considerable magnitude occurs periodically in desert snails. One predator, a song thrush, uses rock anvils to smash the shells of those gastropods (Yom-Tov, 1970; Heller, 1975). Episodes of extensive avian predation of this kind occur infrequently in the Negev desert, which may help to explain why as many as 10%–40% of *Sphincterochila zonata* aestivate on the soil surface under shrubs (where algal crust is most available following rains), while others remain slightly buried in the soil beneath shrubs (Shachak et al., 1975). A similar tactic may be less effective on nearby hillsides for *S. prophetarum,* which is regularly preyed on by rodents. Piles of discarded shells attest to the effects of these carnivores on *S. prophetarum* (Fig. 29) and on *Levantina* spp. (Heller, 1979). Steinberger (1979) observed that the proportion of *S. prophetarum* shells found in front of rodent burrows, compared to the shell proportions of four other snail species, was much greater than that of the others. *S. prophetarum* was also by far the most abundant species in the area. *Helicella seetzeni* and *S. zonata* are likewise heavily predated by rodents in the Negev, especially on south-facing slopes (Yom-Tov, 1970, 1972).

The synchronous emergence of adults of long-lived insect species can also attract predators and lead to decimated populations. An example of this

Fig. 29. Broken and discarded shells of *Sphincterochila prophetarum* after years of predation by rodents. Limestone outcrop, Negev desert. (Photograph by the author)

was noted by Gwynne and Hostetler (1978), who reported that the day after the emergence of hundreds of cerambycid adults from a sand-dune habitat, few living specimens remained. Large numbers of these beetles had instead been the victims of predators.

Other long-term herbivores and detritivores may be less attractive as food items during their development. We know little of the mortality patterns of insects developing underground, but adult tenebrionids—and millipedes at any stage—produce "defensive" secretions that may benefit their survival. These chemicals are certainly noxious to the human observer, but while rather spectacular instances of their repelling effects have been documented (Eisner and Meinwald, 1966), there is little evidence that mammals cannot either solve the problem or learn to put up with it. Grasshopper mice (*Onychomys* spp.) in the southwestern U.S. simply jam *Eleodes* adults, tail down, into the sandy soil and eat their way down to the anal region where the repugnatorial glands are located (Eisner and Meinwald, 1966). In 1978, Slobodchikoff reported that naive skunks rolled adult tenebrionids in the substrate until the beetles' noxious secretions were presumably exhausted. Then they ate the beetles.

However, some *Eleodes* species do seem able to repel ants with their secretions, and Slobodchikoff (1979) found evidence of this in Arizona. There,

a

Fig. 30. Desert coleopterans with convergent defensive behavior. **a** The tenebrionid *Eleodes hispilabris* "headstanding." **b** The cerambycid *Moneilema appressum.* **c** The meloid *Cystedemus* (probably *armatus*). The last two have toxic secretions—as does *E. hispilabris*—and also "headstand" when disturbed. Author's observations apply to **c,** and are inferred for **b** from Raske (1967). (Photographs by the author: **a** and **c** in central New Mexico desert grassland, **b** in Big Bend National Park, Chihuahuan desert)

b

c

three species of *Eleodes* are much more abundant on detritus-rich mounds of the harvester ant *Pogonomyrmex barbatus* than are two sympatric but nonsecreting *Stemomorpha* species. In addition to having a defensive function, secretions from the anal glands of tenebrionids result in aggregations of members of the same species. This was demonstrated experimentally in the Negev using *Blaps sulcata* (Kaufman, 1966).

Sometimes associated with the release of defensive secretions by tenebrionids is the peculiar habit of "headstanding" (Fig. 30a). Tenebrionid-mimicking *Moneilema* cerambycids (Fig. 30b) do this too (Raske, 1967), and I have observed the small meloid shown in Fig. 30c performing likewise. Death feigning and stridulation can also occur when secretions are given off by tenebrionids (see references in Allsopp, 1978).

Owing to their repugnatorial gland emissions, desert millipedes do not appear to be regularly killed or eaten by vertebrates, although occasionally specimens are seen in sections, some still moving. Lizards, birds, or rodents may be responsible for these seemingly infrequent attacks. In the Chihauhaun desert the immature stages of *Zarhippus,* a phengodid beetle, specialize in killing and eating *Orthoporus ornatus* (Fig. 31). Members of the same genus feed on other millipedes in California (Tiemann, 1967).

Fig. 31. A predatory phengodid, *Zarhippus* sp., (late-instar larva) dragging a desert millipede it has just killed by biting along the ventral nerve cord. Southern New Mexico, Chihuahuan desert. (Photograph by the author)

Endoparasites of desert invertebrates appear to be poorly known. Thelasto-matid nematodes often pack the hindguts of *O. ornatus, Archispirostreptus syriacus,* and other spirostreptid millipedes. However, the pinworms are also common in certain other diplopod orders, as well as in numerous detritivore-omnivore insects (Upton et al., in press), and may simply be commensals.

The effects of predation and parasitism on adult insects belonging to this life-history category are also unclear. Assuming that adults in many of these long-lived species are themselves short-lived, they should produce most of their offspring over relatively brief periods. Therefore, unless predator action is timed rather precisely, severe predation on relative massive populations of *Tibicen* cicadas should have negligible effects. While *Sphecius* wasps do indeed provision their nests with large numbers of these insects, the process of capture and transportation of prey is infrequently observed (J. M. Hastings, personal communication). Again, recent experiments suggest that rodents can learn to handle and eat desert cicadas despite the piercing distress calls given out (Smith and Langley, 1978). However, there seems to be no published evidence that these often extremely abundant insects are subject to appreciable predation as adults.

D. Detritus as a Resource

Since the use of food and shelter by herbivores is dealt with at length in Part 4, we now focus briefly on the use of a single resource, namely detritus.

It should be clear that although desert detritus may actually be present in abundance, the constraint of dormancy often interferes with its procure-ment. There may be more to this point than seems intuitively evident. Why, for instance, cannot a true detritus feeder forage efficiently at moderate tem-peratures as long as its water balance is not in jeopardy? An answer based only on some phylogenetically controlled dormancy response may be begging the real issue. One easily overlooked explanation that ought to be explored has to do with the harvesting of microorganisms by detritivores for certain gut-associated functions, including digestion (see Martin and Martin, 1978). Perhaps some detritivores feed mostly under conditions that allow such mi-croorganisms to be functional symbionts. Certainly the microbial gut flora of desert millipedes (Fig. 32) contributes significantly to the digestion of cellulose and pectin; moreover, the millipedes show preferences for some species of fungi over others (E. C. Taylor, personal communication). And, as might be expected, a broad array of carbohydrases is present in the gut of *O. ornatus* (Nunez and Crawford, 1976).

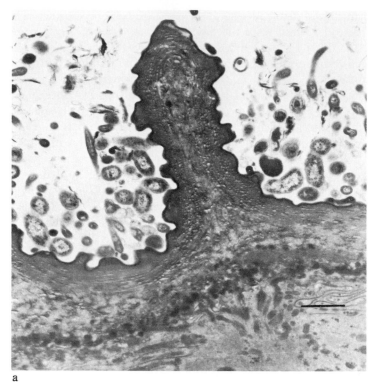

a

Fig. 32. Bacterial morphotypes in the hindgut of the desert millipede *Orthoporus ornatus.* **a** Bacteria adjacent to an intimal protuberance. **b** Details of bacteria near intima. (TEM photographs courtesy of G. P. Minion and M. D. Boyers; *bar* = 1 μm)

Another aspect of detritus that tends to be ignored is its water content. If, as was suggested in Part 2, most water intake in active desert invertebrates occurs during ingestion of food, then whether or not the food is well hydrated may have implications regarding dormancy versus continued activity. We know that detritus absorbs condensation water and that dew formation is common in some deserts like the Negev (Broza, 1979) and the Namib (Tschinkel, 1972). Perhaps the high frequency of dew in such places causes detritus absorbing it hygroscopically to be more nutritious (i.e., a better growth medium for microorganisms) than detritus from deserts that actually experience more annual rainfall but less regular condensation. The chain of events beginning with ingestion of available moisture and proceeding through detritivore water balance and reproductive effort needs to be examined in detail if we are to understand the feeding dynamics of desert detritivores.

Patterns reviewed in the present section suggest that fitness in long-lived desert detritivores and herbivores is strongly dependent on the timing of reproductive, developmental, and other resource-utilizing events in their life

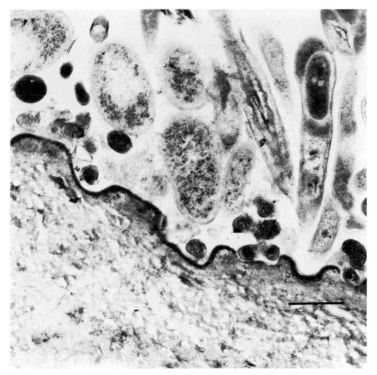

b

Fig. 32. b.

histories. The effects of predation on fitness are difficult to document. Also, there is no strong evidence that the ultimate factor of food per se is even a major influence on the life-history patterns in these animals. On the contrary, timing of critical life-history events seems mainly geared to seasonal levels of moisture occurring in the habitat.

Chapter 11
Long Lives: Carnivores

A. Introduction

Arachnids clearly dominate this category, and are represented mostly by scorpions and certain large-bodied spiders. The few whip scorpions occurring in deserts should also be included, as should some pseudoscorpions. Scolopendromorph centipedes add moderately to the remaining taxa, as most likely do some of the large carabid beetles, but very little is known about the life histories of either in arid regions.

None of these animals is surrounded continuously by its food. Rather, for them nutritional supply tends to be sporadic in time and clustered in space, and to arrive as high-density "pulses" associated indirectly with rainfall. This kind of food relationship means that the predaceous consumers must be phenologically "ready" to take advantage of fairly unpredictable bouts of food availability in order to profit from its presence. Otherwise, such carnivores must be able to do without—to starve as it were—often for long periods.

Long-lived carnivorous invertebrates in deserts are usually obligate predators. A large number of carnivorous desert vertebrates, on the other hand, are capable of switching to other forms of food (Noy-Meir, 1974; Reichman et al., 1979). Hence, tactics of food utilization by the invertebrates are set in a more restrictive evolutionary and ecological framework, a matter to bear in mind as we consider the life-history patterns that follow.

B. Reproductive Patterns

Fecundity variations in these animals seem to be correlated with family—or with higher taxonomic levels. For scorpions in general, a large amount of reproductive data has been brought together by Polis and Farley (1979a), who list an average (± SD) clutch size of 31.3 ± 15.0 for the order. This is somewhat low compared to values given above for long-lived desert herbivores and detritivores, and there seems to be no indication of a clutch size typical of desert species. Since a number of the latter are iteroparous, however, clutch size alone is but one aspect of their reproductive effort. Thus in North America, *Centruroides sculpturatus* can have at least two clutches a year (Williams, 1969), and *Paruroctonus mesaensis* can remain gravid for 3 consecutive years (Polis and Farley, 1979a). In contrast, the Australian scorpion *Urodacus yaschenkoi* appears to be semelparous even though it lives for 6 years (Shorthouse, 1971).

Scolopendromorph centipedes may be similar to scorpions in terms of number and size of clutches. Reports of clutch size in species inhabiting regions with long dry seasons range from about 30 to 60 (Brunhuber, 1970; J. G. E. Lewis, 1969, 1972, 1973), based on eggs present in the ovary. These large and aggressive chilopods can reach maturity in 1 or 2 years, and some apparently live for at least six, so their potential for iteroparity is high. Unfortunately, aside from the studies of Brunhuber and of Lewis, neither of whom worked with truly desert species, practically nothing is known about the reproductive biology of these invertebrates.

Large desert spiders appear to produce more offspring per clutch than do scorpions or scolopendromorphs. This is evident in the North American wolf spider *Lycosa carolinensis,* which averages around 150 eggs per egg sac (Shook, 1978), and in *Aphonopelma chalcodes,* a North American desert tarantula with a known range of about 450–500 eggs per sac (Minch, 1979). Judging from comments made by the authors cited, the potential for iteroparity in these species is high. Clearly, the two spiders have significant clutch-size differences, and D. C. Lowrie (personal communication) feels that these may be partly explained by the greater maternal care shown by wolf spiders. If this view is correct (intensity of maternal care is difficult to quantify), then perhaps it also helps to explain the small clutches of scorpions and centipedes.

The timing of reproduction-associated activities in these long-lived carnivores ranges from well defined to very unpredictable. Thus, birth in a given population of North American vaejovid scorpions can be a highly synchronous event (Williams, 1969), and in *Paruroctonus mesaenis* may result from pulses of available prey (Polis and Farley, 1979a). On a broader basis the picture changes, with mid-to-late summer being the period of birth for 8 out of 9 vaejovid species. On a worldwide basis, however, scorpions can be born in all months of the year (Polis and Farley, 1979a). Mating is another activity showing much variation, with "migrating" swarms of adult males moving about during the warmer months (Williams, 1966), presumably in search of females. Similar behavior takes place in male tarantulas during late summer and early fall in the southwestern United States (personal observation).

C. Developmental Patterns

Some degree of maternal care, or brooding, distinguishes this group from other general categories treated in Part 3. Recall, however, that both *Hemilepistus* isopods and some solifugids brood their offspring as well. In scorpions many studies have shown that brooding is restricted to the period when newborn individuals ascend the mother's back, remaining there until they molt to the second instar (e.g., Stahnke, 1966; Williams, 1969). After that they are able to forage for themselves.

Brooding is manifested similarly in desert populations of *Lycosa carolinensis*. In this wolf spider and in *Geolycosa* spiders as well (see Fig. 33), hatchlings leave the egg sac and stay on the mother's body for a week or so. As with scorpions they do not feed until they molt and descend. Then they too disperse (Shook, 1978). First instars of the tarantula *Aphonopelma chalcodes* remain in the egg sac for over a month after eclosion from the egg. Following that they emerge, remain gregarious for a time, and finally leave the maternal

Fig. 33. Dune-inhabiting *Geolycosa* sp.; female at burrow entrance with hatchlings. (Photograph courtesy of D. T. Gwynne)

burrow for nearby shelters. Mortality at this stage is probably very high (Minch, 1979).

Brooding also characterizes the southern African scolopendromorph *Cormocephalus anceps anceps,* which grooms both eggs and young with its mouthparts. If offspring are separated from the mother in the first month and a half of life they die, apparently of fungal attacks (Brunhuber, 1970). This species eats its eggs if the soil becomes too dry, warm, or moist. Such a tactic is tantamount to postparturition egg resorption, and leads one to wonder if similar physical stresses might not elicit like responses in true desert centipedes—and perhaps in other carnivores being considered.

Postembryonic development is not rapid in these animals. It was mentioned above that scolopendromorphs can mature in 1 or 2 years, and while information from desert species is lacking, we can assume that temperature alone may be an important determinant of growth rate since tropical species appear to complete development more rapidly than do species from temperate regions (J. G. E. Lewis, 1969, 1972, 1973). The higher rate in the tropics can be continuous during the dry season and must result in a relatively rapid lowering of the body's surface:volume ratio. J. G. E. Lewis (1972) speculates that extended foraging time should, therefore, be possible in these centipedes, which are otherwise relatively more susceptible to desiccation than scorpions (see Chapter 4).

It is difficult to generalize about development times in scorpions. On the whole these arachnids average about 6 molts per lifetime and live from about 1 to over 6 years (Polis and Farley, 1979a; O. F. Francke, personal communication). We also know that the large whip scorpion, *Mastigoproctus giganteus,* has 4 instars and molts underground in early summer (Wegoldt, 1971). Adults of this species can be kept alive in captivity for several years.

Lycosa carolinensis in desert habitats develops to reproductive maturity in about 2 years, and females can then live another two (Shook, 1978). A much longer life is typical of tarantulas, however, and after taking about a decade to reach sexual maturity, females may remain alive for a similar duration (Gertsch, 1949).

In the introduction to this chapter, it was implied that phenological readiness to take advantage of episodes of prey arrival should be an important option at any time during ontogeny. The option is of course subject to the constraints of ectothermy, but from my own observations and from records of seasonal respiration in arid-land scorpions and centipedes (Crawford and Riddle, 1975; Riddle and Pugach, 1976), it is clear that when these animals are warmed from sluggishness due to winter cold, they rapidly become active and aggressive. Studies need to be made of the actual "opportunistic" feeding of such species in order to understand the significance of this capacity for rapid arousal. The relationship between feeding bouts in cold seasons and the initiation of ovarian development should also be explored.

The other possible tactic, that of prolonged inactivity, is an alternative that should be adaptive, provided it does not result in a dormancy from which arousal is difficult. Earlier we discussed metabolic changes that increase the efficient use of energy stores in wolf spiders and scorpions during cold periods (Chapter 6). While these changes undoubtedly involve altered enzymatic activity, there is no evidence from desert species that deep dormancies are achieved. It would be useful to study carefully the seasonal metabolic patterns of tarantulas in this regard, because, as Minch (1979) points out, in the desert these animals often remain in plugged burrows for most of the year.

D. Patterns of Resource Utilization

It has been emphasized above that prey to this assemblage of obligate carnivores probably represent a relatively rare resource most of the time. Indeed, this should be a very fundamental aspect of their existence, and whether we are discussing their reproduction, development, or use of shelter, we cannot ignore its reality. Foraging for rare prey in a potentially stressful habitat involves certain obvious liabilities. One is the danger of wasting energy and body water, the rapid replacement of these being improbable at best. A further hazard is that of being eaten by another carnivore, an event that becomes increasingly likely with prolonged exposure in relatively vegetationless landscapes. It is hardly surprising, therefore, to find that so many carnivorous species in deserts are nocturnal, a matter considered also in Parts 2 and 4 of this book.

The two ends of the foraging spectrum for carnivores are characterized by the "sit-and-wait" tactic and by active hunting. These are oversimplifications, because acquiring living animal food usually involves a complex behavioral repertoire; nevertheless, they do help to define the limits of foraging behavior that we can expect of these animals.

Turning first to desert scorpions, it seems from several accounts (e.g., Stahnke, 1966; Hadley and Williams, 1968) that they are often "sit-and-wait" hunters and tend to be broad feeders, or generalists. On the whole they take what is "in season," a tactic that makes sense in a desert. Closer examination, however, reveals that certain feeding restrictions and limitations can be easily overlooked. For example, Stahnke (1966) noted that scorpions tend not to feed on certain isopods (but see below). Again, Hadley and Williams (1968) noted the tendency of some species not to include tenebrionid beetles in their diets, although this is obviously not the case among others (see Chapter 14). Even more restricted is the Australian scorpionid, *Isometroides keyserling,* which specializes on burrowing spiders (Main, 1956). Moreover, an important feeding limitation has to do with the age and size of the scorpion. Thus, while *Paruroctonus mesaensis* is indeed a generalist with at least 100 prey species, there are major age-specific differences in its utilization of prey. Furthermore, even though this scorpion can be classified as a "sit-and-wait" predator, its food has a behavioral classification too, being roughly assorted as 80% cursorial, 10% fossorial, and 10% aerial (Polis, 1979). (Illustrations of predation on these three prey categories are shown in Fig. 34.) The most surprising finding about the food of *P. mesaensis* is that on a biomass basis most of the prey are members of its own species (Fig. 34d) (Polis, 1979; Polis and Farley, 1979b). This has important implications for the regulation of its population size (Polis, 1980b) and raises the question of similar density-dependent regulation in other relatively stationary hunters.

Scorpions in the family Buthidae are well known for their poisonous sting, and some also (e.g., *Centruroides sculpturatus*) for a roaming type of foraging (Hadley and Williams, 1968). Others may be less mobile hunters, an example being *Scorpio maurus palmatus* in the Negev desert. When the burrows of this carnivore are in loess plains, piles of prey remains are seen at burrow entrances (Fig. 35), implying a relatively inactive foraging pattern. The isopod *Hemilepistus reaumuri* is said to constitute 20%–60% of these remains (Shachak, 1981).

Regardless of prey abundance, and in apparent contradiction of our emphasis on taking advantage of prey availability, relatively few scorpions in a population actually seem to forage at any one time. Estimates of feeding frequencies on a given night range from 1% to 5% (Hadley and Williams, 1968) and from 0.5% to 7% (Polis and Farley, 1979a). Likewise, not all individuals of *Urodacus yaschenkoi*, which waits at the mouth of its burrow in Australia, are in foraging position on any given night (Shorthouse, 1971).

Mention should be made briefly here of how prey are detected and captured by scorpions. Much controversy has attended this point, but Brownell (1977) demonstrated convincingly that *P. mesaensis* detects prey as distant as 50 cm on sandy substrates by using sensory structures on its legs to perceive low-velocity compressional and surface waves. Accurate determination of direction and distance is possible within 15 cm (Brownell and Farley, 1979). Bub and Bowerman (1979) point out that some species of scorpion seldom if ever sting their prey during capture, while others such as *Hadrurus arizonensis* do so repeatedly. These authors cite Baerg's (1961) observation that scorpions having large pedipalps and a reduced metasoma probably do not use the sting for immobilizing prey.

Feeding frequency also seems low in large desert spiders. Out of 674 actual field encounters with *Lycosa carolinensis*, Shook (1978) observed feeding 3 times. Perhaps this paucity of observations can be partly explained by the territorial behavior of these animals. They, as well as tarantulas, wait for prey in small, predetermined home ranges around the burrow, and only make short, fast dashes to capture their food.

In Arizona, mature females of *Lycosa santrita* were shown by Kronk and

a

b

Fig. 34. Prey categories of *Paruroctonus mesaensis* in the Mojave desert. **a** Cursorial/
fossorial: an *Arenivaga* cockroach. **b** Cursorial/fossorial: an emerobatid solifugid. **c**
Aerial: an adult myrmeleontid neuropteran. **d** An example of cannibalism. (Photographs courtesy of G. A. Polis; **b** also with permission of John Wiley and Sons,
Inc.)

c

d

Fig. 34. c and d.

Fig. 35. Piles of prey remains outside the burrow entrance of *Scorpio maurus palmatus,* Negev desert. (Photograph by the author)

Riechert (1979) to move to increasingly bare substrates bordering a desert creek. Available prey were relatively abundant there and apparently met the energy requirements for reproduction by the spider.

Most trapdoor spiders are even more restricted in their foraging behavior, and catch their prey without completely leaving the burrow. However, Main (1957) reported that species inhabiting dry *Acacia* and *Casuarina* litter in New South Wales have a decidedly larger search area in this relatively unproductive habitat. There, these mygalomorphs use twigs attached to the rims of their burrows as "feeding lines." Extending up to 25 cm from the burrow entrance, the twigs are followed by the foraging spiders, and thereby expand the area of capture. Ants are specialized on by these carnivores in this habitat.

In contrast, large sparassid spiders in the genus *Carparachne* hunt more openly in the Namib desert (Fig. 36). In that sandy environment, an important prey item seems to be the web-footed dune gecko, *Palmatogecko* (Lawrence, 1959), but actual observations of feeding are difficult to make and much of the evidence is inferential. One large sparassid in the stony Negev desert makes sheet webs with two openings on the sides of stones (G. Levy, personal communication); like its relatives in the Namib, it is very aggressive and presumably does much more chasing of its prey than do the wolf and mygalomorph spiders mentioned above.

Fig. 36. Large sparassid, *Carparachne alba,* from the Namib desert. (Photograph courtesy of M. K. Seely)

It should now be clear that foraging by such carnivores is intimately associated with the temporal and spatial use of habitat, which also provides shelter. There are obviously many kinds of shelter, and we have alluded many times already to burrowing and to the use of burrows. More will also be said about these manipulations of habitat in Part 4; it is sufficient here to remind ourselves that shelter can often be an indispensible resource for carnivores.

The timing of habitat use has also been discussed (Part 2), but it may be instructive at this point to regard such behavior in a context not mentioned earlier, namely that of competition. If we use the term in a broad sense, we may agree with Polis (1980b) that age-specific patterns of seasonal and nightly surface activity in *Paruroctonus mesaensis* probably minimize both cannibalism and intraspecific competition for food. Surface encounters among scorpions and other large invertebrate carnivores, on the other hand, are felt to result in competition at the interspecific level. Thus, Williams (1970) postulates that the low regional diversity of scorpions compared to other arachnid groups may be due to competitive exclusion resulting from similarities in scorpion food sources, habitat requirements, morphology, and generalized behavior. Whether or not competitive exclusion is the assortative mechanism involved, it is now quite evident from a number of thorough studies (e.g., Williams, 1970; Allred and Gertsch, 1976; Warburg et al., 1980) that different habitats provide for unique combinations of these species in deserts.

Thus, it seems probable that food limitations in deserts are more closely linked to the distribution and abundance of long-lived invertebrate carnivores than to those features of their detritivore-herbivore counterparts. The comparative flexibility of the patterns just reviewed appear to reflect this tight association. The argument is supported further by the opportunistic timing of reproduction and foraging shown by these animals, although the picture is admittedly far from clear. Rainfall, which was assumed to prime major events in the life-history categories covered earlier, may be operating more indirectly for the large carnivores. Theirs, we may conclude, is a "bet-hedging" way of life that involves the capacity of quick response in seasonal time and habitat space.

Summary Comments: Part 3

Life-history patterns based on evolutionary "tactics" are as variable among desert invertebrates as they are among invertebrates in other biomes. However, despite this variability patterns of reproduction, development, and resource utilization in many desert species seem to be more closely related to the timing of precipitation and plant growth than they are in more mesic environments. This linkage is particularly strong in multi- and univoltine desert taxa, and it also applies to long-lived herbivores and detritivores in arid regions. The simplest explanation for this kind of relationship is based on the comparatively brief pulses of primary production in deserts. This constraint in turn limits the duration in which plants can directly or indirectly supply their hosts with food and shelter, and simultaneously enhances the value of appropriate timing among the consumers.

Paradoxically, long-lived detritivores tend to have long dormant periods even though these animals are literally surrounded by their food all year. Phylogenetic reasons may account in part for their long dormancies, but the seasonal competence—made possible by moisture—of ingestible gut symbionts to provide digestive enzymes may also be involved.

By way of contrast, long-lived carnivores are apt to experience long periods of absolute food shortage in deserts. Furthermore, the arrival of their prey is unlikely to be regular. As a result, considerable flexibility in breeding, development rates, and prey selection seems generally to occur among these species.

Part 4
Invertebrate Communities: Composition and Dynamics

Introduction: Use of the Community Concept

It is conventional to think of an ecosystem's biota as belonging to discrete communities that have more complex structure and properties than do the populations of which they are composed. Various measures of community species diversity and stability are now cited in textbooks of ecology, and many ecologists subscribe to the view that community structure is in part structured by competition (see Cody and Diamond, 1975). Useful as these concepts may be in allowing one to visualize abstractly the dynamics of biotic assemblages, they were developed by biologists working mostly in comparatively productive, temperate-zone ecosystems. And, for reasons we now mention, they do not seem to apply as easily to less productive ecosystems with more extreme climates.

Indeed, it has been questioned whether the community concept is even necessary to understand the ecology of deserts, where climatic fluctuations have such obvious effects on populations. Noy-Meir (1978), for example, has suggested that desert ecology can be assessed realistically in terms of "sets of populations" reacting independently to their environment without much affecting it. In a similar vein Holdgate (1977) has argued that the different components of Antarctic ecosystems may function as "independent variables." These views perhaps apply best to extreme desert environments; as one approaches semi-arid regions, there should be a progressive increase in biotic interactions and in their consequent feedback effects.

While the merits of de-emphasizing tight interspecific couplings among desert organisms seem fairly obvious, it is useful in a book of this kind to portray groups of invertebrate populations in relation to the spatial resources that dominate their life-history patterns. Accordingly, in this section we shall use the term "community" to describe an association of invertebrates occupying a definable habitat and making use of a distinctive set of resources. With this operating definition in mind, we now consider various types of invertebrate associations found in desert soil, vegetation, and ephemeral waters.

Chapter 12

Soil and Litter Community: Nematodes and Microarthropods

A. Introduction

Many small-to-minute invertebrates permanently inhabit desert soil throughout the year. They include protozoans and possibly rotifers as well as enchytraeid worms—taxa we shall have to ignore owing to our nearly total ignorance about them in arid environments. Instead, we shall emphasize the fauna we do know something about, namely the free-living nematodes, a great variety of mostly prostigmatid mites, and the Collembola (Fig. 37).

On the whole this community is species-poor compared to its counterparts in most other biomes, although densities of Antarctic microarthropods (Tillbrook, 1967a) and Arctic collembolans (Chernov et al., 1977) compare favorably with those of similar taxa from mesic, temperate-zone environments. Within this community the numbers of nematodes greatly exceed those of mites and Collembola combined, as Table 5 clearly shows.

B. Distribution

On a geographic scale the community's composition is a partial reflection of its historical biogeography. In the Antarctic, for example, many microarthropod species appear to be endemic relicts that survived Pleistocene glaciations because of their combined abilities to exploit refugia in warmer coastal habitats (Wallwork, 1976) and to tolerate cold as well (see Chapter 6). However, in the Taimyr Peninsula of extreme north Asia, some members of the

Fig. 37. A nematode and microarthropods from the soil and litter community. **a** *Acrobeloides* sp., a bacterial-feeding nematode from the Mojave desert. **b** Gamassid mesostigmatid mite, a predator from the northern Chihuahuan desert. **c** Brachychthoniid cryptostigmatid mite from California desert grassland. **d** Podurid collembolan from California desert grassland. **e** *Tomocerus* sp., an entomobryid collembolan, common in arid sites generally. **f** *Serianus* sp., an olpiid pseudoscorpion from Joshua Tree National Monument, Mojave desert. [Photograph **a** courtesy of D. W. Freckman (Freckman et al., 1977), with permission; **b–f** courtesy of J. A. Wallwork]

Table 5. Comparative population densities of desert nematodes and microarthropods

Taxon	Desert	Density ($\times 10^3$ m^{-3})	Reference
Nematoda	Mojave	422.59	Freckman and Mankau (1977)
Nematoda	Arctic (under vegetation)	200–400	Chernov et al. (1977)
Nematoda	Arctic (bare soil)	0.1–1.0	Chernov et al. (1977)
Acari: nonpredatory Prostigmata	Mojave	2.48–17.46	Edney et al. (1975)
Acari: total Prostigmata	Chihuahuan (under shrubs)	2.69	Santos et al. (1978)
Acari: Prostigmata	Mojave	0.25–0.68	Wallwork (1976)
Acari: Prostigmata: Nanorchestida	Chihuahuan (open areas)	0.15	Santos et al. (1978)
Acari: Cryptostigmata (Oribatida)	Chihuahuan (under shrubs)	1.85	Santos et al. (1978)
Acari: Cryptosigmata (Oribatida)	Mojave	0.72	Wallwork (1976)
Acari: Cryptosigmata (Oribatida)	Australia	0.15	Wallwork (1976)
Collembola	Chihuahuan (center of arroyo)	0.92	Santos et al. (1978)
Collembola	Chihuahuan (under shrubs)	0.66	Santos et al. (1978)
Collembola	Australia	0.14	Wallwork (1976)
Collembola	Mojave	0.11	Wallwork (1976)

Source: Crawford (1978), with permission.

community may have close evolutionary ties with aquatic life (Chernov et al., 1977).

The comparative youthfulness of polar deserts (see Chapter 1) may be inferred from the composition of their microarthropod faunas. This is because of the preponderance there of Collembola and prostigmatids (see Chapter 2), both of which have "r-selected" characteristics (Addison, 1980; Behan and Hill, 1980). And in these extreme climates it appears that such organisms are ultimately controlled by environmental influences rather than by interspecific competition (Block, 1980). Thus, plant growth form is a more important determinant of collembolan abundance than are plant species in polar "semidesert sites" (Addison, 1980).

In both polar regions microarthropods occur commonly in mosses and lichens at the surface, their establishment much below the surface being precluded by permafrost. Antarctic fumaroles (volcanic vents) are the polar equivalents of warm-desert oases, because they possess a relatively diverse and abundant fauna (Tillbrook, 1967b). In warm deserts mosses constitute habitats in which hygrophilous cryptostigmatid mites (Hammer, 1966) and considerable numbers of microarthropods can exist. Mosses from a volcanic escarpment in the desert grassland of central New Mexico contained cryptostigmatid, prostigmatid, and mesostigmatid mites, as well as collembolans, nematodes, rotifers, tardigrades, and protozoans (S. D. Evans and S. J. Upton, personal communication). Some of the rotifers and tardigrades from this habitat are shown in Fig. 38. Whether or not the relict concept applies to aggregations of soil microfaunas in warm deserts has been minimally explored, although Wood (1971) considered the presence of Collembola and poorly sclerotized prostigmatid mites unexpected in arid Australian shrubland. There, populations of each are about equally dense, collembolans being the more abundant "decomposers" (Wood, 1970; Greenslade, 1975). Explanations for the Australian distribution include the following: (1) regular condensation of moisture in the superficial soil (Wood, 1971) and (2) the ability of these microarthropods to become inactive in dry weather (Greenslade and Greenslade, 1973; Greenslade, 1975).

Because soil does not freeze permanently in warm deserts, there is a vertical distribution among members of this community that extends into the mineral soil (Wallwork, 1972). Their penetration appears to be limited by levels of temperature, availability of moisture, and amounts of organic matter. Generally speaking, the upper 10 cm of soil seems to have a greater concentration of taxa than does the region below (Freckman et al., 1974; Santos et al., 1978; Franco et al., 1979). At times, however, the next 10 cm can actually contain more individuals (Franco et al., 1979). Location of root biomass complicates the picture since—at least in nematodes—it correlates positively with spatial distribution (Fig. 39) (Freckman and Mankau, 1979). The horizontal patchiness among members of the community is likewise dictated partly by physical constraints, a fact made quite evident by the studies just

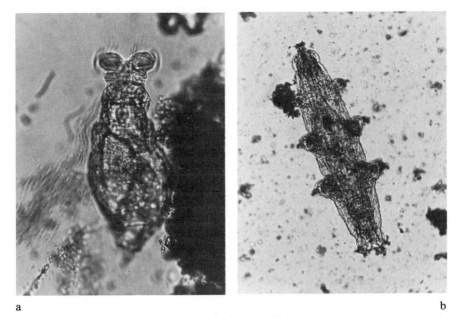

Fig. 38. Some inhabitants of mosses (unidentified) from a volcanic escarpment in central New Mexico desert grassland. a A bdelloid rotifer, *Rotaria* sp. b A cosmopolitan arctiscid tardigrade, *Milnesium tardigradum*. (Photographs courtesy of S. J. Upton)

cited. Factors regulating such dispersion include shrubs, stones, debris, slope aspect, and other topographic features.

Studies of this kind also reveal the influence of season on the spatial distributions of soil microarthropods and nematodes in deserts. There is now little question that changes in population structure within the community take on phenological patterns and that the arrival of rainfall pulses can produce dramatic effects on these populations. Moreover, age structure within mite populations can be a function of season, and reproductive phenologies of cryptostigmatid and prostigmatid mites can be associated with the vertical distribution of these organisms in desert soil (Wallwork, 1972). While Wallwork found both gravid females and eggs most commonly in mineral soil at Joshua Tree National Monument in the Mojave desert, the seasonal age–class distribution of mites in mineral soil and litter suggested to him that immature forms disperse upwards into the litter in late winter. There, their rates of development are quite possibly accelerated by prevailing high temperatures.

In a subsequent review of his earlier Mojave work, Wallwork (1980) argues that this inferred rapid development, together with limited recruitment periods, nonoverlapping generations, and comparatively low "equitability" (distribution of total individuals among total species present) are all factors pointing

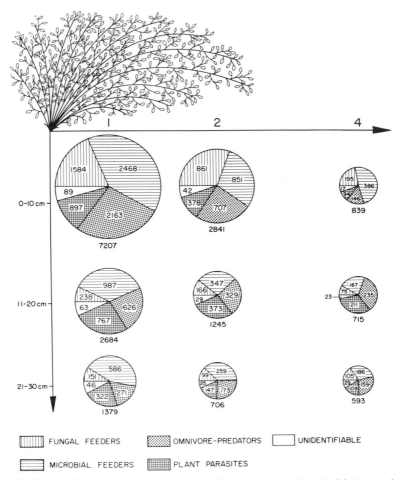

FUNGAL FEEDERS   OMNIVORE-PREDATORS   UNIDENTIFIABLE

MICROBIAL FEEDERS   PLANT PARASITES

Fig. 39. Spatial distribution of nematode trophic groups associated with desert shrubs, Rock Valley, Nevada, Mojave desert. Numbers per 500 cm³ from four desert shrubs. (Freckman and Mankau, 1977; with permission)

to "r-selection." A correlate of this observation is that of high productivity and turnover of biological materials, which Wallwork (1980) equates with rapid release and leaching of soil nutrients. Indeed, the soil profile at his Mojave study site is lacking in discrete fermentation and humus layers. Manipulative experiments testing cause and effect should provide a useful follow-up.

From this brief review it appears, therefore, that despite the usual lack of structure of desert soils, the resident invertebrate community of small, permanent dwellers achieves a structure of its own, this being greatly influenced by the physical environment.

C. Community Roles

I. Trophic Relationships

In his Mojave desert study, Wallwork (1972) found site-specific differences between carnivorous and primary-consumer mites. These are listed in ratio form in Table 6.

Although it is difficult to compare these ratios with values from other studies, we can make the attempt using additional Mojave desert data from the Rock Valley study reported by Edney et al. (1975, 1976). Wallwork considered prostigmatids to be carnivores, while Edney and co-workers classified them in the approximate ratio of nonpredators (5):predators (1). By adding Collembola and crypostigmatids (calculated from Edney et al., 1975:Table 7) and by ignoring mesostigmatids—which were not treated separately—one arrives at a nonpredator:predator ratio from Rock Valley of 8:1. This is not too different from Wallwork's combined ratio and gives us some idea of the numerical assortment into trophic units of individuals in the microarthropod segment of this community. It should be recognized, however, that ratios of this kind are not seasonally constant, and Franco et al. (1979) showed that Rock Valley populations of Collembola decrease after January, while predatory prostigmatids there increase from winter to spring. Their nonpredatory counterparts do so during spring.

D. W. Freckman and her co-workers have provided us with a comparable insight into the temporal population structure of soil nematodes in western North America. A fundamental observation made at Rock Valley in the Mojave desert was that lower densities occurred from late spring to early summer than in winter, which is the wet season (Freckman et al., 1974). Annual mean biomass (dry weight) of these animals was 0.7 g m^{-2} (D. W. Freckman, personal communication).

Trophic levels in desert nematode faunas also have their numerical patterns, and at Rock Valley Freckman and Mankau (1977) obtained relative densities of the following description: microbiovores > omnivores-predators > fungal feeders > plant parasites. Such a pattern does not necessarily hold from desert to desert, however. To illustrate this, in Table 7 we compare percentages

Table 6. Trophic-level ratios of mites from the Mojave desert[a]

Site	Ratio (primary consumer:carnivore)
Litter	1:1
Mineral soil	19.6:1
Combined	4.6:1

[a] Data from Wallwork (1972).

Table 7. Trophic aspects of nematodes from cold and warm deserts[a]

Location	Microbiovores (%)	Plant parasites (%)
Cold desert	18–22	61
Warm deserts	50	6–20

[a] Data from Freckman et al. (1974).

of total nematode populations at 0–10 cm depths that were reported by Freckman et al. (1974) and that apply to a "cold" desert (Great Basin) and to "warm" deserts (Sonoran and Chihuahuan).

Trophic relationships among mites, collembolans, nematodes, and other elements of desert soil communities were elucidated by Santos (1979). He monitored changes in community structure during the early stages of decomposition of buried creosote bush *(Larrea tridentata)* litter in the Chihuahuan desert. By using specific chemical inhibitors, Santos determined the effects of bacteria–nematode–mite interactions on decomposition processes. These processes normally involve the sequential appearance of bacteriophagic nematodes, tydeid mites, and pyemotid mites. Meanwhile, continuously low levels of fungivorous nematodes increase somewhat as the pyemotids that graze upon them begin to colonize the system.

Removal of the mites left the available biomass of fungi unchanged, but increased the population of bacteriophagic nematodes. The latter in turn reduced the numbers of their prey, thereby diminishing the overall amount of decomposition by 40%. In addition, Santos (1979) found that most decomposition occurred in the first 30 days of litter burial and that the sequence of colonizing microarthropods was independent of season. Apparently, therefore, bacteria, nematodes, and mites achieve early importance in the establishment of this detritus food web. More subtle effects undoubtedly occur in later stages of decomposition as biotic diversity within the community increases.

II. Energetics

Another way of assessing the importance of the soil-litter community in the desert ecosystem as a whole is to measure the relative contribution to energy flow made by the community's component trophic units. Several studies allow us to arrive at tentative conclusions. Work with North American desert nematodes by Freckman and her colleagues over the years suggests that the annual respiratory metabolism of nematodes at Rock Valley is about 1160 cal m^{-2}, and that annual production comes to 6940 cal m^{-2}. (D. W.

Table 8. Annual respiratory metabolism of desert soil microarthropods[a]

Trophic/taxonomic category	Annual respiratory metabolism (cal m^{-2})
Saprovore mites	24.80
Collembola	67.76
Predatory mites	151.64

[a] Data from Edney et al. (1976).

Freckman, personal communication). Values derived for microarthropods at Rock Valley by Edney et al. (1976) can be compared with the former figure and are given in Table 8.

Notwithstanding the potential error inherent in most studies of population energetics, two points seem worth noting from the above comparisons. One is that relative to the Rock Valley microarthropods, nematodes there make an enormous contribution to respiratory energy flow. The other point, which may be less reliable because of the rather similar values involved, is that predatory mites seem to make a metabolic contribution out of proportion to their numbers. In fact, Edney et al. (1976) consider that the respiratory expenditure of predatory mites comprises nearly half of the total annual metabolic energy generated by soil invertebrates in the system.

While much more information about the interactive effects of this community's major components must be compiled before the tentative conclusions above can be applied broadly in deserts, it is difficult to dispute the community's importance in decomposition processes. Further testing (by manipulation) of how taxonomic as well as trophic associations control rates of decomposition is necessary on a wide geographic scale if we are to understand deserts in both their natural and altered states.

Chapter 13
Soil and Litter Community: Social Arthropods

A. Sociality in Desert Species: General Comments

Various forms of social existence occur in certain groups of arthropods inhabiting all but the most austere and unproductive landscapes. Numerous categories of sociality in these animals have been erected, ranging from simple forms of cooperation in subsocial embiopterans, cockroaches, beetles, and hymenopterans, to the highly evolved interactions of eusocial insects. The latter use division of labor, complex intracolony communication, and the direct reproductive effort of relatively few individuals. Termites of both sexes and colonies of mostly female ants, bees, and wasps fit this description and are among the most numerous of all animal groups.

In the present treatment of desert species, we shall be less concerned with categorical distinctions than with the ecological significance of sociality in arid regions. Our focus will be on termites and ants, since social bees and most subsocial arthropods are comparatively insignificant in most deserts. Nevertheless, we can begin our discussion by elucidating several general principles that may apply to all social taxa in these regions.

Aside from its inherent advantages in most natural settings, sociality provides members of a colony with a condition that should be of overriding importance in deserts. That condition is a stable microclimate, in which reproduction, communication, and food storage can take place steadily over a long duration. Thus, compared to habitats of most other desert animals, the nests of termite (Fig. 40) or ant (Fig. 41) colonies should be generally much more constant in terms of their temperature and humidity. Parenthetically, a relatively unvarying microclimate is available not only to the social

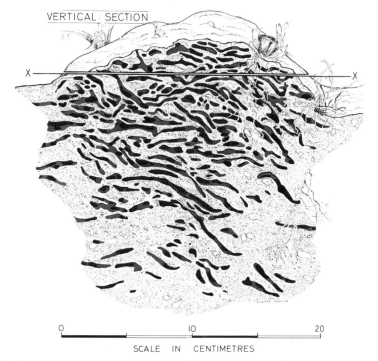

VERTICAL SECTION

SCALE IN CENTIMETRES

Fig. 40. Vertical section through a nest of *Psammotermes allocerus,* a termite species known from the Namib desert. (Coaton and Sheasby, 1973; with permission)

species involved, but also to associated myrmecophilic and termitiphilic species.

Microclimatic stability in such nests is achieved by a combination of factors. An indispensible element is some form of a workable substrate, usually soil but often wood. Thermal constancy is essentially built into the system when the colony is subterranean. Even then the characteristic mound around the entrance to an ant nest can modify temperature in its upper portions (Ettershank, 1971). In the case of termite mounds in arid regions, the orientation, insulation, and general architecture of these complex dwellings has long been known to constitute a fine-tuned system of environmental engineering (Holdaway and Gay, 1948; Noirot, 1970; Weir, 1973). In Australia, *Amitermes meridionalis* builds spectacular mounds with the elongated axis oriented in a north–south plane. By sawing off a nest at the base and rotating its axis in an east–west plane, Grigg (1973) showed that the original orientation allows rapid warming in the morning, avoids excessive heating at noon, and maintains nest warmth late into the day. Besides modifying the microclimates of their occupants, the essentially subterranean nests of *Acanthotermes ahngerianus* in Central Asia are known to increase porosity and to lower evaporation in grey desert soils (Ghilarov, 1960).

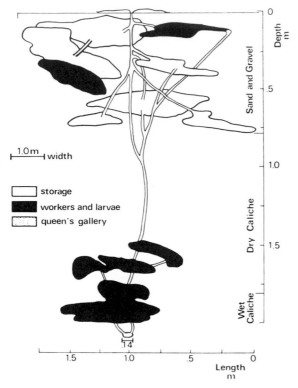

Fig. 41. Vertical section through a nest of the harvester ant *Pogonomyrmex rugosus*, in Chihuahuan desert shrubland, New Mexico. (Whitford et al., 1976; with permission)

The value of cooperation in maintaining constant conditions for a colony can be appreciated by referring to the comparatively simple burrow of a desert isopod (see Fig. 23b). *Hemilepistus reaumuri* illustrates how even a small organizational unit of 100 or so members can create a favorable microclimate. For the most part these unusual crustaceans are guaranteed sufficient energy and nutrition from surrounding vegetation and algal soil crust. However, once the wet winter season has passed and families are established, there is no assurance of adequate moisture either in the soil crust consumed or in the air of the burrow. In the loess soil of the northern Negev desert, a minimum soil moisture of 6% is needed to produce a suitable burrow humidity (Shachak, 1981), but without a certain number of actively digging individuals, the construction of a sufficiently deep burrow of appropriate proportions would apparently not be possible. Hence the need for a relatively high allocation of energy for family digging.

Actual importation of moisture, on the other hand, is characteristic of certain social insects. Founding pairs of *Hodotermes mossambicus* use specialized salivary "water sacs" to provide a water reserve for the newly developing colony during drought (Hewitt et al., 1971), while "honey pot" repletes of certain myrmecine ants in deserts and elsewhere make available both water and nutrients to fellow workers by becoming living containers of sweet liquid (Wilson, 1971:285–288).

Long-term storage of food results from foraging, a highly regulated behavior to be discussed below in some detail. Perhaps there is a lower limit of colony size below which the cost of food storage exceeds its benefits; storage does not occur to any great extent, for example, in *Hemilepistus*. But phylogeny itself has much to do with the practice of storage, which is hardly confined to social species. In fact, solitary females of provisioning bees and wasps effectively "store" prey food after first paralyzing it.

Phylogeny also plays a part in the *use* of environmental stability, and such use provides us with a key ecological distinction between ants and termites. The Isoptera are generally like isopods in that they are poorly adapted to resist desiccation. Normally this does not present a problem since they forage either within the substrate they inhabit or within a contiguous substrate such as wood, or—in some arid regions—dung (Ferrar and Watson, 1970). An exception is *Hodotermes mossambicus* from semi-arid South Africa: Its well pigmented adult workers forage in the open during the day (Coaton, 1958) and, like a common species in the Negev desert (Fig. 42), also have obvious burrow entrances at the soil surface. Ants, on the other hand, usually forage on or above the soil surface and, while being more effective than termites in resisting desiccation, still have to synchronize their foraging with

Fig. 42. Soil surface of loess plain in the Negev desert, just after sunrise, showing two openings (*upper center* and *upper right*) made by termites. Several termites are barely visible in the opening at center. Also visible: two *Hemilepistus reaumuri* isopods foraging at *right,* and considerable plant litter. (Photograph by the author)

climatic conditions they can tolerate. A consequence of this difference is that over a year's time, desert termites may be able to forage much longer than desert ants.

B. Ants

I. Patterns of Distribution

Despite their obvious numerical abundance in some deserts, the species diversity of ants in these regions is not particularly high, a point illustrated by the following statements: There are from 12 000 to 14 000 ant species estimated to exist in the world, diversity being maximal in the tropics and declining sharply with increasing latitude. As a result, only about 455 species are found in the Western Hemisphere north of Mexico (Wilson, 1971). Less than 70 of these occur in deserts (A. C. Cole, 1968), and in the vicinity of Tucson, Arizona, there are no more than 18–33 species (Gaspar and Werner, 1976). Regional distribution of harvester species in parts of the southwestern United States varies, however, and is highly (and positively) correlated with mean annual precipitation (Davidson, 1977).

On a topographic basis we find further that desert species are distributed according to differences in vegetation, soils, and microclimate. An example is that of two seed-harvesting species in southern New Mexico. There, Schumacher and Whitford (1976) showed that *Pheidole* spp. were most common on a moderately sloping bajada supporting an abundance of *Larrea* shrubs, while *Pogonomyrmex* spp. dominated the fringes of an *Ephedra–Prosopis* playa fringe at the base of the bajada. Chew's (1977) findings in southeastern Arizona support the same principle; he ranked the relative frequency of ant species in two plant communities differing in dominant shrubs and found that rankings within a community were generally different.

The seasonal distribution of ant foraging in deserts is also a complex matter. Among the exogenous factors known to affect it are the availability, density, and quality of food. Availability clearly can be important, since Rissing and Wheeler (1976) noted that the main harvester in Death Valley, *Veromessor pergandei,* changes its foraging-column patterns as local plant production varies. Also, Whitford (1978b) found that selective foraging in several harvesting species in New Mexico decreased as their food's abundance diminished. In the Negev desert, foraging intensity of seed harvesters in the genera *Messor* and *Goniomma* is said to be geared directly to seed abundance in the area and to vary greatly from year to year (Ben Mordechai and Kugler, 1978). Foraging on a more condensed time scale was observed in the omnivore *Novomessor cockerelli,* which in the Chihuahuan desert alternates between nocturnal and diurnal feeding, depending on the activity of its prey (Whitford and Ettershank, 1975).

Density and quality of food are difficult to separate in natural settings; however, it has been suggested that group foragers specialize in high density forage and are active during periods of low climatic stress, whereas individual foragers display just the opposite behavior (Davidson, 1977; Whitford, 1978b). The selection of food quality by desert ants was demonstrated by Whitford (1978b), who showed that *Pogonomyrmex desertorum* chooses smaller and less abundant grass seeds over others. While this would appear to discount the importance of food energy as a factor in food selection, Taylor (1977) used unnatural food and an experimental format to show that energy intake is maximized by *Pogonomyrmex occidentalis* in southeastern Arizona. The rate of worker recruitment in this species increased with an increase in seed size and density and with a gain in size of seed "patches." It decreased with distance between colony and "patch."

Seasonal distribution of foraging in desert ants may also be influenced by latitude and altitude. Thus, Bernstein (1974) predicted that since seeds should in general ripen more slowly as latitude and altitude increase, one should expect harvester ant foraging at high latitudes and altitudes to be postponed until relatively late in the year. While the argument probably has merit, it does not go far enough since vegetation and topography also vary with altitude and latitude. Moreover, there may be ecotypic differences among the ants themselves.

Studies of ant distribution in space and time inevitably raise the question of competition within and among species. Wilson (1971) and Matthews (1976) make the point that when social insect colonies mature in a given habitat, they should experience increased intra- and interspecific competition, and as a consequence their colonies should be overdispersed. This prediction is partly supported by the observations of Briese and Macauley (1977) in Australia. These authors examined a fairly large number of species in arid regions and noted some overdispersion, but also some aggregation. They suggested that aggressive interactions were largely responsible for structuring the ant communities they studied.

Surely the potential for aggressive interaction often exists, but it is now becoming evident that mitigating factors can preclude the full expression of that potential. For example, Whitford et al. (1976) made a study of two randomly dispersed *Pogonomyrmex* species having an area of foraging overlap. While some aggression did occur, in the overlap area the temporal foraging patterns of these two species became increasingly different.

In another example of reduced interaction, Brough (1976) found that an Australian desert species of *Calomyrmex* has nests organized into discrete groups and may have colonies occupying more than a single nest. Observations of fighting behavior demonstrated that certain nests were compatible, suggesting that colonies are integrated into social units.

Avoidance of competition can also be conditioned by morphology. Davidson (1977) obtained evidence for this in species of desert harvesters, where body size of workers was highly correlated with size of the seeds they selected, and where coexistence apparently occurred because of species-specific foraging strategies. In a variation on this theme, Whitford (1978a) noted that within a feeding guild of several species there was little overlap in the body length of workers. Chew (1977) also found that within three general feeding categories the mean body weights of most species differed significantly. In a 1980 report Chew and DeVita ascertained that body length correlated with forage size in several foraging guilds of desert ants. So, while it is certainly possible that competition is a function of aggressive interactions of foraging workers, it seems equally possible that behavioral and morphological factors modify the intensity of competition and perhaps also the spatial arrangement of colonies.

Finally, mention can be made of how physiology and the microhabitats of nesting sites can aid coexistence. Hansen (1978) recently determined that among three species of *Pogonomyrmex* in desert grassland, differences in desiccation resistance enabled foragers to be active at different times of day and, as a consequence, to incorporate different amounts of insect prey into their diets. Hansen also concluded that interspecific differences in the microhabitats of nest locations facilitated the division of seeds among these mainly harvesting species.

On a broader scale it has been questioned whether ants compete for seeds in deserts with other granivorous animals. Removal experiments by Brown and Davidson (1977) led those authors to conclude that harvester ants do, in fact, compete with local rodents for available seeds. However, as Davidson et al. (1980) point out, interactions affecting granivory in desert ecosystems are very complex and difficult to describe and test. Moreover, it seems likely that such interactions should be interpreted in a geographical context, since the diversities of granivorous insects, birds, and mammals vary according to the location of the desert concerned (Orians et al., 1977; Morton, 1979).

II. Community Roles

It is still too early to assess the contribution of ants to energy flow in deserts. Only the study by Rogers et al. (1972) of *Pogonomyrmex occidentalis* in the Colorado short-grass prairie comes close to showing what perhaps occurs in the more southerly deserts where this species also lives. In Colorado *P. occidentalis* assimilated between 0.14 and 1.45 kcal m^{-2} in a year. However, this is an order of magnitude lower than the flux reported for *P. badius* in Florida (Golley and Gentry, 1964). Surely a comprehensive energy budget for a desert harvester ant colony must take many factors into consideration. Among these is the effect of constructing deep galleries (see Fig. 41) and elaborate gravel mounds around colony entrances (Fig. 43), a cost that Taylor (1978) feels may be major relative to the actual gathering and storing of seeds. Another factor is the production of alates, which varies considerably

Fig. 43. *Pogonomyrmex* sp. mound in northern Great Basin (Guano Valley, Oregon). Note elevation of mound and cleared area around it. Shrubs are mainly *Artemisia tridentata.* (Photograph courtesy of J. T. Rotenberry)

from one year to the next (Ben Mordechai and Kugler, 1978), and which is undoubtedly an important form of energy output.

A more direct impact by ants on the desert ecosystem probably has to do with the conservation, localization, and turnover of nutrients. Just the cutting and removal of annual plants from nest areas by *P. occidentalis* alone accounts for 157–226 million plants per hectare annually near Reno, Nevada (Clark and Comanor, 1975). Furthermore, Whitford (1978b) reminds us that foraging alone may involve removal of significant fractions of available seeds. Clearly food gathering and nutrient concentration by harvester ants in arid regions constitutes an important influence of these insects on their environment; however, as Wiens (1976:108) suggests, underground storage of food may introduce a considerable delay into the nutrient cycling process. On the other hand, it is also tempting to suggest that the delay may be offset by relatively rapid decomposition of surface debris (Fig. 44) around a colony. Exposure of this material to weathering, to the action of detritivores and decomposers, and to other biotic activity [such as the strutting action of the sage grouse, *Centrocercus urophasianus* (Giezentanner and Clark, 1974)] ought to enchance rates of nutrient cycling.

In the final analysis, it is the relationship between worker activity and nutrient resource that determines how extensively desert ants influence their biotic and abiotic surroundings. If, as seems to be the case, pulses of available nutrients trigger recruitment and foraging responses, then the system is essen-

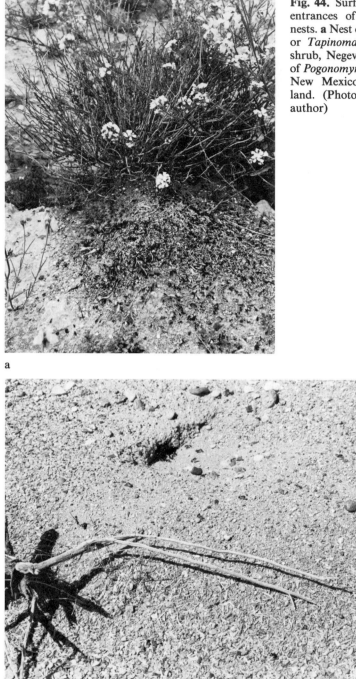

a

b

Fig. 44. Surface debris near entrances of harvester ant nests. **a** Nest of either *Messor* or *Tapinoma* sp. at base of shrub, Negev desert. **b** Nest of *Pogonomyrmex* sp. central New Mexico desert grassland. (Photographs by the author)

tially rainfall-dependent. It should be stressed, however, that different taxonomic and ecological categories of desert ants respond in special ways to microenvironmental factors, as well as to the nature of their food resources.

C. Termites

I. Patterns of Distribution

Like the ants, termites are also heavily concentrated in the tropics. Of the approximately 2200 known species (Wilson, 1971), the number found in deserts is, again, low. At least 48 are said to occur near Alice Springs in central Australia (Watson et al., unpublished), 32 in the Indian desert ecosystem (Roonwall, 1977), 18 on the Arabian Peninsula (Chhotani and Bose, 1979); and about a dozen are found near Tucson, Arizona (Nutting and Haverty, 1976). In arid parts of South-West Africa (Coaton and Sheasby, 1972) and Australia (Calaby and Gay, 1956), mound-building species contribute distinctively to the topography; while in the same regions and elsewhere, e.g., Central Asia (Ghilarov, 1960), strictly subterranean forms may be abundant but are seldom noticed.

It is generally accepted that temperature and moisture are major determinants of the spatial and temporal distribution of termites, and studies in semi-arid (Pomeroy, 1978) and arid (Haverty and Nutting, 1975) areas certainly support this view. In addition soil conditions can have significant effects. This is illustrated by data from Johnson and Whitford (1975) showing that soil structure influences topographic distribution at the Jornada Range in the Chihuahuan desert. There, foraging groups of the predominant species are numerous in deep, sandy soil, but virtually absent in heavy, clay soil and where the caliche layer occurs within 30 cm of the surface. However, in southern Africa *Psammotermes allocerus* is adapted to widely differing conditions of rainfall and soil. Its nests consist of low mounds (see Fig. 40), either within wood set in soil or in desert sand (Coaton and Sheasby, 1973). Likewise, in Central Asia *Acanthotermes ahngerianus* is widespread and inhabits a variety of soils (Ghilarov, 1960).

Substrate moisture also sometimes determines distribution. Collins and Richards (1966) noted that the desert-invading subterranean species, *Reticulitermes tibialis,* has higher rates of transpiration than do several dry-wood species from dry environments. Within its genus *R. tibialis* is better able to resist desiccation than are species from less xeric environments (Strickland, 1950).

The foraging patterns of desert termites, like those of ants, vary seasonally. This is illustrated by data from Johnson and Whitford (1975), who found that a soil temperature threshold of 3°C–5°C must be exceeded if foraging

near the surface is to occur. Their finding is consistent with the report by
Ueckert et al. (1976) that *Gnathamitermes tubiformans* is inactive near the
surface in west Texas arid grassland between December and February. Upper
lethal limits in desert termites are known for several species in Arizona and
range between 49°C and 54°C (Collins et al., 1973; LaFage et al., 1976),
suggesting that foraging during hot summer weather may be generally possible, other factors permitting.

Atmospheric moisture appears to be one of those factors. This is shown
by the correlation between intensity of surface foraging by *Gnathamitermes*
and an increase in soil moisture caused by rain (Ueckert et al., 1976). Johnson
and Whitford (1975) also observed that *Gnathamitermes* did not consume
debris from annual plants that had died during summer until the saturation
deficit of air near the ground became generally low; this only occurred in
the fall of the year.

Whether or not a chemical change in the plant material was instrumental
in delaying the consumption of such debris is not known; however, in the
same study it was noted that woody parts of *Larrea* and *Prosopis* shrubs
were not attacked by termites for some time after they fell to the ground.
The possibility of inhibitory substances in the fresh wood was considered
and may in fact be of general significance in the breakdown of detritus in
deserts. Fowler and Whitford (1980) showed that *Gnathamitermes* built significantly more galleries in litter bags containing senescent *Larrea* leaf litter
than it did in bags containing fresh leaves. Antiherbivore allelochemics in
the fresh leaves may have been inhibitory.

The issue of competition of food resources has been raised for desert termites, as it has for ants. Lee and Wood (1971) inferred from the pronounced
overdispersion of *Amitermes vitiosius* and other termite mounds in arid Australia that competition occurs at inter- and intraspecific levels. Since clear-cut
demonstration of competition involves careful experimentation, it is undoubtedly too early to draw general conclusions in this area.

II. Community Roles

Studies of foraging in arid-land termites have shown that these insects comprise an important fraction of the biota. This is made clear by biomass and
density values compiled mainly by Ueckert et al. (1976) and presented in
Table 9. These are surely conservative estimates because they only measure
workers at or near the surface, where such individuals probably represent
but a small proportion of the entire population. Despite the ingenious use
of toilet paper rolls to measure foraging by subterranean desert termites (La-
Fage et al., 1973; Johnson and Whitford, 1975), any "bait" of this sort artifi-
cializes their usual vertical and horizontal distribution in soil. In fact there

Table 9. Biomass and density of arid-land termites[a]

Taxa	Biomass (g m^{-2})	Density (number m^{-2})
Nasutitermes (Australian mound builder)	3.0	600
Subterranean spp. in Australian grassland and steppe	12.0	2000
Five spp. in shrub-invaded desert grassland (Arizona)	10.2	1025
Gnathamitermes (subterranean in west Texas arid grassland)	5.8–23	2311 ± 854
Macrotermes (Ugandan mound builder)[b]	5.0	0–9127 ± 3837

[a] First four cases taken from Ueckert et al. (1976).
[b] After Pomeroy (1978); density covers a 2-year seasonal range.

is now evidence that termites detect potential surface food by responding to thermal gradients set up beneath such items (Ettershank et al., 1981).

Trophic relationships in desert termites illuminate the importance of these animals. Feeding guilds of wood eaters, harvesters, and omnivores have in common a high consumption of cellulose but also require some nitrogen in the diet (Matthews, 1976). Moreover, because of the presence in the hindgut "paunch" of symbiotic protozoa, bacteria, and probably fungi as well, the assimilation efficiency of termites is in general quite high. Martin and Martin (1978) suggested that digestive enzymes acquired by ingestion may play an important role in the breakdown of recalcitrant substances such as cellulose, chitin, and lignin. Whether the importance of enzyme ingestion is as great in deserts as it may be elsewhere remains to be determined. Research needs to be done on the contribution of free-living fungi to the hydrolysis of plant material once both have been ingested by desert termites.

The demonstration of nitrogen fixation by microbes living in termites (see LaFage and Nutting, 1977:203) has implications for the management of desert ecosystems. By increasing the carbon content in these nitrogen-poor environments, it may be possible to increase the biomass of termites and other detritivores housing nitrogen-fixers, and thus to incorporate more of this valuable element into the soil (W. G. Whitford, personal communication).

It follows from what we presently know about termites in arid regions that they can harvest and/or ingest much more primary production than we previously assumed. For example, in the Chihuahuan desert consumption by termites during July and August may range between 1 and 8 kg ha^{-1} (Johnson and Whitford, 1975); while in western Australia a colony of *Drepanotermes perniger* may harvest a kilogram of grass in a single year (Watson and Gay, 1970). In one hectare the biomass of this species approximates

2g m^{-2} (compare with values in Table 9), and *Drepanotermes* removes 20–25 kg ha^{-1} annually in dry weight of primary production (Watson et al., 1973). Since other termite species occur there too, the total annual harvest must be large indeed. An even greater harvest value (414 kg ha^{-1} yr^{-1}) was reported for ten species in the Sonoran desert by Nutting et al. (1975), while *Gnathamitermes* in Texas averaged 50 kg ha^{-1} over a 3-year period (Bodine and Ueckert, 1975). According to Matthews (1976), the average *Drepanotermes* colony contains from 2 to 5 kg of stored dry grass, which means that storage itself ties up considerable primary production—just as it seems to do in harvester-ant nests.

Additional conservation of organic materials is brought about by the extensive use of feces-incorporating "carton," the substance that covers surface items being consumed by subterranean species in wet seasons. Carton also comprises the durable homes of mound builders, and in semi-arid Uganda mounds of *Macrotermes bellicosus* enhance decomposition by allowing a slow release of exchangable bases and by depressing C:N ratios. As a consequence, nitrogen and cations are taken up by plants almost as rapidly as they are released (Pomeroy, 1978). Without doubt, the mounds have a decided influence on the dynamics of nutrient flow in the local environment.

Termites in deserts and elsewhere also export nutrients and energy directly to other elements of the food web. This is accomplished by the periodic swarming flights of reproductives and by what may be more consistent predation by other animals. In Australia, for example, lizards in the genus *Ctenotus* are frequently dependent on termites as food (Pianka, 1969), as are solifugids (Muma, 1966) and giant *Dinothrombium* mites (Tevis and Newell, 1962) in North American deserts.

A critical element in the flux of nutrients between a termite colony and its surroundings must be the extent to which harvested material is actually stored. Early studies by N. A. Dimo (cited by Ghilarov, 1960) in Central Asia showed that nests of *Acanthotermes* concentrated humus amounting to 1.5 times that found in surrounding grey desert soils. More extensive studies of this kind are needed if we are to appreciate better the dynamics of energy and nutrients in deserts where termite densities are high. Clearly, where termites are abundant, their potential for influencing the flux must

Table 10. Estimates of production of litter and its consumption by termites in a Chihuahuan desert ecosystem[a]

Topographic site	Estimated litter (cal ha^{-1})	Estimated consumption (cal ha^{-1})
Playa	10.3×10^6	3.7×10^6
Bajada[b]	5.3×10^6	3.4×10^6

[a] Data from Johnson and Whitford (1975).
[b] Not inclusive of litter from arroyos.

be significant. This is verified by findings that arid-grassland termites can remove over 20% of the standing crop and about half of the litter produced in a single year (Bodine and Ueckert, 1975). Sheer numbers and a relatively long foraging season are responsible for such an impact, and for the estimates of July–August consumption (Table 10)—expressed in the context of energy flow—of litter by termites in the Chihuahuan desert (after Johnson and Whitford, 1975).

These figures suggest that a large proportion of the net primary production in the Jornada Range is consumed by termites each year. Even more dramatic are data given by Nutting et al. (1975), suggesting that Sonoran desert termites can consume over 90% of the annual production of fallen dead wood. There seems little doubt that where they occur in large numbers, termites play a major role in the movement of energy and nutrients in arid regions.

Chapter 14
Soil and Litter Community:
Temporary Dwellers

A. Comments on the Fauna

The most obvious invertebrates on the floor of the desert are usually ants and beetles, and although these insects contribute significantly to the taxonomic array and ecological importance of that habitat's temporary fauna, many other kinds of invertebrates add to its composition as well. All of the temporary dwellers are transients on the surface, where they consist either of dispersal stages of otherwise relatively immobile species (e.g., solitary bees, asilid flies, adult and triungulin instars of meloid beetles), or of mobile members of nonmetamorphosing species (e.g., snails, solifugids, crickets). Less restricted to soil than nematodes and microarthropods, these usually nonsocial animals encounter new conditions when and if they leave the confines of the soil. And, once on its surface, they often exploit resources quite different from those utilized underground.

The present section is organized around the *use of habitat* by members of this community. The approach taken is to regard the soil and its surface topography as a continuum, which for convenience is separated into three parts: (1) the soil and its burrows, (2) the crevices or spaces beneath and between objects at the soil surface, and (3) the open surface itself. Clearly, all these places can be used by the same animal within a few minutes, and this possibility helps to define the dimensions of the community. Burrows dug by invertebrates are not treated extensively in this section, since they are dealt with in other parts of the book.

B. Habitats and Their Temporary Residents

I. Soil (Including Burrows)

1. Distribution of Invertebrate Species

The soil offers microclimatic stability to developing stages and resting individuals of many invertebrate species. These organisms tend to have nonrandom distributions in space, and when clumped they are frequently found in association with plants. Examples include larvae of hepialid moths that feed on roots of woody vegetation in arid Australia (Common, 1970), assemblages of soil mesofauna associated with *Thymelaca hirsuta* shrubs in the Egyptian coastal desert (Ghabbour and Mikhail, 1978), and members of the sattelite fauna of *Trianthema hereroensis* dune plants in the Namib desert (Seely et al., 1977).

By comparing the invertebrate contents of equal volumes of soil dug from an open area and from beneath a desert shrub, one begins to appreciate the "island effect" provided by such vegetation. The pattern becomes even more pronounced if the soil beneath the shrub is penetrated by rodent burrows. By no means, however, are all animal burrows clumped. This becomes especially apparent in dune fields, where the entrances of many invertebrate burrows are not dispersed in any obvious manner (Fig. 45). Inhabitants of such eolian deposits construct a variety of burrows, some of which are diagrammed in Fig. 46.

On initial examination of a vertebrate burrow, one usually notices spiders, and sometimes opilionids as well. Ectoparasites (e.g., mites, ticks, fleas) of rodents occur in these places too, as do resting adults and detritivorus larvae of a variety of flies. The life cycle of many fleas and of phlebotomine sand flies is spent almost entirely in burrows (Pavlovskii, 1948, cited by Petrov, 1976:334), and bloodsucking triatomid bugs are not uncommon in burrows of mammals found in the Sonoran and Chihuahuan deserts (Ryckman, 1962; Lowe, 1968:592).

Most temporary inhabitants of burrows are less directly involved with rodents and other vertebrates than are ectoparasites, although it is not uncommon to find tenebrionid larvae in the nesting material imported by *Dipodomys*, the kangaroo rat. (These larvae are nearly ubiquitous in desert soils, however, and one can also locate them in ant nests, under stones, and in soil generally.) Many species of adult beetles also occur in burrows. Most of these insects are probably scavengers and, like the pair of tenebrionids shown entering a burrow in Fig. 47, probably use such places for shelter, reproduction, aggregation and feeding.

While little substantive information has been reported on the arthropod fauna of desert mammal burrows, my own observations indicate that the scavenging larvae of flies mainly occur where organic debris accumulates

Fig. 45. Irregular spacing of arthropod burrows. Sand dunes, Sevilleta National Wildlife Refuge, central New Mexico. (Photograph by the author)

at the interface between the air and soil of the burrow cavity, but this needs further study. Certainly burrows are also used by adults of many Diptera, chrionomid and cecidomyiid midges being prominent among these. Higher suborders of flies are well represented in such places during the heat of the day when burrows provide shade and moderate temperatures.

Burrows are by no means the only—nor necessarily the most ideal—habitats for soil-associated invertebrates in deserts. Rather, the substrate itself affords the conditions of high humidity, slowly changing temperature, and resistance to locomotion with which fossorial species are best able to deal. Some of these animals are close to being permanent soil dwellers. Geophilomorph centipedes come to mind, for they inhabit deep and sandy soil of the littoral

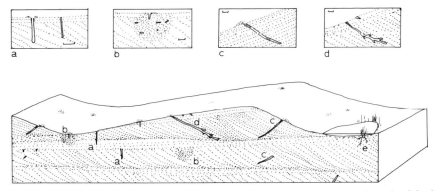

Fig. 46. Bioturbation traces commonly observed in eolian sedimentary deposits (block diagram is not drawn to scale). Items indicated by letters are as follows: **a** Lycosid spider and cicindelid (tiger beetle) burrows, former is larger and with web collar and reinforced (compacted) walls. **b** Burrowing and disruption of sediments by ants. **c** Rhaphidophorine gryllacridid (sand-treader camel cricket) burrow, backfilled at entrance (see also Fig. 17d). **d** Left to right, two trial burrows, a nesting burrow, and a sleeping burrow of nyssonine sphecids. **e** Plant roots nourished from intermittent rains also disrupt sediments. Brackets in enlarged segments indicate 10 cm scale. (Diagram courtesy of S. Andrews)

Fig. 47. A pair of tenebrionids, *Eleodes caudifera*, entering a burrow that was probably dug by a rodent. Central New Mexico desert grassland. (From a photograph by the author)

desert in northern Egypt (Ghabbour et al., 1977), and to my knowledge have not been found on the surface. Occasionally, when the soil is moist in the Negev desert, these elongate carnivores make their way up to the spaces beneath stones (personal observation).

Deeply situated in the soil of deserts is a fauna we know very little about. For the most part it seems to depend on the roots of desert plants. Sand-swimming cockroaches and cicada nymphs are members of this assemblage, and were discussed earlier. Coleopteran larvae found associated with roots of rangeland Compositae in southern Arizona include species of Anobiidae, Buprestidae, Cerambyicidae, Curculionidae, and Scarabaeidae (Hetz and Werner, 1979). To this list we should be able to add the larvae of Elateridae and Tenebrionidae (Rafes, 1960). Known to feed on the roots of *Agave leche-guilla* in the Chihuahuan desert are members of the family Monomidae (Peterson, 1953), and cerambycid beetle larvae in the genera *Mecas* and *Crossidius* are reported to eat the roots of *Artemisia* and *Chrysothamnus* shrubs in arid regions to the north (Linsley, 1957).

Among the Lepidoptera, larvae of certain Hepialidae and Cossidae feed on the roots of woody plants in Australia (Common, 1970), while larvae of some Acrolophidae consume *Prosopis* roots in the American Southwest (Mares et al., 1977b). Other Lepidoptera with larvae that eat roots and tubers of desert plants include species of Sesiidae (Fig. 48), which utilize a number of plant families (Duckworth and Eichlin, 1978), and Megathymidae, which sometimes eat *Yucca* roots (Roever, 1975). Undoubtedly many of the Noctuidae (Crumb, 1956; Rafes, 1960; R. Holland, personal communication), and crambine Pyralidae (Matthews, 1976; personal observation) will also turn out to be significant root consumers in deserts.

Of the Diptera specializing on roots of desert plants not much seems to be known, but anthomyiid species that constitute economic problems to bulb growers certainly ought to have desert relatives that specialize on bulbs of geophytes. A cecidomyid midge forms galls on the roots of *Artemisia ludoviciana,* in the Great Basin (Ranasinghe, 1977), and it would not be surprising to find aphids on the roots of other desert species. Roots are a resource that have up to now largely been ignored by the desert invertebrate ecologist. Fossorial carnivores, of course, feed on the consumers cited above. And while their effects on the root-feeding community are not known, the presence in desert soils of geophilomorph and scolopendromorph centipedes (see numerous discussions in this book) and of carabid larvae (Rafes, 1960)—to name just two groups of predators—indicates active carnivory at some depth.

2. Morphological and Behavioral Adaptations of Soil-Associated Desert Arthropods

Fossorial species often have characteristic morphological traits that enable them to move about in the soil. Some of these features are most conspicuous,

a

b

Fig. 48. *Melittia gloriosa,* a sesiid lepidopteran with a distribution that includes arid regions in southwestern North America. **a** Larva boring in tuber of *Curcubita foetidissima,* on which it appears to specialize. **b** Freshly emerged female with pupal exuvium protruding from sand-covered cocoon. [Photographs courtesy of W. D. Duckworth (Duckworth and Eichlin, 1978); with permission]

examples being the heavy forelegs of cicada nymphs and of burrowing scarab beetles. The scooping "sand baskets" on the tibiae of some rhaphidophorine gryllacridids (see Fig. 17b) and the tarsal-joint brushes of sphegid and musarid wasps in South Africa (Hesse, 1938, cited by Pradhan, 1957) are other structures used to excavate shelters or nests in sandy soil. Likewise, the psammophore organs of some desert ants consist of long curved hairs on parts of the head and are employed to scoop and transport sand (Délye, 1968). Arachnids such as whip scorpions (Crawford and Cloudsley-Thompson, 1971) frequently use their pedipalps for excavating burrows, while solifugids (see Fig. 22) and cockroaches use their legs for this purpose. In *Arenivaga* cockroaches from North America, equilibrium receptors on the cerci provide gravity orientation information via giant interneurons as the animals burrow (Hartman et al., 1979).

Newlands (1972, cited by Newlands, 1978) observed that burrowing behavior in psammophilous scorpionids living in loose sandy habitats in the Namib involves the use of setal combs on the first two pairs of legs. Sand is first loosened by chewing with the chelicerae or by scraping with the anterior pair of legs. The last two pairs of legs are then used to pull the scorpion backwards while it drags a mound of sand along with the front legs. Sand is also leveled and pushed with the tail, "tail scraping" being found as well in psammophilous buthids and vaejovids. Williams (1966) found that *Anuroctonus phaeodactylus* in arid North America also uses its chelicerae and legs in constructing burrows.

Forward movement in loose substrate is facilitated by having a hard-surfaced body that is either elongate and somewhat cylindrical, as in elaterid and staphylinid beetles, or flattened, as in desert cockroaches. Modifications of the legs for rapid digging are not uncommon, and often take the form of flattened segments resembling paddles. These are seen in a variety of desert cockroaches (see *Arenivaga* legs in Fig. 34a) and gryllacridids (see again Fig. 17b) that burrow readily and that have fringe-like hairs on their tibiae and/or tarsi. Such structures are also found on the tarsi of a lepismatid, a large nocturnal cricket, and sparassid spiders in the Namib desert (Lawrence, 1959). Finally, the simple squirming movement of some kinds of caterpillars insures quick entry into sand-dune soil (Fig. 49a,b); other species must labor more tediously as they slowly dig into hard-packed loess soil with their forelegs (Fig. 49c).

Of all the arthropods studied in arid environments, none have been more closely scrutinized than the tenebrionid beetles. Considerable space in this book has already been devoted to various of their physiological and behavioral adaptations, and it should be clear by now that these are often intimately associated with structural peculiarities. Indeed, the morphology of adult tenebrionids in particular has proven fascinating to many investigators, especially students of speciation and adaptation.

Nowhere is morphological variation in tenebrionids more obvious than in the Namib desert. It was from observations in the Namib that Koch and earlier workers (see Koch, 1961, 1962) stimulated a host of later studies of Namib tenebrionids and also of their unique fog-desert ecosystem, and it

Fig. 49. Larvae of Lepidoptera entering desert substrates. **a** Noctuid larvae dug from dune sand beneath a *Prosopis* shrub and placed on surface, Sevilleta National Wildlife Refuge, central New Mexico. **b** Same larvae, a few seconds later. **c** Unidentified larva digging very slowly in relatively compact crust of loess soil, Negev desert. (Photographs by the author)

a

b

c

is from the Namib as well that we have gained some appreciation of adaptive features displayed by larval tenebrionids. Aspects of the water balance of *Onymacris* larvae were considered in Chapter 4; here it is appropriate to summarize briefly the morphological traits of larvae in the tribes Adesmiini and Zophosini—traits that Schulze (1974) associates with sand-dune existence.

Certain of these larvae are "ultra-psammophilous" in that they inhabit loose shifting sand. Apparently locomotion in such a medium is facilitated by their being more slender than species that inhabit firmer substrates. In addition the possession of relatively broad and dorso-ventrally flattened front claws is characteristic of these juvenile forms, as is a comparatively large number of setae on the ventral surface. Yet while these and other features are convergent in the two tribes, they do not represent all possible structural modifications associated with life in shifting sand. This point is made by Schulze (1974), who, in reviewing her earlier work, notes that larvae in "dune-diving" Eurychorini and Opatrini have rounded abdomens.

Adults of these xerophilous insects have been closely examined by biologists in a number of deserts. Koch, as well as Pierre (1958) and Medvedev (1965), pioneered studies of desert tenebrionid faunas generally, and in doing so emphasized in detail certain morphological features of the legs relative to locomotion both within and on the surface of various desert substrates. In general, Koch (1961) found that important modifications for species inhabiting sandy areas involved both hypertrophy of tactile structures maintaining continuous contact with loose sand, and extension of the gripping surface of the tarsi. The dimensions of these structures are understandably quite varied, owing to differing combinations of phylogeny and levels of locomotion.

Features associated with a fossorial way of life among desert tenebrionids are in some respects not unlike those of other kinds of burrowing arthropods. Thus, small, sand-burrowing Dactylocalcarina tenebrionids in southern Africa have strongly dilated tibiae (Fig. 50a) (Penrith, 1974), which is true also for a number of species from Central Asia that inhabit poorly consolidated sands (Fig. 50b) (Medvedev, 1965). (Examples of other fossorial legs with dilated anterior tibiae are diagrammed in Fig. 50c and d.)

According to Koch (1961), other species in the Namib and the Sahara are particularly adept at digging and tunneling in blown sand. These are said to possess laterally compressed tarsal "sand shoes" having long, silky hairs (Fig. 51). Pierre (1958) has correlated the length of such hairs with the texture of the sandy substrate characteristic of the species. Thus, species of *Leptonychus* living in compact and coarse sand dunes in northwest Africa have long tarsal hairs, while others in the same genus that inhabit dunes with finer sand grains possess shorter and more rigid hairs. The position on the tarsi of such hairs is apparently of functional significance: When situated laterally they provide support, but when located on the dorsal or ventral surfaces they are used for "sweeping" sand (Medvedev, 1965). Penrith (1973) also noted that long silky hairs were found on the tibiae of species in the tribe Cryptochilini that live in loose sand in southern Africa.

Still other tenebrionids are adapted to a "gliding" type of movement in

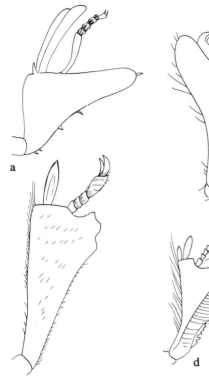

a

b

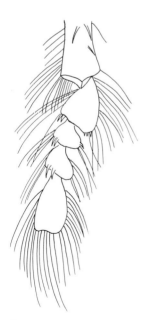

c

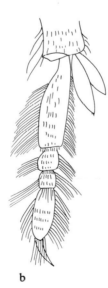

d

Fig. 50. Examples of dilated anterior tibiae of various fossorial, sand-inhabiting desert tenebrionids. Diagrams not drawn to scale, and modified from authors (in parentheses). **a** *Protodactylus inflatus,* Namib desert (Penrith, 1974). **b** *Psammogaster malani,* Namib desert (Koch, 1961). **c** *Pisterogaster kessleri,* central Asia (Medvedev, 1965). **d** *Anemia pilosa,* Sahara desert (Pierre, 1958)

a

b

Fig. 51. Laterally compressed tarsal "sand shoes" with long silky hairs in desert tenebrionids. **a** *Calognathus chevrolati eberlanzi,* which tunnels in blown sand, Namib desert. (After Koch, 1961) **b** *Pisterogaster gigantea,* which digs in slightly consolidated sand, central Asia. (After Medvedev, 1965)

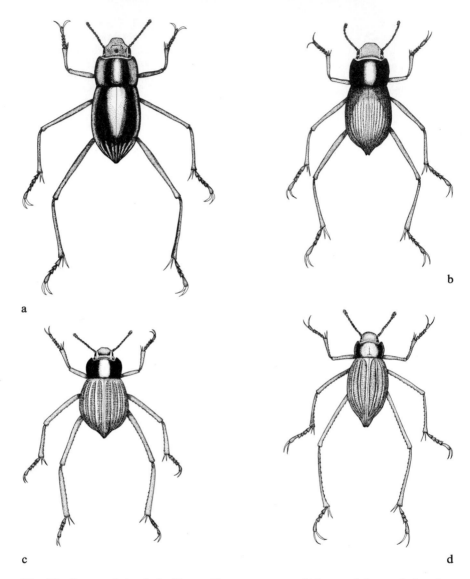

Fig. 52. *Onymacris* tenebrionids, rapid runners on sand dunes, plains, and dry river courses in southern Africa. Note hypertrophied tarsal claws and terminal tibial spines on exceptionally long legs. **a** *O. unguicularis.* **b** *O. laeviceps.* **c** *O. multistriata.* **d** *O. boschimana subelongata.* **e** *O. rugatipennis rugatipennis.* **f** *O. plana plana.* [Courtesy of M.-L. Penrith (Penrith, 1975); with permission]

the sand (Koch, 1961). This group includes tiny *Cardiosis* species that use their elongated tarsi to move rapidly in and on the leeward surface of Namib dunes. In Central Asia, genera that "swim" in sand are found in the tribes Opatrini, Pedinini, and Erodiini; these beetles are small, streamlined, and drop-shaped (Medvedev, 1965).

In southern Africa, *Onymacris* species are found on sand dunes and along

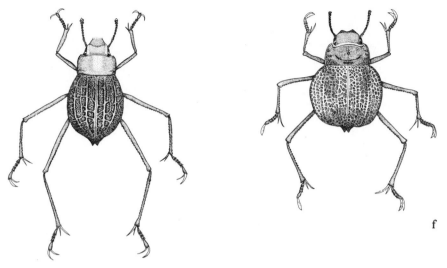

e

f

Fig. 52. e and f.

dry river courses. Rapid runners on the surface of these habitats, they have very long legs. And, as shown in Fig. 52, their tarsal claws and terminal tibial spines are hypertrophied, especially in species inhabiting barchan dunes (Penrith, 1975). In Central Asia and North Africa, the widespread genus *Adesmia* is convergent with *Onymacris* with respect to long legs and running speed. The femora and tibiae of *Adesmia* contribute importantly to limb length, but in other highly mobile forms—especially those often climbing in vegetation—the tarsi are elongate and flexible (Medvedev, 1965).

This review of morphological features associated with movement in and on desert substrates should allow us to appreciate the diversity as well as the subtlety of adaptation to habitat conditions in arid regions. But there are other ways of life in desert soils that should also be mentioned. Certain of these are associated with carnivory, and it is to this topic that we now turn our attention.

3. Adaptations of Soil-Associated Carnivorous Arthropods in Deserts

Some carnivorous insects effectively use the soil just beneath the surface for protection and concealment, while others wait for prey to come close enough to catch after a short run. Larvae of the neuropteran genus *Myrmeleon* are an example of the first group. They and larvae of some other myrmeleontid genera dig a conical pit in sandy soil, and prey falling over the edge are quickly grabbed and subdued by these "ant lions" at the base (Fig. 53). Digging is accomplished in *M. immaculatus* by flicking sand as the insect circles along the bottom of a "digging groove" (Tuculescu et al., 1975). In the South African species, *M. obscurus,* digging is governed by a circadian

a

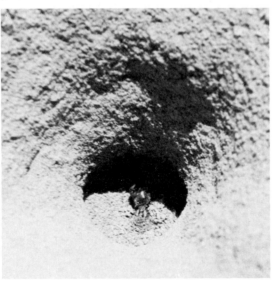

b

Fig. 53. Pits dug by myrmeleontid (ant lion) larvae, *Cueta* sp., in the Negev desert. **a** Series of pits in loose soil on slight, south-facing rise near base of large shrub. **b** An ant being pulled beneath pit base by a larva. (Photographs by the author)

rhythm that peaks at dusk (Youthed and Moran, 1969a); the size of its pits is related to that of the larvae that dig them (Youthed and Moran, 1969b). In the arid part of Costa Rica the dispersion of *Myrmeleon* pits becomes uniform when densities reach five larvae per 100 m²; this apparent way of optimizing foraging (McClure, 1976) could be studied easily in species from true desert areas as well.

A conical pit is also dug in arid sandy regions by larvae of leptid flies in South Africa (Hesse, 1938, cited by Pradhan, 1957), indicating a remarkable convergence with the ant lion way of life. A somewhat different strategy is employed by sand-dwelling larvae of ascalaphid neuropterans in arid portions of Israel (Simon, 1979) and by larvae of the myrmeleontid tribe Brachynemurini in the Mojave and Sonoran deserts (Stange, 1970). Instead of constructing pits, these insects lie—with mandibles spread—on or just beneath the soil surface (Fig. 54). Substrate vibrations set up by potential prey appear to elicit a quick running attack by these well-concealed insects.

Vertical burrows are made—generally in moist sandy soil—by cicindelid tiger beetle larvae in many parts of the world. The predaceous larvae remain just beneath the entrance and, like the insects just described, wait for prey to venture close enough to capture. Rumpp (1961) describes an ecological unit of these burrows from the lee sides of large sand dunes in southern Utah. Adult tiger beetles (Fig. 55a) are also carnivores, but employ short, rapid flights and rapid running in their search and capture behavior.

Less seems known about how staphylinid beetles—also carnivores—make use of desert substrates. Many are very small and occur in litter; I have

Fig. 54. Well-camouflaged larva of an ascalaphid (owl fly) neuropteran, *Ptyngidricerus* n.sp. on soil surface, Negev desert. (Photograph courtesy of D. Simon)

Fig. 55. Predatory beetles. **a** Cicindelid (tiger beetle, *Cicindela* sp.) on sandy bank of Rio Grande River, central New Mexico. **b** First instar, **c** second instar, **d** male adult of the carabid, *Thermophilum sexmaculatum* (all on natural substrate), from the Sahara desert. [Photograph **a** by the author; **b–d** courtesy of W. Paarmann (Paarmann, 1979); with permission]

also found them in soil just beneath stones in the Negev. Hammond (1975) states that species in the arid tropics and subtropics are, like tiger-beetle larvae, generally restricted to moist microhabitats. These places presumably include termite nests—at least in semi-arid regions (Kistner, 1975)—since many genera and tribes of staphylinids are symbiotically associated with termites (Wilson, 1971).

Some species of carabid beetles are also found in deserts, where their predaceous larvae seem to inhabit only extremely moist soils. According to Paarmann (1979), at least one species (Fig. 55b,c) adjusts its developmental phenology to this constraint by reducing the number of larval instars from three to two. This shortens the duration of larval activity—an apparent survival advantage.

Another localized group of predators in desert soils consists if immature insects that depend in part on appropriate placement by the female parent in order to feed on larvae of other species (Figs. 30c, 56). Meloid beetles provide examples of this behavior. Werner et al. (1966) discuss how in arid regions some of the active first instar triungulin larvae locate grasshopper egg pods and the eggs of bees by wandering over the surface, while others attach themselves to flower-visiting bees and are transported to nests. There they parasitize larvae and/or their food, and then molt to a parasitic grub stage.

Larvae of bombyliid bee flies (Fig. 57) are also widely distributed in deserts and are often placed in the vicinity of prey by the female, which flips its eggs into the burrow of a victim (Hull, 1973). Hosts of bee flies include grasshopper egg pods, as well as larvae of ant lions, beetles, moths, and mining bees.

Yet another common strategy of predation in the desert soil is employed by the offspring of provisioning Hymenoptera. Examples in the deserts of North America include larvae of tiphiid wasps in the genus *Brachycistis,* which as eggs are placed on grubs of paralyzed scarab beetles. The adult female is wingless and strongly fossorial (Wasbauer, 1973). Female mutillid wasps are often wingless as well, and Ferguson (1962) notes that they typically select as hosts the larvae of gregarious mining bees.

Numerous sphecid wasps are also provisioners in deserts (Fig. 58). Species of *Larropsis* were found by Gwynne and Evans (1975) to search for burrows of *Ammobaenetes* rhaphidophorine gryllacridids in New Mexico and Colorado sand dunes. Apparently, prey are located and stung underground. Instead of transporting a paralyzed *Ammobaenetes* to a burrow of its own—a common behavior in the Specidae—a female *Larropsis* oviposits directly on the host (Fig. 59) and then departs.

Pepsis pompilids (Fig. 60) are large, dark wasps that are well known for their spectacular attacks on tarantulas, with which they provision their burrows (Gertsch, 1949). Other pompilids preying on *Geolycosa* spiders in the sand dunes of southern Colorado (Fig. 61) form a continuum of habitat—and prey—selection types. Among these, *Anoplius* species modify the burrow of the prey. Such behavior may reduce prey stealing by surface scavengers and by cleptoparasitic pompilids (Gwynne, 1979). A study by McQueen (1979) of another *Anoplius–Geolycosa* relationship in Ontario suggests that *Geolycosa* species close their burrows during periods of greatest wasp activity. Such a tactic may account for the open burrows of *G. raphaelana* in New Mexico only during spring and fall, at which time the young presumably emerge and disperse.

Linsley (1958) summarized the categories of predators and parasites of the larvae of solitary bees in North American deserts. Groups include endopar-

a

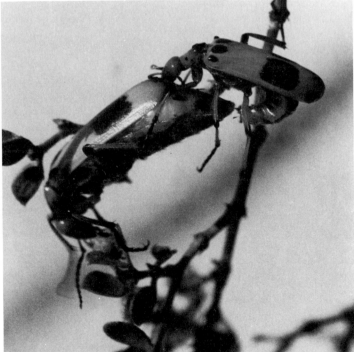

b

Fig. 56. Desert-dwelling meloid beetles. **a** *Megetra sp.* on annual plant, southwestern New Mexico. **b** *Pyrota postica,* mating pair on *Larrea tridentata,* female feeding on inflorescence, Big Bend National Park, Chihuahuan desert. (Photographs by the author)

a

b

Fig. 57. Bombiliid adults (unidentified bee flies), central New Mexico desert grassland. **a** Male following female; their coloration blends well into that of the sandy soil, litter, and dry grass. **b** Very small specimen on flower. (Photographs by the author)

asites such as larvae of rhipiphorid beetles, stylopid strepsipterans, and parasitoid wasps, as well as more direct feeders like larval mantispid neuropterans, clerid and meloid beetles, bombiliid and asilid flies, and mutillid wasps.

II. Crevice-Type Habitats

These provide a compromise between the soil-burrow environment and the surface above. Typified by spaces under rocks and stones (Fig. 62), they

a

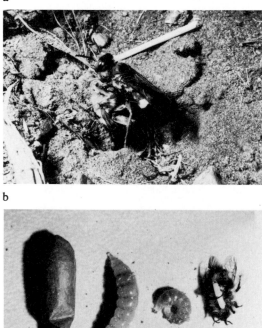

b

Fig. 58. The sphecid digger wasp *Philanthus bicinctus* and its bumblebee (*Bombus* sp.) prey, Great Sand Dunes National Monument, Colorado. **a** Following prey capture. **b** Transporting prey to burrow. **c** Egg on prey, larval stages, and cocoon. (Photographs courtesy of D. T. Gwynne)

c

may be thought of collectively as a sort of environmental "half-way house" having doors to the outside and passages to the basement. Occupants of the house at any one time may have quite diverse life styles. Some are fairly permanent residents—often with private quarters in the basement—and consume food entering or brought in from the soil surface. Sometimes they leave and find new accommodations elsewhere. Others use the place more like an inn (i.e., for food and temporary lodging) but do so at some risk

Fig. 59. Paralyzed *Ammobaenetes phrixocnemoides* bearing the egg of *Larropsis chilopsidis.* *Broad arrow* points to the egg, *slender arrow* to the larva of a miltogrammine sarcophagid fly. The larva shown first consumed the egg, then entered the body of the sand treader prey, upon which it fed for six days prior to pupating. Habitat: sand dunes, Rio Grande Valley, central New Mexico. [Photograph courtesy of D. T. Gwynne (Gwynne and Evans, 1975); with permission]

because of lurking predators. Still others occasionally come up from below to investigate or to use whatever resources might be available at the time.

The behavior of a number of invertebrate types justifies the use of the "half-way house" analogy. Examples of the fairly permanent residents, for example, include scorpions and snails. *Diplocentrus peloncillensis,* mentioned earlier several times, is a scorpion that effectively subdues and consumes visitors arriving from the outside (Fig. 63a), and probably from the soil below as well. Other scorpions appear to make fairly extensive nocturnal use of foraging sites in the vicinity, but typically return to the residence and their burrows beneath it (Tourtlotte, 1974; Crawford and Krehoff, 1975). Certain carnivorous tettigoniid orthopterans also live under stones (Fig. 63b); not much is known about them, but it is doubtful that they stay for long beneath the same one, particularly when a scorpion or centipede is a contemporary inhabitant. Small snails in the genus *Jaminia* are very common on the undersides of stones in the Negev (Fig. 64a) where they graze on algae; seldom are they found in the open.

Members of some gastropod genera, on the other hand, move in and out

Fig. 60. A pompilid tarantula hawk, *Pepsis* sp., emerging from its newly dug burrow in northern Chihuahuan desert shrubland, New Mexico. (Photograph by the author, with permission of John Wiley and Sons, Inc.)

from underneath stones and may be the chief animal importers and exporters of nutrients in stony deserts like much of the Negev (M. Shachak, personal communication) (Fig. 64b). Snails also live under rocks in the arid mountain ranges of the Death Valley area (Jaeger, 1957:137), but their ecology has been ignored. Crickets (Fig. 65a) and thysanurans (see Fig. 7) are examples of other components of the "inn-using" category, and because of their relative vulnerability to predation, these soft-bodied forms, together with numerous insect larvae (Fig. 65b), probably contribute significantly to local food webs. The distribution of desert isopods can also be strongly influenced by the presence of stones (Kheirallah, 1980), under which such crustaceans gain shelter (Fig. 65c) and undoubtedly detritus food.

Termites and ants are necessarily reinjected into the discussion at this point because they illustrate nicely the subcommunity that enters from the subterranean environment. Some ants form relatively permanent nest entrances under surface objects, while entrances of termites (Fig. 65d) are probably more temporary. Fallen vegetation provides a special kind of crevice shelter for termites in that the habitat itself is an object of consumption.

Finally, crevices *between* rocks depart to some extent from the environmental compromise presented by stones, because rock crevices do not always provide access to the soil. Yet these openings may be very extensive and are clearly useful habitats for many transient species, including vertebrates like snakes and lizards. Among the crevice-inhabiting invertebrates, snails

a

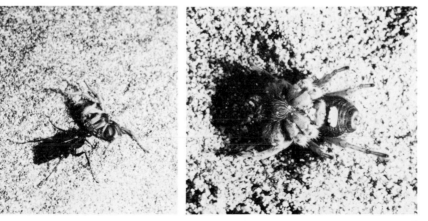

b

c   d

Fig. 61. Predation by pompilid spider wasps of the burrowing lycosid *Geolycosa raphaelana*. Great Sand Dunes National Monument, Colorado. **a** Position of egg of *Anoplius marginalis* on prey: antero-lateral abdomen just behind hind femur in photo. **b** *Pompilus scelestus* digging at its nest entrance. **c** *P. scelestus* dragging prey. **d** Ventral surface of prey abdomen showing position of *P. scelestes* egg. [Photographs courtesy of D. T. Gwynne (Gwynne, 1979); with permission]

Fig. 62. Crevice in limestone rock being entered by a tenebrionid, *Pimelia mittrei,* Negev desert. (Photograph by the author)

can be common in rock-slides in Baja California (Miller, 1972; Christensen and Miller, 1975), and other mollusk species are exceptionally abundant in rock crevices found in arid landscapes of the eastern Mediterranean (Warburg, 1972; Heller, 1975). Rock outcrops in the Judaean and Negev deserts can house large populations of *Archispirostreptus* millipedes in crevices (Fig. 66); in New Mexico volcanic escarpments do the same for *Orthoporus ornatus.* Crevices also enable scolopendromorph centipedes, lepismatid thysanurans, cockroaches, some beetles, and other flat-bodied forms to penetrate deeply into relatively stable microhabitats. Cuteribrid flies that parasitize *Neotoma* wood rats in western North America lay their eggs in rock crevices without regard to the proximity of their hosts (Baird, 1974).

III. Soil Surface Including Litter

Previous passages in this book have already referred to the use of this habitat for foraging, dispersal, reproductive activities, thermoregulation, and the reception of proximate signals. Compared with the restrictive conditions of the soil itself, the open surface allows for an enormous behavioral diversity among invertebrate species. Conversely, the risk of being preyed upon or

Fig. 63. Carnivores beneath rocks, Peloncillo Mountains in southwestern New Mexico. **a** *Diplocentrus peloncillensis* holding tenebrionid prey; note other prey remains nearby. **b** *Eromopedes balli balli,* a tettigoniid. (Photographs by the author)

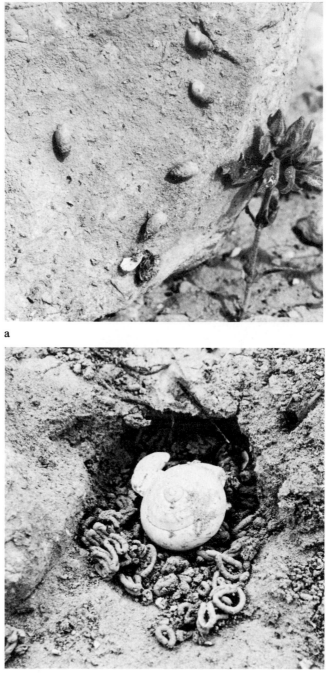

a

b

Fig. 64. Permanent **a** and temporary **b** snail residents beneath stones in the Negev desert. **a** *Jaminia* sp. specimens attached to the underside of a stone, where they feed on algae. **b** *Sphincterochila prophetarum* surrounded by its feces, some of which originated from materials eaten elsewhere. (Photographs by the author)

of being killed by heat and dryness is also high on the surface which, as pointed out in Chapter 1, is subjected to great fluctuations in temperature and moisture. Litter, on the other hand, modifies surface conditions by providing an increased amount of shelter and food, as well as an ameliorated microclimate. Recall, for example, our earlier references to the absorption of dew by surface detritus.

Species living for various periods in litter demonstrate an infinite variety of adaptations to this particular habitat. An example of one kind of adaptive trait involves the cryptic color pattern of the noctuid larva shown in Fig. 67a. Other insects in litter are inconspicuous largely because of their small size and cryptic behavior (Fig. 67b). Yet another kind of adaptation involves the locomotory behavior exhibited by certain litter-inhabiting desert hemipterans. Their movement over the irregular substrate takes the form of rapid, jerky movements. This was reported from southwestern Australia by Slater (1976) for the lygaeid *Fontejus westraliensis,* an insect that inhabits dry, open, hot areas in seed litter, mostly beneath *Acacia laricina.* In the Negev desert at least one species of coreid bug moves in a similar manner. Easily mistaken for a blowing seed (Fig. 67c), this insect may possibly be mimicking plant disemminules as it travels erratically over the desert surface. Perhaps these illustrations will bring to the reader's mind other possibilities or examples of surface-object mimicry by desert arthropods.

This consideration of life on the soil surface would not be complete without some mention of two specialized—and often taxonomically similar—subcommunities: those of the necrophagous and coprophagous arthropods. We know very little about the ecology of these groups in deserts, aside from the fact that they reduce their food substrates in successional stages, as they do elsewhere.

Regional patterns of diversity in necrophagous species are puzzling. Diversity appeared relatively low in a study of decomposing elephant carcasses made following a period of drought in the acacia scrub-grassland of Tsavo (East) National Park in Kenya. There, Coe (1978) judged the main arthropod consumers of soft tissue to be *Chrysomyia* larvae of calliphorid flies, insects similar to those shown in Fig. 68. They in turn were fed upon by ants, staphylinid beetles, and hybosorine scarabs. Other (dermestid) beetles accounted for the removal of most of the skin within a few weeks of the elephants' deaths. Trogine scarabs also fed on the skin, as did larvae of tinaeid moths when the skin was in contact with the ground. Termites slowly removed ligaments and cartilage from the carcass.

A greater diversity of carrion feeders and associated species was recorded by McKinnerney (1978) in a study of rabbit-carcass decomposition in the Chihuahuan desert. From that generally drier and less productive region, some 63 species were identified as members of the rabbit necrovore community. As with the elephant study, a definite succession of feeding groups was observed to concentrate on particular stages of tissue breakdown. This is seen in Fig. 69, which also illustrates the relatively large number of arthro-

Fig. 65. Arthropods relatively vulnerable to predation beneath stones in arid regions. **a** Gryllid cricket (*Gryllus* sp.) southwestern New Mexico. **b** Lepidopteran larva, Negev desert. **c** A porcellionid and two armadillid isopods; also two *Jaminia* snails, Negev desert. **d** Termites at substone nest entrance, Negev desert. (Photographs by the author)

a

b

pod families partitioning the lagomorph-carcass resource. As with the elephant study, specialist feeders were greatly in evidence, with Lepidoptera (not indicated in Fig. 69) and vespid wasps consuming mainly carcass fluids, dipteran larvae working on muscle and internal organs, scarabaeids eating intestinal contents, acridids eating fur, and trogines (= trogids) concentrating on skin. (An illustration of trogine beetles feeding on the dry skin of a desert lizard is shown in Fig. 70a).

Matthews (1976:72) states that in the arid zone of Australia, trogines and dermestids appear earlier on cadavers than they do elsewhere and that as a consequence they have greater relative importance. The limited amount of work done so far on the problem of necrovory in deserts does, in fact, suggest regional patterns of arthropod succession. Whether the species of vertebrate carrion being attacked affects these patterns in a given habitat has not been documented. Certainly, the necrovores themselves include occasional opportunists, and Matthews (1976:73) mentions seeing tenebrionids and dung beetles feeding on dead invertebrates and very small vertebrates that "tend to be consumed mostly by ants." In New Mexico I have noted that desert millipedes *(Orthoporus ornatus)* will scavenge recently dead tenebrionids and

c

d

Fig. 65. c and d.

small rodents; so there is undoubtedly a wide range of species that indulges in this behavior.

Matthews (1976) also treats the question of coprophagy in arid zones, and distinguishes among three sets of behaviors that apply to large detritivores feeding on dung in these and other regions. Thus, dung may be processed initially (before final microbial decomposition): (1) by breeding on it immediately, which takes advantage of existing moisture (as in flies—see Fig. 68—

Fig. 66. *Archispirostreptus syriacus* exposed in a crevice habitat of a limestone outcrop, Judaean desert. (Photograph by the author)

and beetles), (2) by burying it, which tends to conserve moisture (as in dung beetles—Fig. 70b), and (3) by feeding on it after a certain amount of drying has occurred (as in termites and trogine beetles).

Since dung burial depends on the array of available coprophages, which in turn is bound to vary with location, it follows that dung burial may vary greatly in regional importance. Matthews (1976) considers it not to be especially pronounced in the case of Australian scarabaeids, although he notes that several genera transport fecal pellets into shallow soil chambers, from which a vertical shaft is constructed. In North American deserts it is not uncommon to encounter various scarabaeids burying dung balls, although it is not clear whether my impression of the frequency and ubiquity of this practice—as opposed to its comparative rarity in Australia—can be supported.

According to Gordon and Cartwright (1974), some scarabaeine genera utilize preformed dung balls while others form their own. Eventually, the balls are buried and eggs are presumably laid in them. Aphodiine scarabs in the arid mountains of Durango in Mexico depart from this habit. Instead, they inhabit the burrows of gophers *(Thomomys umbrinus)* and either oviposit in fecal chambers of the rodent hosts, or "parasitize" dung balls made by *Onthophagus,* another scarab (Gordon and Howden, 1973). It is surprising that so little of this kind of information has been published for desert-inhabiting dung beetles.

Dried feces are fed upon a great deal by termites in Australia. Ferrar and Watson (1970) recorded many species of *Amitermes* (Termitidae) consuming bovine dung there, especially in the northern and inland parts of the

a   b

c

Fig. 67. Inconspicuous litter-in-habiting insects. **a** Noctuid larva, which when feeding specializes on young leaves of the shrub *Prosopis chilensis* in the Monte desert of Argentina. **b** Lygaeid hemipterans, each about 3.5 cm in length; sometimes extremely abundant in patches of shrub litter in central New Mexico desert grassland. **c** Coreid hemipteran, *Phyllomorpha laciniata,* that looks and moves like a blowing seed, Negev desert. (Photograph **a** courtesy of R. G. Cates; **b** and **c** by the author)

continent. These and the relatively few mastotermitid and rhinotermitid species also feeding on such material are often polyphagous, in contrast to wood-eating and harvester termites that feed on dung infrequently or not at all. It is noteworthy that the dung of placental herbivores is a relatively recent food resource for Australian termites.

In southwestern North America, *Gnathamitermes tubiformans* feeds naturally on grass leaves and cattle dung (Spears and Ueckert, 1976). S. Tucker and W. G. Whitford (personal communication) consider that *Gnathamitermes* spp. in southern New Mexico are of undoubted importance in the removal of cattle and rabbit dung. There, these insects colonize dry dung pats soon after the surrounding soil is wetted. Colonized dung pats lost up to 95% of the original dry weight in a single month compared to pats from which termites were excluded. Obviously, the potential effect of these and previously mentioned species must be considerable in heavily grazed desert grasslands.

Fig. 68. Larvae, probably of calliphorid flies, feeding on the carcass of a cow. South-western New Mexico arid shrubland. (Photograph by the author)

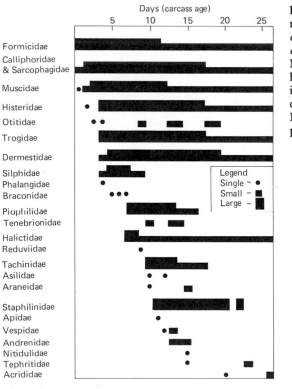

Fig. 69. The community of necrovores on rabbit *(Lepus californicus, Sylvilagus auduboni)* carcasses, Hueco Mountains, Texas, Chihua-huan desert. Legend refers to indices of concentration of dominance over time. (After McKinnerney, 1978; with permission)

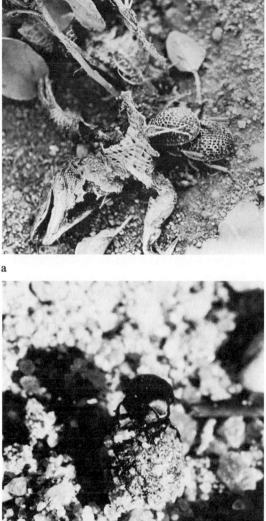

Fig. 70. Examples of necrophagy and coprophagy in the Scarabaeidae. **a** Trogine beetles (*Trox* sp.) feeding on dry lizard carcass, northern Chihuahuan desert, New Mexico. **b** *Boreocanthon melanus,* about 5 cm in length, rolling ball of (probably) rabbit dung; ball will eventually be pulled into the beetle's burrow, and following oviposition and hatching a larva will consume it. Central New Mexico desert grassland. (Photographs by the author)

a

b

Having already noted that *Gnathamitermes* can remove substantial proportions of litter from its habitat (Chapter 13.C.II), we now ask whether other largely detritivorous foragers at the soil surface do likewise. Judging from the report of Ayyad and Ghabbour (1977), the cockroach *Heterogamia syriaca* in northern Egypt may compare well in this respect, since this cockroach comprises nearly a third of the mesofaunal biomass in its habitat. On the other hand, data presented in Table 11 for two other arthropods give much lower consumption values than reported for termites. Moreover, *O. ornatus*

Table 11. Annual consumption of organic matter by two species of desert detritivores

	Organic matter consumed annually		
	Biomass (kg ha⁻¹)	Energy (kcal m⁻²)	Reference
Orthoporus ornatus (Diplopoda)	3.4–8.9	1.3–3.4	Crawford (1979a)
Hemilepistus reaumuri (Isopoda)	—	10.3–38.6	Shachak et al., (1976b)

probably ingests less than 0.5% of its community's net primary production, while *H. reaumuri* may eat up to 4.3% of the plant material available to it.

An overlooked role of these and other desert detritivores has been their potential interaction with microbial decomposers. El-Ayouty et al. (1978) showed that when *Hererogamia* feces are added experimentally to shrub litter and sand-dune soil, a synergistic increase in nitrogen mineralization results. And in *O. ornatus* an enormous number of bacteria inhabit the gut. These comprise a variety of morphotypes as seen by electron microscopy (see Fig. 32) and appear to contribute importantly to digestion of carbohydrates (E. C. Taylor, personal communication). E. C. Taylor (in prep.) has also shown that a large number of fungal species occurs in the gut and that many of these are also present in habitat soil. Since both the desert millipede and *Hemilepistus* consume considerable amounts of habitat soil, the potential for microbial dispersal by these mobile "reservoirs" may be quite significant. Clearly, this is an area where future research will be rewarding.

C. Summary Comments

Soil-associated habitats serve as the major reservoir for biomass in deserts. In these places the arrival of rain is first detected and then channeled into a multitude of biotic events that culminate in productivity. Thus, despite its frequent lack of structure and depth, and partly because of conditions occurring on its surface, soil is the medium through which the tempo of desert life is controlled. This we should keep in mind as we next review the invertebrate communities of plants, because either directly or indirectly, the species comprising such assemblages also depend on the nature and condition of the soil.

Chapter 15
Temporary Vegetation Community: Emphasis on Herbivores

A. Introductory Comments

From the standpoint of herbivory by desert invertebrates, there are two broad groups of plants. One consists of ephemerals, the other of perennial shrubs and trees. We know the drought-evading ephemerals mainly as annuals such as the large number of composites and mustards that bloom quickly and then die, leaving only their seeds and their withered remains. But there are also many other ephemerals in the desert; they consist of deciduous perennial plants like many grasses and members of the Lilliaceae. Bulbs, rhizomes, and underground stems characterize deciduous perennials, which are also called "geophytes."

Desert ephemerals have no aboveground photosynthetic structures that persist, especially during long dry seasons. They are, therefore, only temporary sources of nutrition to the consumer. Plainly, if a desert consumer specializes on one ephemeral species, or even if it feeds broadly on ephemerals collectively present over one or more seasons, it must: (1) be able to track its host plants in time and space by responding to cues associated with plant predation (Joern, 1979), and (2) take compensatory measures in the months or years when its food is not there. These are both problems that we considered in several earlier parts of the book; we also spent some time discussing biotic interactions and adaptations to environmental stress that apply to invertebrates feeding on ephemeral plants or tissues. What we did not treat in any detail now becomes the central issue of the present chapter, namely the relationship of an entire and fairly complex invertebrate community to these transient desert plants.

B. Consumer Array and Dietary Patterns

Any number of categories can be erected to describe the array of consumers of ephemeral desert plants. We shall employ the following arrangement because, although simplistic, it provides a convenient background for the subject at hand.

Fig. 71. Hemipteroid insects on annual plants, central New Mexico desert grassland. **a** Lygaeid, *Melanopleurus delfragei,* feeding on *Lygodesmia* sp. inflorescence. **b** Newly hatched immature hemipterans (not identified) also on *Lygodesmia* inflorescence. **c** Adult and immature membracids attended by ants on *Aster* sp. **d** Thysanopterans (Thripidae) on inflorescence of *Heliotropium* sp. (Photograph **b,** courtesy of S. J. Upton; others by the author)

a

b

I. Direct Consumers

These species feed on living plant tissues and/or seeds. Certain desert snails are included, but insects such as grasshoppers, as well as hemipterans, homopterans, and thysanopterans (Fig. 71) are much more common on ephemerals. Of the holometabolus insect orders, the Coleoptera are often represented

c

d

Fig. 71. c and d.

by adults (Fig. 72) and larvae alike. In the Lepidoptera (see Fig. 24a,b) and Diptera, usually only the larvae feed directly.

Depending on the variety of the host plants consumed, invertebrate herbivores fall somewhere in the specialist–generalist spectrum of feeding types. Referring to grasshoppers in arid grasslands, Joern (1979) asserts that long-lived species feeding on short-lived plants should either be generalists or specialize on highly predictable hosts. According to Cates (1981) and Orians et al. (1977), there should be more generalists than specialists among consum-

a

Fig. 72. Coleoptera on annual plants, central New Mexico desert grassland. **a** Copulating pair of *Tylosis maculata* cerambycids, common on *Sphaeralcea* spp.; note female eating flower bud. **b** Smaller cerambycid, *Bortyle suturale,* and larger meloid (*Nemognatha* sp.) on flower head of composite, probably *Grendelia aphonactis.* (Photographs by the author)

b

Table 12. Insect herbivores from Arizona and Argentina feeding on annuals[a]

| | *Lepidoptera* spp. | | *Coleoptera* spp. | |
Category	No.	%	No.	%
Generalists	10	77	6	66
Specialists	3	23	3	33

[a] Data from Orians et al. (1977).

ers of temporary desert vegetation because the former have more chance to encounter unpredictable edible plants or plant parts. Data reported by Orians et al. (1977: Table 6–8) from a comparison of desert ecosystems are given in Table 12 and support the latter contention, as do more recent data reported by Cates (1981).

II. Pollinators

The chief invertebrate pollinators of desert ephemerals seem to be solitary bees (Fig. 73). Wasps also pollinate, and a case is made below for the ants as well. Adult Diptera and Lepidoptera are probably less important in this regard.

III. Carnivores

These will be mentioned only in passing; more will be said about carnivorous invertebrates on desert vegetation in the next chapter. On temporary vegetation, the most conspicuous carnivores are often certain spiders and hemipterans (Fig. 74a,b). The carnivorous tettigoniid shown in Fig. 74c suggests a larger diversity of predaceous forms on ephemerals than we ordinarily assume to be present.

C. Characteristics of Plants as Resources for Invertebrate Consumers

I. Plant Phenology

Of overriding significance in the phenology of desert ephemerals is their response to rainfall. Heavy blooms during unusually "wet" years are common knowledge, spectacular instances being known especially from winter-rainfall

a

b

c

Fig. 73. Flower visitors on ephemeral plants, central New Mexico desert grassland. **a** Andrenid bee, *Pseudopanurgus aethiops,* a solitary pollinator, on *Senecio longilobus.* **b** Apid bee (*Bombus* sp.) also solitary and on *Zinnia* sp. **c** Acalypterate fly probing nectary on annual blossom. (Photographs by the author)

deserts. There are, however, many species that bloom long after seasonal rains have terminated. In such cases the response is indirect and more subtle; moreover, as we note below, there may be important metabolic differences between winter (or spring) and summer (or fall) annuals.

Microclimate and topography often bring about clumped distributions of ephemerals when these plants occur in large numbers (Goudie and Wilkinson, 1977). As they germinate and grow, water stress is usually at a minimum and blooming occurs in a relatively short time. If water stress is higher than usual, their rate of development may be even more rapid and may produce a smaller than usual amount of tissue and seed (Grenot, 1974). Seeds of desert annuals are generally able to endure long periods of drought, sometimes 10 years or more. Therefore, the timing of their germination is hardly a predictable event. Furthermore, seed depredation in the intervening

a

b

c

Fig. 74. Carnivorous arthropods on ephemeral plants. a Thomicid crab spider barely visible in *Hymenopappus* sp. inflorescence immediately after having captured a fly. b Phymatid hemipterans (copulating pair), showing yellow and dark brown coloration resembling that of *Helianthus petiolarus* flower on which they wait in ambush. c Large tettigoniid grasshopper (*Saga* sp.) on thistle; note raptorial forelegs of the insect. (Photographs by the author: a and b in central New Mexico desert grassland, c in Judaean desert)

duration can be extremely variable, thus contributing to the highly stochastic nature of this food supply.

Deciduous perennials such as geophytes respond on the whole more rapidly than annuals to pulses of rain. Presumably, this is because perennials support more tissue during drought and can, therefore, more quickly marshall large stores of energy and nutrients (Solbrig and Orians, 1977). Hence, when they are present, these plants should provide the "first wave" of primary production to available consumers. Annuals should contribute later on.

The usually small size of new ephemeral tissues restricts the extent to which invertebrate consumers can use them as matching background (Orians et al., 1977) or as shelter. However, leaves of annuals developing in the cooler months are often located close to the ground; clearly they could provide shelter for small animals. Summer annuals on the other hand, at least in North American deserts, tend to lack basal rosettes (Mulroy and Rundel, 1977).

II. Aspects of Photosynthesis

Rates of photosynthesis in developing tissues of all plants are characteristically high. Therefore, other things being equal, rapid production of sugars and other nutrients should render these tissues potentially valuable to many consumers. Physically, too, their initial lack of defense structures such as spines makes them relatively susceptible to consumption by herbivores.

Caswell et al. (1973) presented data suggesting that plants with C_3 photosynthesis provide less resistance to chewing insects than do plants with C_4 photosynthesis. Since most winter annuals in the Mojave and Sonoran deserts are C_3 species, whereas most summer annuals in parts of the Sonoran and adjacent southwestern deserts are C_4 species, the matter becomes of some interest to students of desert insects. Boutton et al. (1978) studied the relationship of insect herbivory to C_3 and C_4 grasses in a semi-arid part of Texas, and concluded that there were no demonstrable differences in the utilization of these plants by major groups of insects. A trend was suggested, however, that among the Orthoptera and Hemiptera, C_3 grasses may be somewhat preferred.

The question is still an important one in the context of the ecology and evolution of insect–plant relationships in deserts, if for no other reason than that many C_3 grasses are said to have higher nitrogen values (Caswell et al., 1973; Boutton et al., 1978; Brown, 1978) and to lack structural tissues found in C_4 plants. Nitrogen is a relatively deficient element in desert food webs (see West and Skujiņš, 1978), yet is also of fundamental importance to developing animals (White, 1978).

D. Characteristics of Invertebrate Consumers

I. Seasonal and Diel Feeding Patterns

There is limited quantitative and somewhat more anecdotal evidence that population buildups of desert insects eating annual plants coincide with pulses of primary production. For example, Shinn et al. (1975) showed that lygaeid bugs were especially dominant during the pre-floral and flowering stages of two important (exotic) annual plants in the northern Great Basin. The plants were succulent at the time (July), when other less significant annuals had withered.

Also, there seems to be a rather clear but poorly documented correlation between vast numbers of lepidopteran larvae and the availability of fast-growing annuals in arid regions (Cates, 1980). In Australia, for example, many species of Noctuidae, Geometridae, and Pyralidae show high rates of larval development on herbaceous vegetation responding rapidly to sporadic rains (Common, 1970). I too have noted this in New Mexico, where after relatively wet winters an abundance of spring annuals is matched by many caterpillars feeding on them. Especially striking are larvae of the migratory butterfly *Vanessa cardui* on lupines (Fig. 75a) and of the sphinx moth *Hyles lineata* on a number of annual species. Cates (1981) documents large variations in larval abundance over time for these two—as well as for four other lepidopteran species, and Casey (1976, citing Grant, 1937) reports "outbreak years" in the Mojave for *H. lineata*. The comparatively wet winter of 1980 in the Negev desert was such a time, with unusually large numbers of caterpillars feeding on ephemeral vegetation in early spring (Fig. 75b). Heavy fall rains in the Sudan are associated with much the same effect (Cloudsley-Thompson and Idris, 1964).

Further indication of the importance of climate in regulating populations of insects on desert annuals was given by Rainey (1967). His study showed that eastward-moving troughs of low-pressure air may have been associated with two separate but temporally coinciding events in desert regions of the Middle East. The incidents were: (1) invasions of *Agrotis ypsilon* cutworm moths, and (2) large migrations of desert locusts.

II. Patterns of Pollination

Of interest to desert biologists is the timing of nectar and pollen gathering by solitary bees relative to the blooming of annual plants. In North America the geographic and phylogenetic affinities of these bees appear to govern patterns of this timing. Thus, a rich fauna of specialist bees with Holarctic

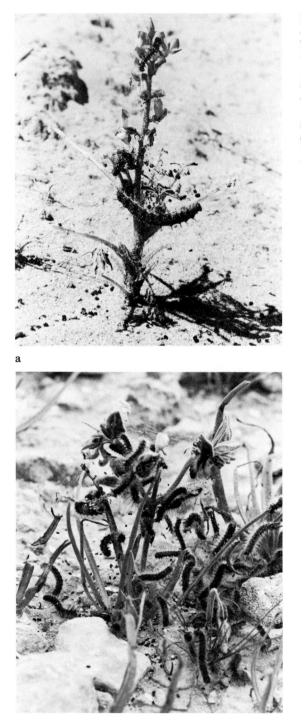

a

b

Fig. 75. Rapid consumption of annuals following outbreaks of lepidopteran larvae. **a** Nymphalids, *Vanessa cardui,* decimating *Lupinus* sp., central New Mexico desert grassland. **b** Arctiids, *Ocnogyna loewii,* doing the same to *Allium* sp., Negev desert, after an unusually wet winter. (Photographs by the author)

origins makes full use of the usually extensive bloom of spring annuals in the southern deserts, while another set of bees with largely tropical and cosmopolitan affinities concentrates on xerophytic shrubs no matter when they bloom (Michener, 1944).

Some very precise mechanisms have evolved in regard to the timing of bee visits to desert annuals. An example demonstrated by Wainwright (1978a) showed the effects of a "banner spot" on the floral parts of two lupine species in the Colorado desert of southern California. A yellow and white spot elicited a positive response prior to pollination, but after pollination the spot turned a deep purple-red, causing wild bees to avoid the plant. Wainwright (1978b) also showed that since *Lupinus arizonicus* sometimes occurs in the overlapping territories of male *Anthidium* and *Anthophora* bees, and since female *Anthidium* and *Anthophora* bees are its major pollinators, the pollination ecology of the plant may be influenced by territorial behavior.

A number of questions about pollinating insects in deserts deserve thought. One has to do with whether or not ants can be important desert pollinators. The matter was raised by Hickman (1974), based on his own studies and on the cited view of Hagerup (1943) that extreme deserts may be the best habitats for ant pollinators. This reasoning has to do with energetics, a low volume of nectar being needed to satisfy the energy requirements of ants (in comparison to flying insects). Also, an ant-pollinated plant needs to produce less nectar; hence its investment in other aspects of development and reproduction ought to be enhanced. The question has obvious implications and should be followed up.

The taxonomic position of a pollinator may also be related to a plant's energy output in nectar. During a study conducted in the western Great Basin, Gut et al. (1977) found that nectar used by three groups of insects has the following average concentration: solitary bees—37%, butterflies—44%, and sphingid moths—57%. One wonders if this trend holds in other arid regions, if it transcends seasons, and if it reflects the relative abundances of pollinating insects.

III. Patterns of Behavior and Development

It is in the evolutionary interest of species feeding on ephemeral desert plants to make the most of their opportunity in a nutritional sense, and at the same time to insure their evolutionary fitness. On balance, this cannot be done without some sort of tradeoff. A partial example of how such a system can work comes from the study of Casey (1976), who showed that in the process of maximizing its consumption of annual plants in the Mojave, the larva of *Hyles lineata* keeps its body temperature relatively high for as long as possible by a series of vertical trips between the ground and the short-lived vegetation on which it feeds. This form of travel may amount to "maxithermy" behavior because the larva's feeding rate is proportional to its body temperature. Presumably, the other side of the tradeoff is that available food plants are not overeaten, partly because the larva is a generalist feeder, and perhaps also because the adult is a highly mobile moth that disseminates its eggs broadly.

The generalist herbivore should be less constrained in its development by a tight feeding schedule than a specialist feeding only on annuals. Thus, larvae of the butterfly *Papilio machaon* (see Fig. 76a) in Iraq are known to feed from April until June on a series of at least five annual species (Pradhan, 1957), thereby insuring themselves of a relatively long developmental period. A similar pattern is true for larvae of the arctiid moth, *Estigmene acrea,* in New Mexico (Cates, 1981). A specialist, in contrast, needs to phase its oviposition more precisely, allowing as much time as possible for its offspring to maximize their consumption of a restricted set of host species or, according to Cates (1981), of a specific tissue such as young leaves.

Parenthetically, it is worth mentioning once more that recourse to migration or to some form of dormancy is needed during seasons when host plants are no longer present. One would expect such escape to be an especially stringent requirement of specialists. The caterpillar shown digging laboriously in Fig. 49c has little choice: It has finished its larval development and must now enter a habitat suitable for aestivation, since the surrounding vegetation will dry up in a few weeks.

E. Coevolution of Temporary Desert Vegetation and Its Herbivores

The pattern of give and take referred to above reflects a balance between temporary vegetation and its consumers. The pattern is erratic in the ecological context but should even out in evolutionary time. For the producing plant the evolutionary problem is that of allocating an appropriate proportion of its energy and nutrient supplies to tissue defense, versus the requirement of maintaining fitness (Rhoades and Cates, 1976; Cates and Rhoades, 1977; Cates, 1981).

As predicted by Orians et al. (1977), the plant's investment should be proportional to several features related to the depredations of herbivores. These features include the intensity of grazing, the time over which tissues not eaten contribute to the plant's fitness, and the importance to the plant of the loss of such tissues. Corollaries arising from the prediction have to do with the system of defense. If the system is to require a minimal investment (a condition that makes sense in a short-lived, rapidly growing plant), and if the investment is to be chemical (an assumption borne out by the facts), then the defense system should have several unique characteristics.

Fig. 76. Aposematic displays on ephemeral vegetation. Each of the following insect species has some combination of black or brown and red or orange, in addition to other colors. **a** Larva of the papilionid, *Papilio machaon,* on its umbellifer food plant, *Ferula communis.* **b** The acridid grasshopper, *Dactylotum bicolor,* probably on *Melanopodium* sp. **c** Aggregation of pyrrhocorid hemipterans, *Scantius aegyptius,* probably on *Lithospermum* sp.; most are adults, some are copulating, others are feeding or simply moving about. (Photographs by the author: **b** in central New Mexico desert grassland, **a** and **c** in the Negev desert)

One of these is for it to be of low concentration and to have specific deterrent effects (Rhoades and Cates, 1976). The chemical nature of toxins and enzyme inhibitors found in ephemeral plants and tissues in deserts conforms to this general characteristic. Another is for the system to be chemcially diverse (see Cates and Rhoades, 1977) or antigeneralist in its effects, since the chance of succumbing to well-timed attacks by specialist consumers is not as great as the chance of being eaten by generalists (Cates, 1981).

The issue, however, is not as clear-cut as the above discussion may seem to imply. We referred earlier (Chapter 9,D), for example, to growth stimulation and drought resistance in *Larrea* shrubs resulting from feeding by *Bootettix* grasshoppers. This finding indicates that certain levels of grazing intensities may in fact benefit both parties. This was also suggested by an experimental study of mirid bugs feeding on the grass *Agropyron desertorum* from the Great Basin desert. Norton and Smith (1975) were able to show that the bugs caused a temporary increase in shoot nitrogen without effecting a net decrease in shoot biomass. Surprisingly, there seems to be little research effort in this direction, considering the potential for competition that exists between range animals and insects that feed on annual plants in arid regions.

Finally, we should mention some subtle—although not always demonstrably coevolutionary—relationships between toxic plants and certain herbivorous insects in desert zones. The insects are aposematic, and aggregations of these and similarly patterned species on toxic and nontoxic plants are not uncommon.

A case in point involves a grasshopper feeding exclusively on milkweeds, namely the widespread North African and Asian pyrgomorphid, *Poekilocerus bufonius*. Fishelson (1960) found that secretions from its abdominal repellent gland are an effective deterrent against both vertebrate and invertebrate predators. Despite the tendency of this insect to hide in the foliage of ascepliad plants or to remain motionless on the ground, it is aposematic, having a dark bluish-grey body with yellow spots, and orange hind wings. Its host plant provides toxic cardenolides that are ejected defensively by the immature hoppers, or produced as conspicuously colored foam by adults (Euw et al., 1967). Aposematic coloration is also evident in the acridid grasshopper shown in Fig. 76b; whether or not it possesses chemical defenses does not seem to be known. However, the pungent odor produced by the osmaterium in papilionid larvae sometimes accords well with their bright color patterns (Fig. 76a).

Another example concerns the chrysomelid beetle *Timarcha punctella,* which appears to specialize on *Plantago albicans* in arid parts of Morocco. According to Joviet (1965), this insect's hemolymph is extremely toxic and is reflexly released from several parts of the body following disturbance.

Irrespective of their own toxicities, some brightly colored insects aggregate on desert plants in large numbers. An illustration of this in a single species of hemipteran is shown in Fig. 76c, and complex mimetic assemblages were described by Linsley et al. (1961) from mountain canyons in southwestern

North America. There, on local flowers the dominant models seem to be toxic lycid beetles in the genus *Lycus*. They are aposematic, being colored yellow or orange, and black. And as they feed and mate on flowering annuals and perennials, they are accompanied by a series of apparent mimics, including cerambycid beetles as well as pyromorphid, lithosiid, and geometrid moths.

Such plant–herbivore relationships have been poorly investigated in arid regions, which is surprising because of the abundance of obviously aposematic herbivorous insects that feed on desert annuals.

Chapter 16
Perennial Shrub Community

A. Introductory Comments

There are many ways to classify perennial desert shrubs; some methods are based on functional morphology, others on more ecological considerations (e.g., Noy-Meir, 1973). Since our present emphasis is on the interactions of these plants with invertebrate consumers and not on their inherent variation, we shall divide the plants broadly into two groups: xerophytic shrubs and succulents. Both have aboveground parts persisting for at least several years. Xerophytes are usually woody, and may also be deciduous or evergreen. They sometimes occur in tree form, and their root systems range from shallow to deep (deep roots characterize phreatophytes). However, in this section we shall concentrate on what goes on aboveground.

B. Consumer Array and Dietary Patterns

As in the case of ephemerals, there are direct consumers, pollinators, and carnivores associated with perennial desert plants. And, depending on the mobility and food preferences of these invertebrates, some can utilize both plant categories. If there is a major distinction to be made between the faunas of temporary and more permanent vegetation in deserts, it has mainly to do with their respective diversities. Perennials usually provide a more complex habitat than do ephemerals, and since perennials are also more persistent, the establishment of specialized niches by their users should be expected.

Most of the categories of users listed below are modified from the arrangement of Sleeper and Mispagel (1975):

Defoliators: Especially common are larvae of Lepidoptera, Diptera, and Coleoptera (Fig. 77), adult Coleoptera such as chrysomelid beetles, and all feeding stages of acridid Orthoptera and certain Gastropoda.

Flower feeders: Examples are adult meloid beetles (see Fig. 56b) and thrips.

Fruit (including seed) eaters (after Kingsolver et al., 1977): Internal feeders consist of lepidopteran larvae and bruchid, cerambycid, and curculionid (Fig. 78) beetle larvae. External feeders include nymphs and adults of Hemiptera, and also larvae of Lepidoptera.

Pollen and nectar feeders: Many of these are effective pollinators as well; they include adults of bees, wasps, beetles, flies, butterflies, and moths (Fig. 79).

Sap feeders: Most frequent are mites, and sucking insects such as a variety of hemipterans, homopterans (Fig. 80), and thrips.

Gall formers: Here one finds cynipid and chalcidoid wasps, tephritid (Fig. 81) and cecidomyid flies, and psyllid homopterans. Several families of Lepidoptera tunnel in galls as well (Common, 1970).

Borers and girdlers: Cerambycid and buprestid beetles feed on the cambium and bark of many woody species. Some of these insects also bore into stems.

Given this array, it is not surprising that Orians et al. (1977:Table 6–8) were able to present data from their comparison of similar desert ecosystems, showing that species feeding on woody perennials are more evenly divided between specialists and generalists than they seem to be when feeding on annuals (see Table 12). Values are given in Table 13. Otherwise, data presented by Cates (1981) suggest that up to 85% of the lepidopteran larvae (23 of 27 species) on woody perennials may be specialists.

The cacti are another group of perennial plants with a distinct fauna of specialist herbivores. Generalists rarely attack these plants (Mann, 1969).

C. Characteristics of Plants as Resources for Invertebrate Consumers

I. Plant Phenology

Seasonal patterns of flowering, fruiting, leaf production, and leaf fall vary considerably among desert perennials. This fact constitutes an important time dimension in the use of flowers, fruits, and leaves by invertebrates.

a

b

Fig. 77. Flower-feeding and defoliating larvae on perennial shrubs. **a** Undetermined lepidopteran consuming flowers of *Zygophyllum dumosum,* Negev desert. **b** Chrysomelid beetle larvae ingesting secretions from the surface of a gall (formed by a tephritid fly larva) on *Chrysothamnus nauseosus,* a shrub it occasionally defoliates severely, central New Mexico desert grassland. **c** Heavy infestation of psychid lepidopterans on *Acacia aroma,* Monte desert, Argentina. **d** Psychid larva (*Amicta* sp.) moving over Negev desert terrain. (Photograph **c** courtesy of R. G. Cates; others by the author)

Solbrig et al. (1977:85) predicted that xerophytic shrubs lacking deep roots should bloom in response to rain and produce fruit at the end of the rainy season, while phreatophytes and succulents should bloom according to photoperiod and in advance of the rainy season. Flowering does, in fact, seem to be predictable in these terms and has surely contributed to the temporal

c

d

Fig. 77. c and d.

diversity of the pollinating fauna. Simpson et al. (1977) concluded that the overlapping and intensive use of *Prosopis* flowers undoubtedly results in competition for floral rewards. This circumstance should in turn select for finely-tuned behavior among flower feeders and pollinators.

a

Fig. 78. Curculionid beetles, probably associated trophically with perennial shrubs. **a** *Ophriastes* sp. on *Larrea tridentata,* Sonoran desert. **b** *Ammocleonus hieroglyphicus;* these large insects are abundant in spring in parts of the Negev desert. (Photograph **a** courtesy of R. G. Cates; **b** by the author)

b

Leaf production by *Prosopis* shrubs in the Western Hemisphere seems to be relatively independent of rainfall pulses and more subject to genetic control (Mooney et al., 1977). Therefore, ecotypic patterns of leaf production occur, and at high latitudes these also reflect photoperiod. Leaf drop at high latitudes appears to be associated with photoperiod as well, but at low latitudes temperature plays an increased role in this event. It follows that specialist defoliators of *Prosopis* should have also evolved developmental responses to the interplay of the exogenous factors affecting the leaf production and leaf fall of *Prosopis* species.

Orians et al. (1977) claim that compared to the spatial positioning of photosynthetic tissues in desert annuals, that of perennials is less predictable and more broadly distributed on a vertical plane. Moreover, the comparatively large leaf size in perennials (a statement some may dispute) should provide matching backgrounds and hiding places for herbivores and carnivores alike.

Fig. 79. Pollen and nectar feeders of perennial shrubs. **a** Andrenid bee (*Perdita* sp.) visiting *Dalea scoparia* flower, central New Mexico desert grassland. **b** Hesperiid skipper, *Pyrgus communis* visiting *Fendlera rupicola*, central New Mexico; larvae of this species feed on Malvaceae, the adult has a broad distributional range, including deserts (R. Holland, personal communication). (Photographs by the author)

a

b

II. Aspects of Photosynthesis

Photosynthetic rates are comparatively low in perennials (Solbrig and Orians, 1977). New, growing tissue should provide an exception to this rule, but the photosynthetic parts of most evergreen shrubs and succulents are tough and not easily chewed. In contrast, desert deciduous shrubs appear more easily chewed (Orians et al., 1977).

Photosynthetic pathways of desert perennials broadly cover the known range. C_4 shrubs are certainly common in deserts, but a large number of C_3 species occur there as well. Cacti and other groups having crassulacean

Fig. 80. Sap feeders on perennial shrubs. **a** Lygaeid hemipterans on cholla cactus (*Opuntia* sp.) central New Mexico desert grassland. **b** Fulgorid homopteran on *Dalea scoparia,* same general area. **c** Membracid homopteran, *Enchenopa binotata* on *Koeberlinia spinosa,* Big Bend National Park, Chihuahuan desert. **d** Coccid homopterans, *Icerya rileyi,* attended by *Myrmecocystus* ants, on *Larrea tridentata,* northern Chihuahuan desert, New Mexico. (Photographs by the author)

a

Fig. 81. A gall-forming tephritid fly, *Aciurina bigeloviae,* on *Chrysothamnus nauseosus,* central New Mexico desert grassland. **a** Typical infestation. **b** Gall sectioned to show larva inside. (Photographs by the author)

b

Table 13. Insect herbivores from Arizona and Argentina feeding on woody perennials[a]

	Lepidoptera spp.		Coleoptera spp.		Orthoptera spp.		Hemiptera spp.	
Category	No.	%	No.	%	No.	%	No.	%
Generalists	4	27	17	52	7	54	5	45
Specialists	11	73	16	48	6	46	6	55

[a] Combined data from Orians et al. (1977).

acid metabolism (CAM) are well established in deserts, too. However, the implications for herbivory are less clear than in the case of annuals.

D. Characteristics of Invertebrate Consumers

I. Seasonal and Diel Feeding Patterns

Because of the typically complex structure and phenology of perennial desert shrubs, correlations involving their seasonal biology with invertebrate biomass may obscure significant interactions unless additional analyses are undertaken. Examples of such correlations are given for shrubs in the Chihuahuan desert by Whitford (1975), who found a weak relationship ($r^2 = 0.33$) between insect density and biomass on *Prosopis* in July and the peaking of that shrub's primary production. Clearly other factors have a lot to do with arthropod visitors to *Prosopis*. In the case of *Larrea,* most insects were present in May; this correlated well ($r^2 = 0.80$) with peak production of flowers and fruit.

In the *Prosopis* study, about 90% of the insect biomass consisted of psyllid bugs. A similar arthropod biomass on *Larrea* in February was composed of chermid aphids in Chew's (1961) study of spiders on shrubs in southwestern Arizona. Still other examples show how dramatically herbivore densities can change from year to year. One instance involves the complete disappearance of bee fly (bombyliid) populations from Mojave desert shrubs in 1974 (Sleeper and Mispagel, 1975). This occurrence was temporally and perhaps causally associated with a simultaneous decline in the proportion of parasites and predators from the previous year. It happens that 1974 was a comparatively dry year and also marked an increase in mealybugs (coccids) on these shrubs; this in turn may have been due to a rise in soluble nitrogen compounds caused by moisture stress.

The phenology of herbivorous insects may be related to that of a plant other than its initial host. An example is that of the gelechiid moth *Aroga websteri,* whose larvae defoliate *Artemisia* shrubs in the Great Basin early in the season, concentrating on terminal leaves. The adults eventually emerge from the pupa in time to feed at *Chrysothamnus* flowers later in the year (Hsiao and Kirkland, 1973).

The seasonal appearance of a herbivore on a desert shrub may be due partly to a combination of the animal's resistance to desiccation and to the moisture content of its food. Orians et al. (1977) made several predictions based on this interesting possibility. One was that in deserts desiccation-sensitive herbivores ought to occur on young leaves (high in moisture) during the cool early growing season. The example of *A. websteri* seems to confirm this prediction, which certainly warrants testing. A second prediction is that desiccation-resistant herbivores should be active later in the growing season. Again, this needs to be demonstrated experimentally, but since insects, including full-grown grasshoppers and adult chrysomelid beetles—on the basis of their surface:volume ratios at least—are inclined to be more resistant than their immature stages, the idea makes sense. A third prediction is that sap-feeders should be present as long as the shrubs are actively transpiring, and regardless of ambient temperatures. The presence of scale insects on desert shrubs for much of the year (personal observation) supports this possibility.

II. Patterns of Behavior and Development

Here it is appropriate first to discuss the behavior of a specialist, much as was done for a generalist in a similar context in the previous chapter. *Manduca sexta* is an example of a sphingid moth that as a larva feeds on *Datura* shrubs in the Mojave desert. Casey's (1976) study reveals how its behavior and development on this plant can be rationalized in terms of its "specialist" designation. Compared to the generalist *Hyles lineata* in the same region, *Manduca* feeds on a relatively rare but predictable host plant, but one that also provides a well-shaded microhabitat. Thermoregulation is, therefore, not at a premium and plays a minor role in the behavioral repertoire of *Manduca* larvae, unlike the situation with *Hyles*. Body and air temperatures are as a consequence fairly similar in the case of the specialist. While *Hyles* is a late-spring feeder and may be quite abundant, *Manduca* occurs in low numbers some months later, when it feeds at night and on the undersides of leaves.

Presumably, the food preferences of generalists feeding on perennials reflect not only plant availability but also changing nutritional needs. Thus Burkhart (1978) observed that in halophytic plant communities of the Sonoran desert, the acridid *Anconia integra* moves from *Atriplex canescens* to *Suaeda torreyana* in the hot summer, and that such a shift may provide it with a more concentrated source of calories and possibly water. Burkhart estimated that this grasshopper consumed from 2.6%–5.2% of the net primary production of perennials in its community.

Perennial shrubs offer conditions suitable for use by cryptic species, and Orians et al. (1977) found a higher proportion of such insects on perennials (and their old stems) than on annuals (and younger stems of perennials). According to these authors, cryptic species should be specialists, and we find that *Manduca* is cryptic in regard to both its color and behavior. Other cryptic herbivores (not all of which are specialists) on perennials occur among the grasshoppers (Fig. 82a and b) and phasmatids (see Fig. 25). Among carnivorous desert invertebrates, cryptic species such as crab spiders (Figs. 74a, 82c) may have relatively broad feeding habits, although this matter needs to be carefully documented. Also, whether the same cryptic species of carnivore occurs on both annuals and perennials does not seem to have been well explored.

Not all specialists on perennial shrubs in deserts are cryptic, and examples of aposematic coloration can be found at least in the adults of some Lepidoptera whose larvae are shrub feeders (Fig. 83). Aposematic patterns are also known in flower-feeding meloid adults (see Fig. 56b).

In contrast to specialists, many generalist feeders must risk exposure as they move from one microhabitat to another. One such generalist is *Onymacris plana,* the dune-inhabiting Namib tenebrionid, which is said to depend heavily on two perennials (the curcubit *Acanthosicyos horrida* and the grass *Stipagrostis sabulicola*) for food and shade (Roer, 1975). Here again, aposematic coloration, whether it be black or some pattern involving dark and warm colors, might be expected. *Onymacris plana* is indeed black, while the wandering generalist larva of *Hyles lineata,* a sphingid, is brightly colored (see Fig. 24b). Whether aposematic coloration among generalist herbivores is more common in desert species than in comparable taxa from other biomes remains an open question.

Some herbivores of shrubs are capable of interesting threat displays. *Hyles* is a relatively passive example, and a number of carnivores, some of which hunt in desert shrubs, also produce threat displays. Thus, Pradhan (1957) cites the example of a desert mantid from Baluchistan that faces its attacker by standing on its hind legs and exposing the brightly colored ventral surface of both pairs of wings. Some desert asilid flies mimic stinging Hymenoptera in body shape and color (Fig. 84a); others are less obvious and appear to feed on a variety of prey that they often capture and eat in shrubs (Fig. 84b). One species, *Epheria tricella,* is able to discriminate the size and color of its tiger beetle prey. Large tiger beetles with orange abdomens are significantly less predated by these robber flies than are small tiger beetles with dark abdomens (Shelly and Pearson, 1978).

Yet another plant (frequently shrub)–insect relationship found in deserts involves the occasional "sleeping aggregations" of solitary bees and wasps. The selective value of their behavior is unclear (Evans and Linsley, 1960), and the puzzle is compounded by the more frequent presence—in my experience—of individual "sleepers" (Fig. 85).

a

Fig. 82. Cryptic arthropods on perennial shrubs. **a** Tettigoniid grasshopper, *Eromopedes bilineatus,* on *Ephedra* sp. northern Chihuahuan desert, New Mexico. **b** Proscopiid grasshopper, *Astroma quadrilobatum,* on *Larrea cuneifolia,* Monte desert, Argentina; this insect also feeds on leaves of at least four other woody perennials (Rhoades, 1977). **c** Thomicid spider with beetle prey on *Artemisia filifolia,* central New Mexico desert grassland. (Photographs **a** and **c** by the author; **b** courtesy of R. G. Cates)

b

c

a

b

Fig. 83. Aposematic coloration in shrub-utilizing specialist Lepidoptera. **a** Saturniid, *Hemileuca hera magnifica,* on *Artemisia filifolia,* its larva's food plant (Cates, 1980a), central New Mexico desert grassland. **b** Citheroniid, *Eacles imperialis* on *Larrea* sp.; its larva feeds on the perennial *Ximenia americana* (Cates, 1980), Monte desert, Argentina. (Photograph **a** by the author; **b** courtesy of R. G. Cates)

Fig. 84. Asilid flies preying on insects in shrubs. **a** Undetermined species resembling a wasp eating captured meloid, *Pyrota postica,* on *Larrea tridentata,* Big Bend National Park, Chihuahuan desert. **b** Probably *Proctacanthus micans* with captured acridid grasshopper in *Dalea scoparia* shrub, central New Mexico desert grassland. (Photographs by the author; **b** with permission of John Wiley & Sons, Inc.)

a

b

E. Coevolution of Perennial Desert Shrubs and Their Herbivores

The general prediction that the investment by a plant species in its tissue defense should be proportional to the level of herbivory it experiences (Orians et al., 1977) applies to perennials as well as to annuals. Since the proportion

a   b

Fig. 85. "Sleeping" Hymenoptera on *Dalea scoparia,* central New Mexico desert grassland. Note use of mandibles. **a** Anthophorid bee, *Melissodes* sp. **b** Sphecid wasp, *Ammophila* sp. (Photographs by the author)

of specialist herbivores seem relatively high on perennials, one might expect that the quality of defense in such plants has evolved to cope with both specialists and generalists (Rhoades and Cates, 1976).

Cacti, and many xerophytes as well, possess thorns and spines believed to deter vertebrate herbivory. Against arthropods, however, chemical systems should be more effective than such structures. And since many shrub-feeding species are predictable specialists, the evolution of a relatively "costly" defense strategy was apparently needed to maintain a balance between consumer and producer.

Cates and Rhoades (1977) reasoned that specialists feeding on desert shrubs should possess more potent detoxifying mechanisms than are characteristic of generalists. They expected, therefore, to find antispecialist chemicals produced by such plants. These substances, moreover, were anticipated to have digestion-reducing properties and to exhibit a functional convergence in unrelated perennial species. The expectations of Cates and Rhoades were confirmed in several warm deserts, but it was also found that some perennials (sympatric woody legumes) contained a high diversity of alkaloids, which are more specific toxins having antigeneralist effects. Both deterrents can, therefore, exist in the same plant. In *Prosopis,* for instance, young leaves were found to be both high in alkaloids and preferred by specialists (3 species), while mature leaves were low in these toxins and consumed by generalists (2 species).

Coevolutionary relationships also exist between pollinators and the plants they visit. The well-known story of the incurvariid prodoxine yucca moths, *Tegeticula* spp., is a classic example of insects requiring specific hosts for pollen, and of the host plants in turn depending entirely on the moths for pollination (see Baker and Hurd, 1968). Actually, the interaction is somewhat more complex in the case of *Yucca whipplei,* since moth larvae in three different families utilize different parts of that plant for their development. Only one of these insect species really accomplishes pollination (Powell and Mackie, 1966).

Finally, a mutual maximizing of coevolutionary benefits is illustrated by the association of *Bombus* bees with the phreatophyte *Chilopsis linearis,* a tree growing along dry water courses in North American deserts. The floral parts of *Chilopsis* are so constructed that nectar (the sole floral "reward") is dispensed early in the day via "grooves" into "pools," according to Whitham (1977) who studied the system. Pool nectar can be extracted more rapidly than groove nectar by *Bombus,* which visits 40% more flowers when the former source is abundant than when it is not. This means that the bee ought to maximize its reward by visiting early in the morning.

Now if *Bombus* flies from some distance away its energy needs will be relatively high, so an early arrival at *Chilopsis* flowers appears to be the best strategy. It is to the advantage of the tree, however, to spread pollinators out over a period of time, and Whitham postulated that even as the supply of pool nectar diminishes, groove nectar should be available to more local bees with their lower energy needs. Indeed, time–energy budgets constructed from field data suggest that bees use both sources as morning wears on and as total nectar production declines. This arrangement should satisfy the energy requirements of bees arriving from varying distances and should at the same time maximize the fitness of the plant.

Chapter 17

The Invertebrate Community
of Ephemeral Waters

A. The Habitat

At intervals dictated by regional or local patterns of precipitation, runoff from rain or melting snow collects in shallow depressions and closed desert basins (Fig. 86). These sites often remain dry for years, but the process of filling can be rapid. Channeled runoff and sheet flooding (Fisher and Minckley, 1978; Eriksen, Patten and Rappoport, in prep.)—both of which can transport considerable sediment loads—seem to account for most of the inflow. Direct rainfall can contribute as well.

Total dissolved solutes are low at first in desert ephemeral waters. Within a relatively short time, however, wind action causes sediments from the surface soil to mix with the water (Hutchinson et al., 1932; Eriksen and Brown, 1980a). This in turn produces a solution of evaporite salts that continually increases in concentration (Friedman et al., 1976). Then, as drying is initiated, the concentration of salts increases markedly; in one summer Brown and Carpelan (1971) recorded a progression of from 0.5% to 34% salinity. Depending largely on thermal conditions, the oxygen concentration may also undergo severe changes and become too low to support certain species. Even-

---

Fig. 86. Temporary waters in deserts. **a** Small pool of runoff water, Algodones Dunes, Sonoran desert; such sites are rapidly colonized by aquatic Coleoptera. **b** Playa with standing water following an April storm, Eureka Valley Dunes, extreme western Great Basin; note snow on dunes in background. **c** Same playa without water; dense vegetation in foreground borders playa. [Photographs courtesy of F. G. Andrews (Andrews et al., 1979)]

a

b

c

tually, the basin dries completely. Duration of drying depends on how full the basin was to begin with, on the permeability of its soil, and on a variety of meteorological conditions.

Accumulation sites vary greatly in size, and as might be expected they are known by different sorts of names. Some are large evaporative basins such as northwestern Nevada's Carson Sink, which has measured 40 x 23 km (Hutchinson, 1937). At the other extreme are rock pools only a few centimeters deep that may last but a few days. Many temporary bodies of water in arid regions, however, are of an intermediate size and are often called "playas" (North America) or "pans" (southern Africa). Most pans are approximately circular (Hutchinson et al., 1932), a fairly common shape, apparently, for these waters. In North Africa a variety of terms (e.g., "chottes," "sebkhas," "r'dirs," or "dayas") are used to describe various kinds of depressions that occasionally fill with water (Gauthier, 1928). Regardless of shape and surface area, the depth of these waters is usually less than 1 m (C. H. Eriksen, personal communication).

The basins are formed initially by an uneven distribution of alluvial outwash (Hutchinson, 1937), by wind deflation of loose surface materials, and by tectonic forces. The majority of the many temporary ponds on the high plains of New Mexico and Texas were produced by wind and may have been present since the Pliocene (Sublette and Sublette, 1967). More recently, shallow temporary pools have been formed in deserts by irrigation practices (e.g., Gunstream and Chew, 1967) and are providing increasingly important habitats for aquatic species. Cattle tanks and the wallows of large ungulates are also places where aquatic invertebrates occur.

The amount of precipitation required to fill these sites varies according to local soil conditions and also depends on temperature, runoff, and wind. Eriksen, Patten, and Rappoport (in prep.) noted that winter rains ranging from 23 mm (no runoff) to 101 mm (runoff) filled Rabbit Dry Lake in the Mojave desert for 1 week and for 2 months, respectively. The bed of this basin consists of hard-packed clay. Again, about 50 mm must arrive before one well-studied basin in southern New Mexico can become an effective habitat for most aquatic organisms (W. G. Whitford, personal communication). And in the scrub desert of northern Sudan, it takes at least 15 mm of rain to create pools in clay soils overlain by sand (Rzóska, 1961).

The salinities of these aquatic systems depend on a number of factors, including size, duration, soil conditions, temperatures, seasonal patterns of rainfall, and the contribution of feces and urine by vertebrates. Large evaporation basins, as well as small basins that remain filled for relatively long durations—or that are located in saline geological deposits—seem to maintain comparatively high salinities. These high-salinity waters tend also to be clear because their colloidal particles are precipitated; thus, wind mixing does not cause them to be as turbid as smaller ponds and puddles with comparatively low salinities (C. H. Eriksen, personal communication).

Another effect of size is related to thermal stratification. In the calm of early morning, stratification may become established in larger bodies of water. Later in the day, when wind develops on the large fetch of a lake or playa, stratification disappears (Brown and Carpelan, 1971). Smaller bodies of water, which as we just noted are often turbid, respond quite differently to the effects of surface heating in the early morning hours. These effects can be so severe in small ponds and puddles that despite the influence of winds on the small fetch of these waters, the density layers remain stable. Moreover, continual establishment of thermal layering allows for chemical and biological stratification as well (Eriksen and Brown, 1980a). Levels of dissolved oxygen are therefore influenced indirectly by the surface area of an ephemeral body of water. And once large ungulates like cattle utilize such a habitat, its temperature levels and oxygen concentrations are further affected.

Since water temperature varies inversely with the amount of dissolved oxygen, it is useful to recognize that there are both warm-season and cool-season desert ponds, depending on the season of major precipitation. Hence, in North American ephemeral waters located in the Great Basin and the Mojave desert, seasonal temperatures may range from 0°C–39°C (Brown and Carpelan, 1971). However, regions with largely summer rainfall would not be expected to have waters with near-freezing temperatures.

B. The Invertebrate Fauna

Being highly changeable habitats, ephemeral waters in arid regions are populated by invertebrate species whose life histories and adaptations are suited for uncommonly stressful conditions. Therefore, it may be surprising that species assemblages in the temporary waters of deserts are often relatively rich (Cole, 1968). Examples of such assemblages in North Africa were given by Gauthier (1928), who distinguished mutually exclusive invertebrate communities in the "zone pluvieuse" from those in the "zone steppique." The influence of climate on species diversity in such cases seems well established, since fossil evidence from Permian strata suggests that comparatively great geographic fractionation of pond-dwelling conchostracan crustaceans occurred when climates were arid (Tasch and Zimmerman, 1961).

Most nonarthropodan invertebrates in desert temporary waters have received little attention from investigators. Among the few reports that list other taxa are those of Rzóska (1961), who observed ciliates, nematodes, and rotifers in rainpools in the Sudan; and Sublette and Sublette (1967), who discovered a turbellarian flatworm, as well as oligochaetes, leeches, and gastropods in playas on the high plains of the New Mexico–Texas border.

Again, Buxton (1923:95) stated that many operculate mollusks inhabit temporary pools in central Australia. Dussart (1966) also mentioned that operculate mollusks may be present in such places if the dry season is not too long. Doubtless more major groups of protozoans, as well as additional rotifers, will be found in these waters.

Crustaceans and insects are much more common in ephemeral desert waters and have been recorded many times. A list of the major taxa of these arthropods includes the following:

Class Crustacea
  Subclass Branchipoda (phyllopods)
    Division Eubranchiopoda
      Order Anostraca (fairy shrimp) (Fig. 87a)
      Order Conchostraca (clam shrimp)
      Order Notostraca (tadpole shrimp) (Fig. 87b,c)
    Division Oligobranchiopoda
      Order Cladocera (water fleas)
  Subclass Ostracoda (seed shrimps)
  Subclass Copepoda (copepods)
  Subclass Malacostraca
      Order Isopoda (aquatic sow bugs)
      Order Decapoda (crabs, crayfish)
Class Insecta
      Order Odonata (dragonflies and damselflies)
      Order Ephemeroptera (mayflies)
      Order Hemiptera
        Family Corixidae (water boatmen)
        Family Notonectidae (backswimmers) (Fig. 87d)
      Order Coleoptera
        Family Dytiscidae (predaceous diving water beetles)
        Family Hydrophilidae (water scavenger beetles)
      Order Diptera
        Family Ceratopogonidae (biting midges)
        Family Chironomidae (midges)
        Family Culicidae (mosquitoes)
        Family Syrphidae (syrphid flies)
        Family Ephydridae (shore flies)
        Family Tabanidae (horseflies)

Of the above taxa, phyllopods are by far the most prominent, and may also be the only invertebrates present (C. H. Eriksen, personal communication). Yet, as will be seen below, the longer a body of water of this type lasts, the greater is the possibility of invasion by insects from distant refugia.

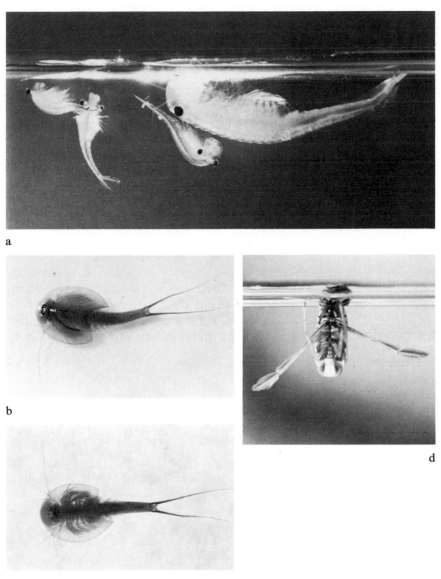

Fig. 87. Arthropods from a playa in south-central New Mexico. **a** Anostraca, possibly *Streptocephalus* sp. **b** Notostraca (*Triops* sp.) dorsal view. **c** *Triops,* ventral view. **d** Undetermined species of notonectid. (Photographs courtesy of J. M. Evans)

C. Reproduction and Development

I. Reproductive Potential

Comparatively high fecundities are known in some invertebrate species from desert temporary waters, but the extent to which such environments may have selected for this trait remains open to question. Thus, Cole (1968) cites reports indicating that clutch sizes of certain copepods in these habitats exceed those of conspecifics in permanent ponds. However, the greater fecundities of the former copepods may be explained in part by their greater body sizes. Likewise, Belk (1974, cited in Belk and Cole, 1975) showed that anostracans from relatively unpredictable rain-filled ponds had larger clutches than did species from snow-melt pools that generally contained water long enough to allow completion of life cycles. Relatively high fecundities of corixids breeding in Baltic archipelago rock pools subject to drying are also known (Pajunen, 1970); yet the influence of refugia conditions on the reproductive potential of these insects may have been important—a point to consider in future studies of desert corixids. The need to avoid simplistic assessments is evident also from the observation of Barnard and Mulla (1978) that non-gravid *Culiseta inornata* mosquitoes from the Colorado desert sometimes reach 40% of the adult population. Whether these low population reproductive potentials have anything to do with larval habitats seems not to be known.

II. Embryonic Development and Survival

Once produced, "eggs" (here the term is also used for shelled embryos of phyllopods) of the invertebrates in question either enter dormancy or soon hatch. Both options are used simultaneously by some crustaceans in desert ephemeral pools (Cole, 1968). Egg dormancy is probably facultative in such uncertain conditions (Belk and Cole, 1975). Moreover, it is characterized by resistance to prolonged drying, heating, and freezing. Dormant eggs of the notostracan *Triops granarius* can, for example, survive temperatures of up to 98°C for many hours (Carlisle, 1968). Resting eggs of phyllopods have been kept in dried pond mud for up to 15 years (Pennak, 1953:335).

Among cladocerans, the ability of their eggs to survive drying is attributed to properties of the embryonic tissues; shells and other coverings probably play a secondary role in adapting these and other crustaceans to desiccating conditions in deserts (Belk and Cole, 1975). Tissue tolerance appears to reach an extreme in the eggs of *Dorylaimis* nematodes. These eggs are said to undergo cryptobiosis in their temporary rain pool habitats of New South Wales (Bishop, 1974).

III. Hatching

Clearly, it is advantageous for eggs in such places to hatch as soon as habitat conditions become conducive to juvenile development. Rapid hatching in response to pond filling has in fact been documented for a number of crustacean species. Other factors as well may promote hatching. For example, in a study of phyllopods from prairie and alpine ponds in Wyoming, Horne (1967) made the point that ranges of temperature and salinity tolerated by adults of a species may govern the hatchability of their eggs. This principle should also apply in North American desert ponds, since the Wyoming taxa occur there too. Levels of salinity permitting hatching of dehydrated "cysts" (eggs for our purpose) of the fairy shrimp *Branchinecta mackini* were studied by Brown and Carpelan (1971) in a Mojave desert playa. Hatching in these anocostracans continues as long as salinities remain below 1.0°/oo, which is the case for only a short time after basin filling. Above 1.0°/oo, *B. mackini* shows a dramatic osmotic decrease in a few days. However, as pond drying begins, salt concentrations increase—sometimes exceeding 30°/oo. Assuming that rising salinities are indicative of potentially short-lived and deteriorating habitats, one would expect hatching at only low salinity levels to be a general pattern among many invertebrate species in such places.

Temperature also seems to have a controlling influence on the hatching of some desert pond species (Belk and Cole, 1975). In fact there appear to be two hatching-temperature ranges characteristic of desert-pond phyllopods. Thus *Branchinecta mackini, B. lindahli,* and the notostracan *Lepidurus lemmoni* hatch and swim near 0°C (Horne, 1967; Brown and Carpelan, 1971; Eriksen and Brown, 1980a,b). In contrast, the following species hatch and swim at higher temperatures: the notostracan *Triops longicaudatus* (13°C–15°C), and the anostracans *Streptocephalus taxanus* (13°C) and *Thamnocephalus platyurus* (17°C) (Horne, 1967), as well as the conchostracan *Cyzicus californicus* (10°C) (Eriksen and Brown, 1980c). How rigidly some of these species adhere to such temperature levels at different seasons is a question needing additional study.

The absence of light inhibits hatching in some cases (Belk and Cole, 1975). Inhibition by light implies that the depth of egg burial may well determine whether or not hatching occurs when a desert pond fills. Considering the potential for soil-surface agitation during filling, it may be that a spectrum of burial depths increases the chances of hatching into an aquatic environment that lasts long enough to insure adult development. Here salinity enters the picture once again, since soil-water salinities in playas increase with soil depth, and as such should progressively inhibit hatching.

IV. Posthatching Development and Survival

Rates of development can be rapid whenever conditions occur that promote hatching and/or release from dormancy. Thus, only 4 days after rain pools filled near Khartoum, Rzóska (1961) recorded a rich fauna, including many copepods, cladocerans, rotifers, and some conchostracans. Of these organisms, the copepod *Metacyclops minutus* developed from egg to mature adult in 72 h, while the conchostracan *Leptestheria aegyptica* matured in 5 days. The notostracan *Triops* was slower, occurring as large individuals 16–20 days after pool initiation.

Other examples of relatively rapid development include durations of 76–126 h for the mosquito *Psorophora confinnis* in irrigated date groves of southern California's Coachella Valley (Gunstream and Chew, 1967), and about 10 days for the anostracan *Branchinecta mackini* in a Mojave desert playa (Brown and Carpelan, 1971). A range of 19–31 days was given for the ceratopogonid *Culicoides* in Israel (Braverman et al., 1974), and it takes roughly a month to develop for the mosquito *Culiseta inornata* (Bernard and Mulla, 1978) and the water scavenger beetle *Hydrophylus triangularis* (Hallmark and Ward, 1972) in arid regions of California and Texas, respectively. Citing Hodgkin and Watson's (1958) study of comparatively rapid maturation by dragonflies in Australian temporary waters, Cole (1968) postulates that selection for increased speed of development may have occurred in temporary-pond faunas.

Owing to the erratic patterns of filling and drying in ephemeral water bodies, the ability to switch between phases of growth and dormancy should be of obvious survival value. Thus, chironomid larvae (Chapters 3, 6; also see Edward, 1964, 1968, cited by Belk and Cole, 1975) use what amounts to anhydrobiosis when their rock pool habitats dry up. Less dramatic, but also effective as a means of enduring long dry periods, is the copepodial stage of *Metacyclops minutus,* which resists exposure to hot, dry weather for at least 9 months in the Sudan (Rzóska, 1961).

Some degree of dormancy is probably also common among aquatic insects spending portions of their lives in these transitory habitats. The water scavenger beetle *Hydrophylus triangularis* is said, for example, to hibernate at any time of year in moist soil and to remain there until the next rain occurs (Hallmark and Ward, 1972). And in adult females of the mosquito *Culiseta inornata* from the Colorado desert, aestivation occurs regardless of the state of ovarian development (Bernard and Mulla, 1978).

Again we return to the alternative to dormancy, which up to now we have termed "migration." Later on in this chapter we shall indeed address migration in flying insects, but now we digress briefly and consider a more passive form of dispersal. In effect, this involves the carrying of any drought-resistant stages of an invertebrate by dust storms, migrating insects, and birds. Avocets are examples of potential transport agents in the intermountain west of North America, since they commonly feed on phyllopods in alkaline, opaque waters. If eggs in gravid phyllopods are not digested, their deposition in feces at other sites should effect successful dispersal (C. H. Eriksen, personal communication). Nothing seems to be known about the proportions of eventual faunal complexes in desert pools that are created by the arrival of such disseminules. Interested biologists may wish to approach this matter experimentally.

D. Adaptation to Abiotic Stress Conditions

Salt concentrations in ephermeral waters increase with evaporation. When this happens, organisms that cannot depart must adjust physiologically if they are to survive. One type of accommodation is to conform osmotically to the wide amplitude of salinities occurring in such habitats. The alternative is to osmoregulate. These options are not mutually exclusive, nor do they preclude regulation of specific ion fluxes between the organisms and their aquatic milieu.

Species managing to survive over a broad range of salinities are called "euryhaline." The anostracan brineshrimp *Artemia salina* is a spectacular example of a euryhaline crustacean; it inhabits both large permanent bodies of salty water and small temporary desert ponds (e.g., Bayly, 1972). Moreover, it survives in these places partly because of its pronounced ability to regulate hyposmotically (Croghan, 1958). This attribute is possessed as well by larvae of the ephydrid shore fly *Ephydra* (Prosser, 1973:35), which is also found in highly saline desert waters.

Certain phyllopods from North American desert waters may be relatively effective osmoconformers, judging from the reports of Horne (1967, 1968). Some of these species are euryhaline and eurythermal as eggs and as adults, while others have such capacities only as adults. Still others occur only under restricted environmental conditions, and are stenohaline (i.e., they survive only in a narrow salinity range) and stenothermal in both stages (Horne, 1967).

Another problem involves adapting to heat. High insolation, particularly during summer months, raises water temperatures to levels that many aquatic species cannot tolerate.

As might be expected, considerable variation exists among nondormant arthropods in desert waters with regard to temperature tolerance. *Potaocypris* ostracods from the Great Basin can survive 5 h at 49°C ± 0.5°C (Wickstrom and Castenholz, 1973), which must be close to the upper limit of temperature tolerance for active aquatic crustaceans. Not far below that level are pupae of the mosquito *Psorophora confinnis*, which can metamorphose after a 15-h exposure to 46°C (Gunstream and Chew, 1967). The upper lethal temperature for *Triops* in Arizona is somewhat lower at 42°C over a 2-h period (Cloudsley-Thompson, 1965b) and is only 34°C in a 24-h period (Cloudsley-Thompson, 1966). Breeding in *Culcoides puncticollis* occurs in a variety of sites in the northern Negev, where habitat temperatures range from 7°C–37°C (Braverman et al., 1974). Larvae of *Culiseta inornata* die at 29°C (Fanara and Mulla, 1974), while those of the relatively eurythermal *C. longiarielata* occur in Negev rain pools at temperatures between 8°C and 31°C. In one such pool, C. Dimentman and J. Margalit (personal communication) also found larvae of *Culex adairi,* which occurs only at water temperatures between 25°C and 28°C.

Reference was made above to temperatures at which phyllopods in desert ephemeral waters hatch and swim. We now extend that discussion to the general matter of temperature sensitivity. In this regard, C. H. Eriksen (personal communication) feels that there may be two classes of playa inhabitants: those adapting to cold-to-moderate temperatures (0°C to ~30°C) and those adapting to moderate-to-warm temperatures (10–15°C to 35–40°C). Adaptation in relatively warm-water species [*Triops longicaudatus, T. platgarus* (Hillyard and Vinegar, 1972); *Cyzicus californicus* (Eriksen and Brown, 1978c)] is manifested by a switch from high respiratory Q_{10}'s, as these species emerge from cold sluggishness, to Q_{10}'s of 1.0–1.6 over a 10°C–15°C range later on.

Another form of tolerance to high temperatures is illustrated by *C. californicus,* which exhibits greater than 50% survival at 35°C for 16 h. This temperature is well above those in the range of its peak oxygen consumption (20°C–24.5°C) (Eriksen and Brown, 1980c).

An interesting case of temperature adaptation in a predator–prey *(Lepidurus lemmoni–Brachinecta mackini)* relationship was recorded by Eriksen and Brown (1980b). These species commonly co-occur in playas of southern California and exhibit oxygen-consumption peaks at similar temperatures. However, the predator does not tolerate high temperatures as well as the prey does. Presumably, there should be no selective advantage for an obligate predator such as *L. lemmoni* to achieve greater temperature tolerance than achieved by its prey.

Rates of oxygen consumption by the Mojave phyllopods studied by Hillyard and Vinegar (1972) varied both with water temperature and with stage of development. Thus, high respiratory Q_{10}'s of 4–12 occurred in larvae at water temperatures of 26°C–30°C. Above 30°C larval Q_{10}'s approached unity. Adults, on the other hand, had lower and more stable Q_{10}'s between 26°C–42°C. Explanations of the adaptive significance of low Q_{10}'s were discussed in Chapter 7, and included the possibility of energy savings at preferred temperatures. Another possibility brought up by Eriksen and Brown (1980b) is that species demonstrating low Q_{10}'s at comparatively high temperatures are able to tolerate these temperatures for longer periods than other phyllopods, and also to tolerate (and inhabit) warmer waters.

Tolerance of low levels of dissolved oxygen seems to characterize crustaceans found in ephemeral desert ponds (Belk and Cole, 1975). Even so, oxygen concentration may be a less important determinant of seasonal distribution and habitat occurrence for certain phyllopod species than temperature and salinity (Horne, 1967).

There is a point, however, at which low oxygen concentration evokes noticeable responses among some phyllopods. Horne (1971b) observed that frequent surfacing by an anostracan and a notostracan in certain Texas playas probably enhanced survival in these species. Phyllopods in the Sonoran desert were also shown to swim to the surface of oxygen-depleted water, which they stirred with their appendages (Hillyard and Vinegar, 1972). Parenthetically, it should be added that other behavioral responses appear to promote survival in phyllopods. One of these is the tendency of *Triops granarius* to swim against the current (positive rheotaxis), which should keep it from being stranded on the leeward side of pools by strong winds (Cloudsley-Thompson, 1966).

In passing, we cannot totally ignore other physical variables with which aquatic invertebrates in desert ponds must contend. These factors include concentrations of cations and anions, and also pH. Although they are obviously important, relatively little is known about these in ephemeral desert waters. For further information the interested reader should consult sources including Hutchinson (1937), Prophet (1963), Cole and Brown (1967), and Eriksen and Brown (1980a,b,c). As might be expected, different species—and most likely different stages of those species—exhibit specific tolerances to ion concentrations and pH in the habitat.

E. Production, Competition, and Seasonal Colonization

Primary production is greatly limited in turbid playa-type pools (C. H. Eriksen, personal communcation). However, some phytoplankton species have been recorded from pans in steppe regions of southern Africa (Hutchinson et al., 1932), from nonturbid saline ponds in Arizona (Cole, 1968), and from desert playas in southern California (Busch and Kubly, 1980). Anderson and Rushforth (1976) reported an abundance of several genera of green algae from cryptogam crusts on dry playas in southern Utah, but whether these organisms survive in playa waters after filling occcurs is apparently not known. Filamentous green algae were observed attached to *Scirpus* and *Eleocharis* grasses (also primary producers, of course) invading waters near the shores of Big Alkali Lake in California, and benthic species in shallow waters of this sort were considered a possibility despite the tenuous nature of such habitats (C. H. Eriksen, personal communication). Despite the indication by J. R. Zimmerman (personal communication) that corixids and *Berosus* hydrophilids—both of which are considered to be algal feeders—occur in large numbers in Lake Texoco, a playa in the Valley of Mexico, the presence of photosynthetic organisms, especially in turbid ephemeral waters, seems in general to be of little consequence to energy flow.

It stands to reason that the main nutritional base for consumers in desert ephemeral waters is more likely to be detritus. This point is supported by data from Eriksen, Patten, and Rappoport (in prep.). Their study shows that the particulate organic fraction in water from direct rainfall into Rabbit Dry Lake can be very small and undissolved. Following runoff from the watershed, however, the particulate organic fraction can rise dramatically, although dissolved organic matter increases only slightly. The particulate fraction increases further with more rain and decreases as anostracan biomass becomes significant.

These authors also find that the alimentary tract of the suspension feeder, *Branchinecta mackini,* is always full of material similar in appearance to that in the water. It seems appropriate, therefore, to view these habitats as repositories of dead biomass that supply largely detrital food webs, and it is useful to keep in mind that the trophic dynamics of these often short-lived systems are strongly constrained by the physical conditions discussed previously in this chapter.

Not all of the stresses experienced by invertebrate species in ephemeral desert waters are physical, since both vertebrate and invertebrate predators occur there as well. Judging from the successional studies referred to below, populations of some predaceous insects, and perhaps of amphibians as well, undergo a time lag associated with searching for—and colonizing—widely separated ponds. Predators present to begin with (e.g., some phyllopod species) may also exhibit such lags.

Flexible reproductive schedules may help some predators track their aquatic prey. The example of *Hydrophylus triangularis* comes to mind. This aquatic beetle has predaceous larvae and was shown by Hallmark and Ward (1972) to produce more than one annual generation, depending on the availability of water between June and September. Each time basins filled, adults appeared and laid eggs. Once more, timing is shown to be of great importance in the life histories of species inhabiting uncertain environments. The timing of a predator's arrival at a desert pond should, one imagines, allow it and/or its progeny to make optimal use of available prey. Likewise, the arrival of species having detritivore larvae should coincide with the appearance of materials that can be ingested by filter-feeders. (Dormant stages of both predatory and detritivorous crustaceans are of course likely to be present to begin with.) Since detritus and accompanying bacteria are surely present at the onset of filling, we might expect the sequence of colonization and reproduction by such insects to precede that of predators.

If such a temporal pattern in fact occurs, then two additional factors are necessarily introduced: competition and succession. Competition for detrital food seems possible among increasingly crowded populations of posthatch or postdormant crustaceans and among larvae produced by immigrant dipterans like mosquitoes and chironomid midges. Cole (1968:460, 467) addressed this point and implied that competition may be weak in desert ponds, since the inherent instability of such systems may not allow enough time for selection of competitiveness. Of course, the great abundance of organic debris in these often turbid waters may alone be sufficient to explain weak competition—or indeed its absence altogether among detritus feeders. Competition among predators is a different matter and has received little study in playas. Collins (1977) points out that benthic insects of (permanent) brine lakes usually lack larval predators and competitors.

With regard to succession, certain units of the animal community in temporary waters clearly replace—or at least add to—other units during the life of a desert pond. Evidence for this is given by a number of authors, including Gauthier (1928) and Rzóska (1961). Doubtless succession under such conditions is governed by species-specific patterns of fecundity, development, and longevity, as well as by rates of immigration and emigration. These elements should in turn be subject to influences from the physical environment. As a result, one might anticipate that while certain broad patterns of faunal succession hold for a given kind of pond, the species associations present at any one time may be highly variable.

Indeed, this suggestion is supported by the sequential options given by Sublette and Sublette (1967) for aquatic species in playa lakes of Texas and New Mexico. There the approximate sequences are as follows:

1. Phyllopods and amphibians→→phyllopods, amphibians, and insects→→ either:
2. Coleoptera, Hemiptera, Odonata, and chironomids plus oligochaetes and/ or leeches, or:
3. Chironomids alone plus oligochaetes and leeches.

The influence of just one physical factor—temperature—on the seasonal appearance of phyllopods from the same region was documented by Horne (1971b), who showed that appearance times of such crustaceans correlated with mean maximum and minimum weekly air temperatures.

In other regions the successional sequences are likely to be quite different, and comparative studies should be done to determine if area- or pond-specific patterns of succession occur. More investigation of arrival times by flying insects would also be informative; their colonization has been interpreted as a way to penetrate deep into arid regions from more permanent dispersal centers (C. Dimentman and J. Margalit, personal communication).

In summary, perhaps an appropriate view of ephemeral waters in deserts is as small aquatic islands in a vast sea of aridity. The "islands" are populated largely by relatively "endemic" invertebrates that can survive long periods of drought. When that drought is broken by the arrival of water and the influx of particulate organics that fuel the food webs, these organisms switch from a variety of dormant stages to stages characterized by rapid development and reproduction. At varying interludes thereafter, winged insects arrive and make direct or indirect use of the now life-sustaining habitat.

Part 5

Invertebrates in Desert Ecosystems: Summary Remarks

A. Introduction

Part 1 of this book established a "desert perspective" to serve as a background for the material to follow. It also introduced an underlying theme, namely the contribution of invertebrates to the structure and function of desert ecosystems. Yet up to now, this inclusive concept has been treated only indirectly in the book's three major units: adaptations to the physical environment (Part 2), life-history patterns (Part 3), and community dynamics (Part 4).

Each of these units produced generalizations about how invertebrates utilize resources in arid regions. Clearly, resource use by some of these animals (e.g., nematodes, termites) can have profound immediate or regulatory effects on rates and processes occurring in desert ecosystems. Now, in summary, we focus on the collective involvement of desert invertebrates with their resources—at first, in time and space (sections B and C below). This relationship is then presented by way of simple compartment models that emphasize roles of consumer and producer groups in deserts (section D). Questions and thoughts raised by these and earlier discussions are couched finally as comments on future studies (section E).

B. The Temporal Dimension

Given the uncertainty of food and shelter required by many desert invertebrates, the survival of these animals may depend largely on how effectively they synchronize their life cycles with environmental events. Consequently,

their morphological and physiological adaptations (e.g., waterproofed integuments of many species, regulated respiratory Q_{10}'s of certain terrestrial and
aquatic species) are likely to be of little day-to-day value unless the uses of
such traits are timed to meet restrictive habitat conditions (e.g., low humidities, high temperatures). Correspondingly, behavioral adaptations involving
exposure (e.g., sun-basking in cicadas) are likely to be hazardous unless they
coincide with diminished predator activity. In contrast, seasonal patterns
of reproduction and development in desert invertebrates reflect a temporal
continuity of adaptations. Manifested in one or a few seasons by short-lived
organisms, these adaptive sequences can recur year after year in animals
with long lives.

Optimizing resource use in diel as well as seasonal time is clearly vital
to the survival of invertebrates in habitats when food and shelter are limited
or unpredictable, and when microclimates are stressful. Temporal expressions
of resource use vary, moreover, according to the life-history patterns and
trophic levels of the consumers. We would expect, for example, short-lived
carnivores such as asilid flies to track the availability of food and shelter
more closely than do long-lived carnivores such as scorpions.

Since asilids and scorpions are occasional members of faunal assemblages
on desert vegetation, it follows that the temporal meshing of their activities
helps to characterize the organization of such communities. But community
organization also has its spatial attributes, a matter to which we now turn.

C. The Spatial Dimension

Organisms affecting the dynamics of desert ecosystems operate above and
below the soil surface. Thus, perennial plants function simultaneously in
both horizontal zones, while geophytes and many animals make intermittant
use of either stratum. Plainly, the surface itself marks the ecotone between
the two major kinds of desert habitats.

Soil is the great reservoir of desert ecosystems. As the prime sink for
water and nutrients in these unproductive regions, it also anchors and sustains
virtually all plant biomass. Furthermore, its relatively moderate microclimate
provides a comparatively stable habitat for resident organisms. And, under
shrubs in particular, the fairly continuous presence of living and nonliving
food materials frees many species (e.g., microarthropods, larvae of cicadas
and scarabaeid beetles) from a direct dependence on resources located at
the soil surface. As a result, pulses of rainfall and primary production should
have relatively minor and indirect effects on the lives of many soil-bound
species.

The linkage between those organisms and surface conditions should never
be totally absent, however, because even at depths of about a meter slight

seasonal variations in temperature and moisture do occur. Also, food webs on which such taxa depend are characterized by vertical as well as horizontal transport. The life-history patterns of nematodes in desert soils reflect these relationships and illustrate them nicely as well, since nematodes undergo anhydrobiosis when their habitats begin to dry and their food supplies diminish. Conversely, nematodes, in addition to many other dormant invertebrates, become active upon excessive soil wetting at appropriate temperatures. These and other examples of the linkage in question bear a stochastic element, too, depending on the heterogeneity of soil conditions and on the age distributions and physiological states of soil organisms.

The above examples suggest that spatial structuring in desert ecosystems partly reflects the degree to which invertebrate life cycles and activities mesh with the vicissitudes of climate and resources. They also suggest that the life history–resource connection is apt to be relatively loose among invertebrates having strong affinities for the soil habitat. Yet for species depending heavily on resources available on or above the surface, a more finely tuned linkage is expected. This distinction obviously has its limits, since a plethora of life-history patterns occurs among desert species. Nevertheless, its application to cases where the biota is fairly well known may be useful in generating models of seasonal activity.

D. Models of Invertebrate Activity in Desert Ecosystems

The above evaluation of desert invertebrates represents one means of summarizing their collective activities in time and space. A different approach to how these animals function in their desert setting is now presented in the form of a simple compartment model (Fig. 88). The model portrays relationships in such a way that processes, rather than dimensions, are emphasized. Like any description of this kind, the model has definite limitations, one being that it can also apply to certain nondesert systems like grasslands. Still, it does have the virtue of revealing—in highly condensed form—some of the main invertebrate activities covered in this book.

Then too, the model provides a broad trophic-level context in which these activities may be viewed. Consequently, nowhere in the model is the word "invertebrate" used, nor are the names of any invertebrate taxa mentioned. These omissions are justifiable, because in terms of energy flow invertebrates are heterotrophs, as are all other animals. After pondering the simplistic nature of the model, readers may wish to supply its animal compartments with the names of invertebrate species discussed in previous chapters. An exercise of this kind may indeed prove to be a salutary review.

Another shortcoming of the model is that it does not reveal the relative importance of any biotic group to the overall flow of energy and nutrients.

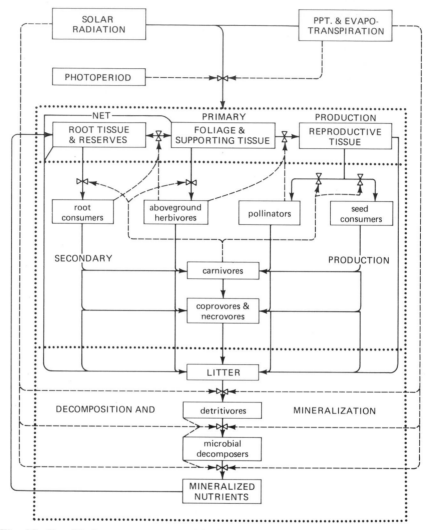

Fig. 88. Simplified compartment model of a desert ecosystem emphasizing roles of consumers *(lower case)* as they utilize and contribute to biotic and abiotic resources. Specific roles are discussed in some detail in the text. Major inputs and processes are seen as driving or otherwise regulating variables. Energy and/or nutrient flow: ————→; major regulatory pathways: — — — →

This deficiency can be rectified by the use of other formats. Examples are tables comparing relevant data within feeding guilds or within and among trophic levels. Reference is made to tabular comparisons involving termites (Chapter 13) and different trophic classes of consumers (Chapter 7). Other data on consumer activities are found in the text of Part 4.

A review of these earlier comparisons suggests, among other things, that termites may account for much more of the energy and nutrient flux in deserts than is accounted for by most other metazoans. However, nematodes may turn out to be at least as important in this role in some deserts—a matter that needs further study. In a similar vein, it is clear from information cited in Chapter 15 that solitary bees are undoubtedly the major pollinators of North America's subtropical deserts. But this last example in particular also brings up several reasons why the comparative approach is only moderately useful at this point in time.

Its utility is obviously hindered by a lack of data from the many deserts of the world. Certainly, an exceedingly useful beginning was made by Orians and Solbrig (1977b) and their co-workers in comparing two structurally similar deserts in the Western Hemisphere. Yet there is a great deal more of this sort of work to be accomplished before broad generalizations can be made about resource use by desert invertebrates. Another current limitation of the comparative approach—and one that relates to a second reason why the model in Fig. 88 cannot reveal the importance of specific taxa in the dynamics of ecological processes—is that very little comprehensive, published information on *single* desert ecosystems exists.

A major exception to this statement is a thorough analysis of the Namib dune ecosystem by Seely and Louw (1980). In that cool, coastal desert, fog supplies what little water organisms can routinely acquire. Occasionally, however, relatively heavy rains produce dramatic responses in the biota. Water is therefore demonstrably a supremely limiting factor in the Namib dunes (as are nitrogen and phosphorus). Potential energy, in contrast, does not seem to be limiting—at least to omnivores and herbivores. However, in dry years the protein content of detritus probably limits the growth and reproduction of species that feed upon organic debris. These species are mainly tenebrionid beetles and their larvae, animals discussed extensively in this book. In the Namib, it seems that they (or their symbiotic gut flora) are responsible for most of the nutrient cycling stemming from accumulated detritus, since there is said to be a virtual absence of microbial decomposers elsewhere in that dune ecosystem.

A generalized scheme given by Seely and Louw (1980) for the flow of energy and nutrients through animals in the Namib dune system is shown in Fig. 89. A single major food web is presented, showing the complexity of these movements even in a "simple" desert ecosystem.

Still another way of indicating energy and nutrient flow in deserts is to begin with a single organism. This can be done ad nauseum, of course, but if pursued on a comparative basis, especially with taxonomically similar or ecologically convergent species in different deserts, it may reveal convergence (or a lack of it) among components of such webs. An example of a partial species-centered food web was formulated by Hadley and Szarek (1981) and is given in Fig. 90. Again, it is evident that the involvement of even a single

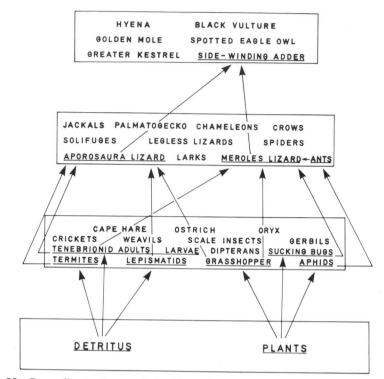

Fig. 89. Generalized scheme of the flow of energy and nutrients through animals in the Namib dune ecosystem. Only a single major food web, ending in *Bitis peringueyi,* the side-winding adder, is indicated. (Seely and Louw, 1980; with permission)

species—in this case a Sonoran desert grasshopper—in the trophic dynamics of a desert ecosystem has potentially far-reaching effects.

E. Future Studies

Models, whether they take the form of verbal descriptions, flow charts, or equations, are not ends in themselves. Rather, they serve as springboards both for verifying established concepts and for investigating new questions. In this concluding discussion, I have tried to bring together, from material presented in this book, suggestions that address both issues in regard to desert invertebrates. The suggestions derive mainly from discussions in the present chapter and many earlier chapters. So far as possible the suggestions are considered in the framework of topics covered in Parts 2, 3, and 4. They represent, of course, a distillation of my own views, and while they do not deal specifically with the need for further taxonomic studies of desert invertebrates, surely the urgency of such a task remains implicit.

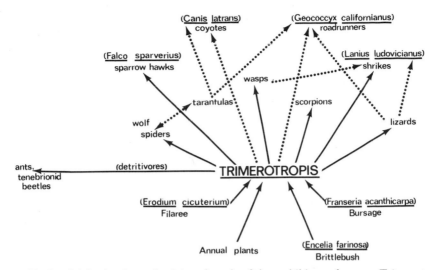

Fig. 90. Partial food web emphasizing the role of the acridid grasshopper, *Trimerotropis pallidipennis,* in the Sonoran desert. *Arrows* indicate direction of energy and nutrient transfer. *Solid lines* indicate preferred items of the grasshopper and its principal predators. *Dotted lines* indicate infrequent or presumed predators and predator–prey relationships between representatives of the higher trophic levels. (After Hadley and Szarek, 1981)

I. Adaptation

Description and evaluation of adaptive traits in desert invertebrates should and will continue. Furthermore, these efforts should be expanded to include taxa heretofore neglected in experimental studies (e.g., solifugids, scarabaeoid coleopterans, immature stages of many species). Behavioral and physiological responses to natural and controlled regimes of light, moisture, and temperature should also be examined to test the relevance of such factors (particularly light) to diel timing of activity patterns and to seasonal patterns of life-history events.

Long-term studies will be especially useful in illustrating seasonal patterns. We obviously know very little, for instance, about seasonal metabolism and water balance in arid-adapted species. Yet without such information we will be unable to make sensible generalizations about physiological and ecological efficiencies in these animals, compared to the efficiencies of ecologically equivalent species in other environments.

II. Life-History Patterns

Life histories of most desert invertebrates remain entirely unknown. Plenty of purely descriptive work will therefore be most welcome, particularly if

students concentrate on species representing major taxa such as the Tenebrionidae. If organized along classical ecological lines, these descriptive efforts
can also lead to the construction of life tables, which will be helpful for
eventual studies of the population dynamics of these species. Currently, aside
from recent investigations of agelinid spiders by Riechert and her colleagues
(cited mainly in Chapter 9), and of desert scorpions by Shorthouse (1971),
and Polis and Farley (cited mainly in Chapter 11; also see Polis and Farley,
1980), we know little of the details of carnivore life history and population
biology. Other trophic groups have received variable attention in this regard,
but much of what is published appears in the older literature and often
lacks quantitative rigor. Exceptions involve species with economic impacts
(e.g., bushflies and desert locusts).

Models of life-history patterns should be made of desert invertebrates to
test whether deserts are really as "risky" and "unpredictable" to organisms
living there as we often casually assume (this author is as guilty as anyone
in this regard). Unfortunately, until more basic studies are reported, it will
be difficult to develop meaningful models of this sort.

The reproduction and development of desert invertebrates could afford
intensive scrutiny from the points of view of ecology and evolution. Comparative studies of reproductive effort by broadly dispersed conspecifics, and between and among convergent species (closely or distantly related) in different
deserts will help to elucidate patterns applying to taxonomic as well as trophic
categories.

The timing of resource use by desert invertebrates is another sphere of
endeavor awaiting serious application. Results of studies concentrating on
users of highly ephemeral resources (e.g., herbivore guilds associated with
annual plants) should be especially appropriate for models emphasizing the
tight temporal restrictions of many desert environments. Likewise, it will
be useful to look carefully at species that because of life-history constraints
use apparently abundant resources for comparatively short periods each year
(e.g., many herbivores on perennial plants, also certain long-lived detritivores).
Fundamental questions relating to optimal foraging over time by both groups
of consumers have to do with the limitations of available food energy and
the use of symbiotic organisms in processing ingested materials.

III. Community Dynamics

As desertification increases and as deserts become increasingly exploited for
resources desired by the human community, the need to comprehend the
organizational dynamics of desert biotas takes on special significance. Moreover, if, as is commonly suggested, there is a need to manage desert ecosystems,
then it will be necessary to predict the outcome of man-made perturbations.
Predictions of this kind can only be accomplished, however, by having a

prior knowledge of the successional trends that follow controlled modifications of relatively undisturbed habitats.

Hence, the effects of many kinds of manipulations should be monitored and compared against "control" situations. Various forms of vegetation removal, ranging from gathering of detritus (and dung of grazing animals) to grazing by ungulates, should be studied for their effects on components of the affected communities. And the opposite approach, namely the regulated addition of water and nutrients, should also be performed for the same reasons. By such means we should not only come up with practical answers affecting desert management, but also we should learn much about biotic interactions relative to resource availability in deserts. More specifically, perturbation and amendation studies should, if properly planned, tell us something about the roles of competition and predation in structuring invertebrate assemblages. They should also reveal something of the dependence on time and space of coevolved relationships between desert plants and their herbivores. Other by-products of these approaches may occur as well to the reader who, at this juncture, will hopefully be inclined to contribute further to our knowledge of desert-invertebrate biology.

F. Final Comments

In the last analysis, despite the recent surge of facts and interpretations so evident in the pages of this book, we are plainly still far from a comprehensive understanding of the roles of desert invertebrates. One wonders, too, whether some of their patterns of adaptation, life history, and community interaction—patterns so readily portrayed in the text above—are not more apparent than real. Only continued study, which to many of us is more of a delight than a chore, will bring us closer to the truth in such matters.

And what of our central theme: the contribution of desert invertebrates to the structure and function of their arid ecosystems? Do the data available really support the idea of significant contributions? I for one believe they do, at least in some instances in which conditions are carefully defined. But with deference to the tradition of healthy scepticism in my craft, I would be the first to promote further inquiry of this fundamental question.

References

Adams PA, Heath JE (1964) An evaporative cooling mechanism in *Pholus achemon* (Sphingidae). J Res Lepid 3: 69–72

Addison JA (1980) Influences of individual plant species on the distribution of Arctic Collembola. In: Dindal DL (ed) Soil biology as related to land use practices. Proc VII Int Colloq Soil Zool. Office of Pesticide and Toxic Substances EPA, Washington DC, pp 704–718

Ahearn GA (1970a) Water balance in the whipscorpion, *Mastigoproctus giganteus* (Lucas) (Arachnida, Uropygi). Comp Biochem Physiol 35: 339–353

Ahearn GA (1970b) The control of water loss in desert tenebrionid beetles. J Exp Biol 53: 573–595

Ahearn GA, Hadley NF (1977) Water transport in perfused scorpion ileum. Am J Physiol 233: R198–207

Ahlbrandt, TS, Andrews S, Gwynne DT (1978) Bioturbation in eolian deposits. J Sediment Petrol 48: 839–848

Alcock J (1975) The behaviour of western cicada killer males, *Sphecius grandis* (Sphecidae, Hymenoptera). J Nat Hist 9: 561–566

Alexander AJ, Ewer DW (1958) Temperature adaptive behaviour in the scorpion *Opisthophthalmus latimanus* Koch. J Exp Biol 35: 349–359

Allred DM (1965) Note of phalangids at the Nevada Test Site. Great Basin Nat 25: 37–38

Allred DM (1971) Ecological notes on recently described myriapods from Nevada. Great Basin Nat 31: 161–163

Allred DM, Beck, DE (1967) Spiders of the Nevada Test Site. Great Basin Nat 27: 11–25

Allred DM, Gertsch WJ (1976) Spiders and scorpions from northern Arizona and southern Utah. J Arachnol 3: 87–99

Allred DM, Mulaik S (1965) Two isopods at the Nevada Test Site. Great Basin Nat 25: 43–47

Allsopp PG (1978) Defensive behaviour of adult *Pterohelaeus darlingensis* Carter (Coleoptera: Tenebrionidae). Aust Entomol Mag **5:** 1–4

Anderson DC, Rushforth SR (1976) The cryptogam flora of desert soil crusts in southern Utah, U.S.A. Nova Hedwigia Z Kryptogamentol **27:** 691–729

Anderson JF (1970) Metabolic rates of spiders. Comp Biochem Physiol **33:** 51–72

Anderson RL, Muchmore JA (1971) Temperature acclimation in *Tribolium* and *Musca* at locomotory, metabolic, and enzyme levels. J Insect Physiol **17:** 2205–2219

Andrewartha HG, Birch LC (1954) The distribution and abundance of animals. Univ of Chicago Press, Chicago London, p 782

Andrews FG, Hardy AR, Giuliani D (1979) The coleopterous fauna of selected California sand dunes. Report: BLM Contract CA-960–1285–1225-DEOO. Calif Dep of Food and Agric, Sacramento p 142

Arlian LG, Veselica MM (1979) Water balance in insects and mites. Comp Biochem Physiol **64A:** 191–220

Axelrod DI (1979) Desert vegetation, its age and origin. In: Goodin JR, Northington DK (eds) Arid land plant resources. Int Center for Arid and Semi-Arid Land Studies Tex Tech Univ, Lubbock, pp 1–72

Axelrod DI, Raven PH (1978) Late Cretaceous and Tertiary vegetation history of Africa. In: Werger MJA (ed) Biogeography and ecology of southern Africa, vol I. Dr Junk Publishers, The Hague, pp 77–130

Ayyad MA, Ghabbour SI (1977) Systems analysis of Mediterranean desert ecosystems of northern Egypt (SAMDENE). Environ Conserv **4:** 91–101

Baird CR (1974) Field behavior and seasonal activity of the rodent bot fly, *Cuterebra tenebrosa,* in central Washington (Diptera: Cuterebridae). Great Basin Nat **34:** 247–253

Baker HG, Hurd PD Jr (1968) Intrafloral ecology. Annu Rev Entomol **13:** 385–414

Balsbaugh EU Jr, Tucker WL (1976) Geographical variation in *Pachybrachis nigricornis* (Coleoptera: Chrysomelidae). Coleopt Bull **30:** 117–131

Bamberg SA, Volmer AT, Kleinkopf GE, Ackerman TL (1976) A comparison of seasonal primary production of Mojave desert shrubs during wet and dry years. Am Midl Nat **95:** 398–405

Barnard DR, Mulla MS (1978) The ecology of *Culiseta inornata* in the Colorado Desert of California: Seasonal abundance, gonotrophic status, and oviparity of adult mosquitoes. Ann Entomol Soc **71:** 397–400

Bateman MA (1972) The ecology of fruit flies. Annu Rev Entomol **17:** 493–518

Baust JG, Miller LK (1970) Seasonal variation in glycerol content and its influence in cold hardiness in the Alaskan beetle, *Pterostichus brevicornis.* J Insect Physiol **16:** 979–990

Bayly IAE (1972) Salinity tolerance and osmotic behaviour of animals in athatassic saline and marine hypersaline waters. Annu Rev Ecol Syst **3:** 233–268

Beck DE, Allred DM (1968) Faunistic inventory—BYU ecological studies at the Nevada Test Site. Great Basin Nat **28:** 132–141

Behan VM, Hill SB (1980) Distribution and diversity of North American Arctic soil Acari. In: Dindal DL (ed) Soil biology as related to land use practices. Proc VII Int Colloq Soil Zool. Office of Pesticide and Toxic Substances EPA, Washington DC, pp 717–740

Belk D, Cole GA (1975) Adaptational biology of desert temporary-pond inhabitants.

In: Hadley NF (ed) Environmental physiology of desert organisms. Dowden Hutch-
    inson & Ross Inc, Stroudsburg Pa, pp 207–226
Bell FC (1979) Precipitation. In: Goodall DW, Perry RA (eds) Arid-land ecosystems,
    vol I. Int Biol Programme 16. Cambridge Univ Press, Cambridge London New
    York Melbourne, pp 373–392
Ben Mordechai Y, Kugler J (1978) The adaptation of the food collecting seasons
    and the occurrence of the nuptial flight of ants to the ecological conditions in
    the desert loess plain of Sede Boqer (Sde-Zin). Abstr 4th Int Congr Ecol, Jerusalem,
    p 36
Bentzien MM (1973) Biology of the spider *Diguetia imperiosa* (Araneida: Diguetidae).
    Pan Pac Entomol **49:** 110–123
Bequaert JC, Miller WB (1973) The mollusks of the arid southwest. Univ of Arizona
    Press, Tucson, p 271
Bernstein RA (1974) Seasonal food abundance and foraging activity in some desert
    ants. Am Nat **108:** 490–498
Berry L, Cloudsley-Thompson JL (1960) Autumn temperatures in the Red Sea Hills.
    Nature (London) **188:** 843
Bishop JA (1963) The Australian freshwater crabs of the family *Potamonidae* (Crusta-
    cea: Decapoda). Aust J Mar Freshwater Res **14:** 218–238
Bishop JA (1974) The fauna of temporary rain pools in eastern New South Wales.
    Hydrobiology **44:** 319–323
Blackith RE, Blackith RM (1969a) Observations on the biology of some morabine
    grasshoppers. Aust J Zool **17:** 1–12
Blackith RE, Blackith RM (1969b) Variation of shape and of discrete anatomical
    characters in the morabine grasshoppers. Aust J Zool **17:** 697–718
Block W (1979) Cold tolerance of micro-arthropods from Alaskan taiga. Ecol Entomol
    4: 103–110
Block W (1980) Aspects of the ecology of Antarctic soil fauna. In: Dindal DL (ed)
    Soil biology as related to land use practices. Proc VII Int Colloq Soil Zool. Office
    of Pesticide and Toxic Substances EPA, Washington DC, pp 741–758
Block W, Young SR (1978) Metabolic adaptations of Antarctic microarthropods.
    Comp Biochem Physiol **61A:** 363–368
Block W, Young SR, Conradi-Larsen EM, Sømme L (1978) Cold tolerance of two
    Antarctic terrestrial arthropods. Experientia **34:** 1166–1167
Blower JG (1969) Age-structure of millipede populations in relation to activity and
    dispersion. In: Sheals JG (ed) The soil ecosystem. Syst Assoc Publ **8:** 206–216
Bodenheimer FS (1953) Problems of animal ecology and physiology in deserts. Israel.
    Ha-móatsah Ha-lé umit Le mehkar Ule Fituah. Spec Publ **2:** 205–229
Bodine MC, Ueckert DN (1975) Effect of desert termites on herbage and litter in a
    shortgrass ecosystem in west Texas. J Range Manage **28:** 353–358
Bohm BC, Hadley NF (1977) Tritium-determined water flux in the free-roaming
    desert tenebrionid beetle, *Eleodes armata.* Ecology **58:** 407–414
Bornemissza GF (1970) Insectary studies on the control of dung breeding flies by
    the activity of the dung beetle, *Onthophagus gazella* F. (Coleoptera, Scarabaeinae).
    J Aust Entomol Soc **9:** 31–41
Borror DJ, DeLong DM, Triplehorn CA (1976) An introduction to the study of
    insects, 4th edn. Holt Rinehart and Winston, New York, p 852
Borut S (1960) An ecological and physiological study on soil fungi of the northern
    Negev (Israel). Bull Res. Counc Isr **3D:** 65–80

Boutton TW, Cameron GN, Smith BN (1978) Insect herbivory on C_3 and C_4 grasses. Oecologia **36:** 21–32

Bowden J (1978) Diptera. In: Werger MJA (ed) Biogeography and ecology of southern Africa, vol II. Dr Junk Publishers, The Hague, pp 775–796

Braverman Y, Galun R, Ziv M (1974) Breeding sites of some *Culicoides* species (Diptera, Ceratopogonidae) in Israel. Mosq News **34:** 303–308

Briese DT, Macauley BJ (1977) Physical structure of an ant community in semi-arid Australia. Aust J Ecol **2:** 107–120

Brough EJ (1976) Notes on the ecology of an Australian desert species of *Calomyrmex* (Hymenoptera: Formicidae). J Aust Entomol Soc **15:** 339–346

Brown JH, Davidson DW (1977) Competition between seed-eating rodents and ants in desert ecosystems. Science **196:** 880–882

Brown LR, Carpelan LH (1971) Egg hatching and life history of a fairy shrimp *Branchinecta mackini* (Crustacea: Anostraca) in a Mojave desert playa (Rabbit Dry Lake). Ecology **52:** 41–54

Brown RH (1978) A difference in N use efficiency in C_3 and C_4 plants and its implications in adaptation and evolution. Crop Sci **18:** 93–98

Brownell PH (1977) Compressional and surface waves in sand: Use by desert scorpions to locate prey. Science **197:** 479–482

Brownell P, Farley RD (1979) Prey-localizing behavior of the nocturnal desert scorpion, *Pararoctonus mesaensis:* Orientation to substrate vibrations. Anim Behav **27:** 185–193

Broza M (1979) Dew, fog and hygroscopic food as a source of water for desert arthropods. J Arid Environ **2:** 43–49

Broza M, Borut A, Pener M (1976) Osmoregulation in the desert tenebrionid beetle *Trachyderma philistina* Reiche during dehydration and subsequent rehydration. Isr J Med Sci **12:** 868–871

Brunhuber BS (1970) Egg laying, maternal care and development of young in the scolopendromorph centipede *Cormocephalus anceps anceps* Porat. Zool J Linn Soc **49:** 225–234

Bud K, Bowerman RF (1979) Prey capture by the scorpion *Hadrurus arizonensis* Ewing (Scorpiones, Vaejovidae). J Arachnol **7:** 243–253

Burkhart JT (1978) Ecological energetics of the alkali grasshopper *(Anconia integra).* PhD Thesis, Arizona State Univ, Tempe, p 165

Bursell E (1974) Environmental aspects—temperature. In: Rockstein M (ed) The physiology of insecta, vol II, 2nd edn. Academic Press, London New York pp 1–41

Burton RF (1966) Aspects of ionic regulation in certain terrestrial pulmonates. Comp Biochem Physiol **17:** 1007–1018

Busch DE, Kubly DM (1980) Diatoms from desert playas in southern California. J Arid Environ **3:** 55–62

Büttiker W (1979) First records of eye-frequenting and anthropophilic Lepidoptera from Saudi Arabia. In: Wittmer W, Büttiker W (eds) Fauna of Saudi Arabia, vol I. Pro Entomologia co/Natural History Museum Ciba-Geigy Ltd, Basle, p 372

Buxton PA (1923) Animal life in deserts—A study of fauna in relation to environment. Edward Arnold & Co, London, p 176

Byalynitskii-Birulya AA (1965) Scorpions. In: Nasonov NV (ed) Fauna of Russia and adjacent countries—Arachnoidea. (Translated from Russian by Munitz B) Israel Programme for Scientific Translations, Jerusalem, p 154

Cable DR (1967) Fire effects on semidesert grasses and shrubs. J Range Manage
  20: 170–176
Calaby JH, Gay FJ (1956) The distribution and biology of the genus *Coptotermes*
  (Isoptera) in Western Australia. Aust J Zool 4: 19–39
Calaby JH, Gay FJ (1959) Aspects of the distribution and ecology of Australian
  termites. In: Keast A, Crocker RL, Christian CS (eds) Biogeography and ecology
  in Australia. Dr Junk Publishers, The Hague, pp 211–223
Campbell GS (1977) An introduction to environmental biophysics. Springer, Berlin
  Heidelberg New York, p 159
Carlisle DB (1968) *Triops* (Entomostraca) eggs killed only by boiling. Science 161:
  279–280
Casey TM (1976) Activity patterns, body temperature and thermal ecology in two
  desert caterpillars (Lepidoptera: Sphingidae). Ecology 57: 485–497
Casey TM (1977) Physiological responses to temperature of caterpillars of a desert
  population of *Manduca sexta* (Lepidoptera: Sphingidae). Comp Biochem Physiol
  57A: 53–58
Caswell H, Reed F, Stephenson SN, Werner PA (1973) Photosynthetic pathways
  and selective herbivory: A hypothesis. Am Nat 107: 465–480
Cates RG (1980) Feeding patterns of monophagous, oligophagous, and polyphagous
  insect herbivores: The effect of resource abundance and plant chemistry. Oecologia
  46: 22–31
Cates RG (1981) Host plant predictability and the feeding patterns of monophagous,
  oligophagous, and polyphagous insect herbivores. Oecologia 48: 319–326
Cates RG, Rhoades DF (1977) Patterns in the production of antiherbivore chemical
  defenses in plant communities. Biochem Syst Ecol 5: 185–193
Causey NB (1975) Desert millipedes (Spirostreptidae, Spirostreptida) of the southwest-
  ern United States and adjacent Mexico. Occas Pap Mus Tex Tech Univ 35: 1–12
Chamberlin RV (1943) On Mexican centipeds. Bull Univ Utah 33: 55
Charney J, Stone PH, Quirk WJ (1975) Drought in the Sahara: A biophysical feedback
  mechanism. Science 187: 434–435
Cheke RA (1978) Theoretical rates of increase of gregarious and solitarious populations
  of the desert locust. Oecologia 35: 161–171
Chernov Jr, Striganova BR, Aranjeva SI (1977) Soil fauna of the Polar desert at
  Cape Cheluskin, Taimyr Peninsula, USSR. Oikos 29: 175–179
Chew RM (1961) Ecology of the spiders of a desert community. J NY Entomol
  Soc LXIX: 5–41
Chew RM (1977) Some ecological characteristics of the ants of a desert-shrub commu-
  nity in southeastern Arizona. Am Midl Nat 98: 33–49
Chew RM, Chew AE (1970) Energy relationships of the mammals of a desert shrub
  (Larrea tridentata) community. Ecol Monogr 40: 1–21
Chew RM, DeVita J (1980) Foraging characteristics of a desert ant assemblage: Func-
  tional morphology and species separation. J Arid Environ 3: 75–83
Chhotani OB, Bose G (1979) Isoptera. In: Wittmer W, Büttiker W (eds) Fauna of
  Saudi Arabia, vol I. Pro Entomologia co/Natural History Museum Ciba-Geigy
  Ltd, Basle, pp 75–83
Chopard L (1938) Les orthopteres desertiques de l'Afrique du Nord. Soc Biogeogr
  (Paris) 220–230
Christensen CC, Miller WB (1975) Genital anatomy and phylogeny of the snails,

Berendtia Crosse and Fischer and *Spartocentrum* Dall (Stylommatophora: Bilimulidae). Nautilus **89**: 43–46

Clark WH, Comanor PL (1975) Removal of annual plants from the desert ecosystem by western harvester ants, *Pogonomyrmex occidentalis.* Environ Entomol **4**: 52–56

Cloudsley-Thompson JL (1956) Studies in diurnal rhythms. VI. Bioclimatic observations in Tunisia and their significance in relation to the physiology of the fauna, especially woodlice, centipedes, scorpions and beetles. Ann Mag Nat Hist **9**: 305–328

Cloudsley-Thompson JL (1959) Studies in diurnal rhythms. IX. The water relations of some nocturnal tropical arthropods. Entomol Exp Appl **2**: 249–256

Cloudsley-Thompson JL (1962a) Some aspects of the physiology and behaviour of *Dinothrombium* (Acari). Entomol Exp Appl **5**: 69–73

Cloudsley-Thompson JL (1962b) Lethal temperatures of some desert arthropods and the mechanism of heat death. Entomol Exp Appl **5**: 270–280

Cloudsley-Thompson JL (1964a) Terrestrial animals in dry heat: Arthropods. In: Dill DB (ed) Handbook of physiology, Sect 4. Am Physiol Soc, Washington DC, pp 451–465

Cloudsley-Thompson JL (1964b) On the function of the sub-elytral cavity in desert Tenebrionidae (Col.). Entomol Mon Mag **100**: 148–151

Cloudsley-Thompson JL (1965a) The scorpion. Science J 35–41

Cloudsley-Thompson JL (1965b) The lethal temperature of *Triops granarius* (Lucas) (Branchiopoda: Notostraca). Hydrobiology **25**: 424–425

Cloudsley-Thompson JL (1966) Orientation responses of *Triops granarius* (Lucas) (Branchiopoda: Notostraca) and *Streptocephalus* ssp. (Branchiopoda: Anostraca). Hydrobiology **27**: 33–38

Cloudsley-Thompson JL (1967) The water-relations of scorpions and tarantulas from the Sonoran Desert. Entomol Mon Mag **103**: 217–220

Cloudsley-Thompson JL (1968) Spiders, scorpions, centipedes and mites. Pergamon Press, Oxford, p 278

Cloudsley-Thompson JL (1970) Terrestrial invertebrates. In: Whittow GC (ed) Comparative physiology of thermoregulation, vol 1. Academic Press, London New York, pp 15–77

Cloudsley-Thompson JL (1973) Factors influencing the supercooling of tropical Arthropoda, especially locusts. J Nat Hist **7**: 741–780

Cloudsley-Thompson JL (1974) The expanding Sahara. Environ Conserv **1**: 5–14

Cloudsley-Thompson JL (1975) Adaptations of Arthropoda to arid environments. Annu Rev Entomol **20**: 261–283

Cloudsley-Thompson JL (1977a) Adaptational biology of the Solifugae (Solpugida). Bull Br Arachnol Soc **4**: 61–71

Cloudsley-Thompson JL (1977b) Diurnal rhythms of locomotory activity in isolated desert locusts (*Schistocerca gregaria* (Forsk.)). J Inter-discip Cycle Res **8**: 27–36

Cloudsley-Thompson JL (1977c) The black beetle paradox. Entomol Mon Mag **113**: 19–22

Cloudsley-Thompson JL (1978a) Biological clocks in Arachnida. Bull Br Arachnol Soc **4**: 184–191

Cloudsley-Thompson JL (1978b) Diurnal rhythms of supercooling in locusts. Int J Biometeorol **22**: 112–115

Cloudsley-Thompson JL (1979) Adaptive functions of the colours of desert animals. J Arid Environ **2**: 95–104

Cloudsley-Thompson JL, Chadwick MJ (1964) Life in deserts. Dufour Editions, Philadelphia, p 218

Cloudsley-Thompson JL, Crawford CS (1970) Water and temperature relations, and diurnal rhythms of scolopendromorph centipedes. Entomol Exp Appl **13**: 187–193

Cloudsley-Thompson JL, Idris BEM (1964) The insect fauna of the desert near Khartoum: Seasonal fluctuation and the effect of grazing. Proc R Entomol Soc London Ser A **39**: 41–46

Coaton WGH (1958) The hodotermitid harvester termites of South Africa. Union S Afr Dep Agric Entomol Ser No 43, p 112

Coaton WGH, Sheasby JL (1972) Preliminary report on a survey of the termites (Isoptera) of South West Africa. Cimbebasia **2**: 129

Coaton WGH, Sheasby JL (1973) National survey of the Isoptera of Southern Africa. 3. The genus *Psammotermes* Desneux (Rhinotermitidae). Cimbebasia Ser A **3**: 19–28

Cody ML, Diamond JM (eds) (1975) Ecology and evolution of communities. Harvard Univ Press, Cambridge London, p 545

Coe M (1978) The decomposition of elephant carcases in the Tsavo (East) National Park, Kenya. J Arid Environ **1**: 71–86

Cohen AC, Pinto JD (1977) An evaluation of xeric adaptiveness of several species of blister beetles (Meloidae). Ann Entomol Soc **70**: 741–749

Cohen D (1966) Optimizing reproduction in a randomly varying environment. J Theor Biol **12**: 119–129

Cole AC (1968) *Pogonomyrmex* Harvester ants: A study of the genus in North America. Univ of Tennessee Press, Knoxville p 585

Cole GA (1968) Desert limnology. In: Brown WG Jr (ed) Desert biology, vol I. Academic Press, London New York, pp 423–486

Cole GA, Brown RJ (1967) The chemistry of *Artemia* habitats. Ecology **48**: 858–861

Cole LC (1954) The population consequences of life history phenomena. Q Rev Biol **29**: 103–137

Colless DH, McAlpine DK (1970) Diptera. In: The insects of Australia. Univ Press, CSIRO Melbourne, pp 656–740

Collins MS, Richards AG (1966) Studies on water relations in North American termites. II. Water loss and cuticular structures in Eastern species of the Kalotermitidae (Isoptera). Ecology **47**: 328–331

Collins MS, Haverty MI, LaFage JP, Nutting WL (1973) High-temperature tolerance in two species of subterranean termites from the Sonoran desert in Arizona. Environ Entomol **2**: 1122–1123

Collins NC (1977) Ecological studies of terminal lakes—their relevance to problems in limnology and population biology. In: Greer DC (ed) Desertic terminal lakes. Utah State Research Laboratory, Logan, pp 411–420

Common IFB (1970) Lepidoptera (Moths and butterflies). In: The insects of Australia. Melbourne Univ Press, CSIRO Melbourne, pp 765–866

Common IFB, Waterhouse DF (1972) Butterflies of Australia. Angus and Robertson, Sydney, p 498

Congdon JD, Vitt LJ, Hadley NF (1978) Parental investment: Comparative reproduc-

tion energetics in bisexual and unisexual lizards, genus *Cnemidophorus.* Am Nat
112: 509–521

Connell JH (1975) Some mechanisms producing structure in natural communities:
A model and evidence from field experiments. In: Cody ML, Diamond J (eds)
Ecology and evolution of communities. Belknap Press of Harvard Univ, Cambridge
London, pp 460–490

Corbet PS (1966) The role of rhythms in insect behaviour. In: Haskell PT (ed) Insect
behaviour, Symp No 3. R Entomol Soc, London, pp 13–28

Coutchié PA, Crowe JH (1979) Transport of water vapor by tenebrionid beetles.
II. Regulation of the osmolarity and composition of the hemolymph. Physiol Zool
52: 88–100

Cox BC, Healy IN, Moore PD (1976) Biogeography—an ecological and evolutionary
approach, 2nd edn. John Wiley, New York, p 194

Crabill RE (1960) A new American genus of crytopid centipede, with an annotated
key to the scolopendromorph genera from America north of Mexico. Proc US
Natl Mus **III:** 1–15

Cracraft J (1974) Continental drift and vertebrate distribution. Annu Rev Ecol Syst
5: 215–261

Crawford CS (1972) Water relations in a desert millipede *Orthoporus ornatus* (Girard)
(Spirostreptidae). Comp Biochem Physiol **42A:** 521–535

Crawford CS (1976) Feeding-season production in the desert millipede *Orthoporus
ornatus* (Girard) (Diplopoda). Oecologia **24:** 265–276

Crawford CS (1978) Seasonal water balance in *Orthoporus ornatus,* a desert millipede.
Ecology **59:** 996–1004

Crawford CS (1979a) Desert detritivores: A review of life history patterns and trophic
rôles. J Arid Environ **2:** 31–42

Crawford CS (1979b) Assimilation, respiration and production: (a) invertebrates. In:
Goodall DW Perry RA (eds) IBP 16, Arid land ecosystems, vol I. Cambridge
Univ Press, Cambridge Engl, pp 717–729

Crawford CS, Cloudsley-Thompson JL (1971) Water relations and desiccation-avoid-
ing behavior in the vinegaroon *Mastigoproctus giganteus* (Arachnida: Uropygi).
Entomol Exp Appl **14:** 99–106

Crawford CS, Dadone MM (1979) Onset of evening chorus in *Tibicen marginalis*
(Homoptera: Cicadidae). Environ Entomol **8:** 1157–1160

Crawford CS, Krehoff RC (1975) Diel activity in sympatric populations of the scorpions *Centruroides sculpturatus* (Buthidae) and *Diplocentrus spitzeri* (Diplocentri-
dae). J Arachnol **2:** 195–204

Crawford CS, Matlack MC (1979) Water relations of desert millipede larvae, larva-
containing pellets, and surrounding soil. Pedobiologia **19:** 48–55

Crawford CS, Riddle WA (1974) Cold hardiness in centipedes and scorpions in New
Mexico. Oikos **25:** 86–92

Crawford CS, Riddle WA (1975) Overwintering physiology of the scorpion *Diplocentrus spitzeri.* Physiol Zool **48:** 84–92

Crawford CS, Wooten RC Jr (1973) Water relations in *Diplocentrus spitzeri,* a semi-
montane scorpion from the southwestern United States. Physiol Zool **46:** 218–
229

Crawford CS, Riddle WA, Pugach S (1975) Overwintering physiology of the centipede
Scolopendra polymorpha. Physiol Zool **48:** 290–294

Croghan PC (1958) Osmotic and ionic regulation in *Artemia.* J Exp Biol **35:** 219–233

Crowe JH, Cooper AF Jr (1971) Cryptobiosis. Sci Am **225:** 30–36

Crumb SE (1956) The larvae of the Phalaenidae. US Dep Agric Tech Bull 1135: 356

Curry A (1974) The spiracle structure and resistance to desiccation of centipedes. Symp Zool Soc London **32:** 365–382

Dadd RH (1960) Observations on the palatability and utilization of food by locusts, with particular reference to the interpretation of performances in growth trials using synthetic diets. Entomol Exp Appl **3:** 283–304

Danilevsky AS, Goryshin NI, Tyshchenko VP (1970) Biological rhythms in terrestrial arthropods. Annu Rev Entomol **15:** 201–244

Davidson DW (1977) Species diversity and community organization in desert seed-eating ants. Ecology **58:** 711–724

Davidson DW, Brown JH, Inouye RS (1980) Competition and the structure of granivore communities. BioScience **30:** 233–238

Deboutteville CD, Rapoport E (1968) Biologie de l'Amérique Australe, vol V. CNRS, Paris, p 472

Délye G (1968) Rescherches sur l'écologie, la physiologie et l'éthologie des fourmis du Sahara. Doctororal thesis, Univ Aix-Marseille, Marseille, p 155

Délye G (1969) Permeabilité du tegument et resistance aux temperatures elevées de quelques Arthropodes sahariens. Bull Soc Entomol Fr **74:** 51–55

Demange J-M, Mauriès J-P (1975) Données de morphologie, tératologie, développement postembryonnaire, faunistique et écologie des Myriapodes Diplopodes nuisibles aux cultures du Sénégal. Bull Mus Natl Hist Nat 333 Zool **235:** 1243–1256

Dingle H (1972) Migration strategies of insects. Science **175:** 1327–1335

Doyen JT (1973) Systematics of the genus *Coelocnemis* (Coleoptera: Tenebrionidae)—A quantitative study of variation. Univ Calif Publ Entomol **73:** 1–110

Doyen JT, Somerby R (1979) Phenetic similarity and Müllerian mimicry among darkling ground beetles (Coleoptera: Tenebrionidae). Can Entomol **106:** 759–772

Doyen JT, Tschinkel WF (1974) Population size, microgeographic distribution and habitat separation in some tenebrionid beetles (Coleoptera). Ann Entomol Soc Am **67:** 617–626

Duckworth WD, Eichlin TD (1978) The clearwing moths of California (Lepidoptera: Sesiidae). Occas Pap Entomol No 27. Calif Dep Food Agric, Sacramento, p 80

Dussart B (1966) Limnologie-L'étude des Eaux Contintales. Gauthier-Villars, Paris, p 677

Edney EB (1937) A study of spontaneous locomotor activity in *Locusta migratoria migratorioides* (R. & F.) by the actograph method. Bull Entomol Res **28:** 243–278

Edney EB (1960) The survival of animals in hot deserts. Smithsonian Rep 1959; 407–425

Edney EB (1966) Absorption of water vapor from unsaturated air by *Arenivaga* sp. (Polyphagidae, Dictyoptera). Comp Biochem Physiol **19:** 387–408

Edney EB (1968) The effect of water loss on the haemolymph of *Arenivaga* sp. and *Periplaneta americana.* Comp Biochem Physiol **25:** 149–158

Edney E B (1971a) Some aspects of water balance in tenebrionid beetles and a thysanuran from the Namib desert of southern Africa. Physiol Zool **44:** 61–76

Edney EB (1971b) The body temperature of tenebrionid beetles in the Namib desert of southern Africa. J Exp Biol **55**: 253–272

Edney EB (1974) Desert arthropods. In: Brown G W Jr (ed) Desert biology, vol II. Brown, Academic Press, Condon New York, pp 311–384

Edney EB (1977) Water balance in land arthropods. Springer, Berlin Heidelberg New York, p 282

Edney EB, Barrass R (1962) The body temperature of the tsetse-fly *Glossina morsitans* Westwood (Diptera, Muscidae). J Insect Physiol **8**: 469–481

Edney EB, McFarlane J (1974) The effect of temperature on transpiration in the desert cockroach, *Arenivaga investigata,* and in *Periplaneta americana.* Physiol Zool **47**: 1–12

Edney EB, Haynes S, Gibo D (1974) Distribution and activity of the desert cockroach *Arenivaga investigata* (Polyphagidae) in relation to micro-climate. Ecology **55**: 420–427

Edney EB, McBrayer JF, Franco PJ, Phillips AW (1975) Abundance and distribution of soil microarthropods in Rock Valley, Nevada. US/IBP Desert Biome Res Memo **75–29**: 39–46

Edney EB, Franco PJ, McBrayer JF (1976) Abundance and distribution of soil microarthropods in Rock Valley, Nevada. US/IBP Desert Biome Res Memo **76–24**: 11–27

Edney EB, Franco P, Wood R (1978) The responses of *Arenivaga investigata* (Dictyoptera) to gradients of temperature and humidity in sand studied by tagging with technetium 99M. Physiol Zool **51**: 241–255

Edwards CA, Lofty JR (1977) Biology of earthworms, 2nd edn. Chapman and Hall, London, p 333

Eisner T, Meinwald J (1966) Defensive secretions of arthropods. Science **153**: 1341–1350

Eisner T, Hurst JJ, Keeton WT, Meinwald Y (1965) Defense mechanism of arthropods. XVI. *Para*-benzoquinones in the secretion of spirostreptoid millipedes. Ann Entomol Soc Am **58**: 247–248

El-Ayouty EY, Ghabbour SI, El-Sayyed NAM (1978) Rôle of litter and the excreta of desert fauna in the nitrogen status of desert soils. J Arid Environ **1**: 145–155

El-Duweini AK, Ghabbour SI (1968) Nephridial systems and water balance in three oligochaete genera. Oikos **19**: 61–70

Ellis PE, Carlisle DB (1965) Desert locusts: Sexual maturation delayed by feeding on senescent vegetation. Science **149**: 546–547

Emlen JM (1973) Ecology: An evolutionary approach. Addison-Wesley, Reading Menlo Park London Don Mills, p 493

Emmel TC, Emmel JF (1973) The butterflies of Southern California. Sci Ser 26, Nat Hist Mus LA County, p 148

Engelmann MD (1966) Energetics, terrestrial field studies, and animal productivity. Adv Ecol Res **3**: 73–115

Eriksen CH, Brown RJ (1980a) Comparative respiratory physiology and ecology of phyllopod Crustacea. II. Anostraca. Crustaceana **39**: 11–21

Eriksen CH, Brown RJ (1980b) Comparative respiratory physiology and ecology of phyllopod Crustacea. III. Notostraca (including a summary discussion). Crustaceana **39**: 22–32

Eriksen CH, Brown RJ (1980c) Comparative respiratory physiology of phyllopod Crustacea. I. Conchostraca. Crustaceana **39**: 1–10

Ettershank G (1971) Some aspects of the ecology and microclimatology of the meat ant, *Iridomyrmex purpureus* (Sm.). Proc R Soc Victoria **84:** 137–151

Ettershank G, Whitford WG (1973) Oxygen consumption of two species of *Pogonomyrmex* harvester ants (Hymenoptera: Formicidae). Comp Biochem Physiol **46A:** 605–611

Ettershank G, Ettershank JA, Whitford WG (1981) Location of food sources by subterranean termites. Environ Entomol **9:** 645–648

Euw JV, Fishelson L, Parsons JA, Reichstein JA, Rothschild M (1967) Cardenolides (heart poisons) in a grasshopper feeding on milkweeds. Nature (London) **214:** 35–39

Evans HE (1966) The comparative ethology and evolution of the sand wasps. Harvard Univ Press, Cambridge Mass, p 526

Evans HE, Linsley EG (1960) Notes on a sleeping aggregation of solitary bees and wasps. Bull South Calif Acad Sci **59:** 30–37

Fanara DM, Mulla MS (1974) Population dynamics of larvae of *Culex tarsalis* Coq. and *Culiseta inornata* (Will.) as related to flooding and temperature of ponds. Mosq News **34:** 98–104

Fautin RW (1946) Biotic communities of the northern desert shrub biome in western Utah. Ecol Monogr **16:** 251–310

Ferguson WE (1962) Biological characteristics of the mutillid subgenus *Photopsis* Blake and their systematic values. Univ Calif Berkeley Publ Entomol **27:** 1–82

Ferrar P, Watson JAL (1970) Termites (Isoptera) associated with dung in Australia. J Aust Entomol Soc **9:** 100–102

Fishelson L (1960) The biology and behaviour of *Poekilocerus bufonius* Klug, with special reference to the repellent gland (Orth. Acrididae). Rev Esp Entomol **36:** 41–62

Fisher SG, Minckley WL (1978) Chemical characteristics of a desert stream in flash flood. J Arid Environ **1:** 25–33

Fitzpatrick EA (1979) Radiation. In: Goodall DW, Perry R A (eds) Arid-land ecosystems, vol I. Int Biol Programme 16. Cambridge Univ Press, Cambridge London New York Melbourne, pp 347–371

Fleissner G (1977a) Entrainment of the scorpion's circadian rhythm via the median eyes. J Comp Physiol **118:** 93–99

Fleissner G (1977b) Scorpion lateral eyes: Extremely sensitive receptors of Zeitgeber stimulus. J Comp Physiol **118:** 101–108

Fleissner G (1977c) The absolute sensitivity of the median and lateral eyes of the scorpion, *Androctonus australis* L. (Buthidae, Scorpiones). J Comp Physiol **118:** 109–120

Fowler HG, Whitford WG (1980) Termites, microarthropods and the decomposition of senescent and fresh creosotebush *(Larrea tridentata)* leaf litter. J Arid Environ **3:** 63–68

Fox LR, Macauley BJ (1977) Insect grazing on *Eucalyptus* in response to variation in leaf tannins and nitrogen. Oecologia **29:** 145–162

Franco PJ, Edney EB, McBrayer JF (1979) The distribution and abundance of soil arthropods in the Northern Mojave desert. J Arid Environ **2:** 137–149

Freckman DW (1978) Ecology of anhydrobiotic soil nematodes. In: Crowe JH, Clegg JS (eds) Dried biological systems. Academic Press, London New York, pp 345–357

Freckman DW, Mankau R (1977) Distribution and trophic structure of nematodes in desert soils. Ecol Bull (Stockholm) **25:** 511–514

Freckman DW, Mankau R (1979) Nematodes and microflora in the root rhizosphere of four desert shrubs. In: Harley JL, Russell RS (eds) The soil-root interface. Academic Press, London New York, p 423

Freckman DW, Kaplan DT, Van Gundy SD (1977) A comparison of techniques for extraction and study of anhydrobiotic nematodes from dry soils. J Nematol 9: 176–181

Freckman DW, Sher SA, Mankau R (1974) Biology of nematodes in desert ecosystems. US/IBP Desert Biome Res Memo **74–35:** 90–98

Friedman I, Smith GI, Hardcastle KG (1976) Studies of Quaternary saline lakes— II. Isotopic and compositional changes during desiccation of the brines in Owens Lake, California, 1969–71. Geochim Cosmochim Acta **40:** 501–511

Friedmann EI, Galun M (1974) Desert algae, lichens, and fungi. In: Brown GW Jr (ed) Desert biology, vol II. Academic Press, London New York, pp 165–212

Friedmann EI, Ocampo R (1976) Endolithic blue-green algae in dry valleys: Primary producers in the Antarctic desert ecosystem. Science **193:** 1247–1249

Fuchs M (1979) Atmospheric transport processes above arid-land vegetation. In: Goodall DW, Perry RA (eds) Arid-land ecosystems, vol I. Int Biol Programme 16. Cambridge Univ Press, Cambridge London New York Melbourne, pp 393–408

Fuller WH (1974) Desert soils. In: Brown GW Jr (ed) Desert biology, vol II. Academic Press, London New York, pp 31–101

Gaspar C, Werner FG (1976) The ants of Arizona: an ecological study of ants in the Sonoran desert. US/IBP Desert Biome Res Memo **73–50:** 1–14

Gates DM (1962) Energy exchange in the biosphere. Harper & Row, New York, p 151

Gates GE (1967) On the earthworm fauna of the Great American Desert and adjacent areas. Great Basin Nat **27:** 142–176

Gauthier H (1928) Recherches sur la faune des eaux continentales de L'Algérie et de la Tunisie. Minerva, Algiers, p 419

Gertsch WJ (1949) American spiders. D van Nostrand, New York, p 285

Ghabbour SI, Mikhail WSA (1977) Variations in chemical composition of *Heterogamia syriaca* Sauss. (Polyphagidae, Dictyoptera); a major component of the Mediterranean coastal desert of Egypt. Rev Biol Écol Mediterr **4:** 89–104

Ghabbour SI, Mikhail WZA (1978) Ecology of soil fauna of Mediterranean desert ecosystems in Egypt. II. Soil mesofauna associated with *Thymelaea hirsuta.* Rev. Ecol Biol Sol **15:** 333–339

Ghabbour SI, Mikhail W, Rizk M (1977) Ecology of soil fauna of Mediterranean desert ecosystems in Egypt. I.—Summer populations of soil mesofauna associated with major shrubs in the littoral sand dunes. Rev Ecol Biol Sol **14:** 429–459

Ghilarov MS (1960) Termites of the USSR, their distribution and importance. Proc New Delhi Symp. UNESCO, Paris, pp 131–135

Giezentanner KI, Clark WH (1974) The use of western harvester ant mounds as strutting locations by sage grouse. Condor **76:** 218–219

Gillon D (1971) The effect of bush fire on the principal pentatomid bugs (Hemiptera) of an Ivory Coast savanna. In: Proc Annu Tall Timbers Fire Ecol Conf, no 11. Tall Timbers Research Station, Tallahassee, pp 377–414

Gillon Y (1971) The effect of bush fire on the principal acridid species of an Ivory Coast savanna. In: Proc Annu Tall Timbers Fire Ecol Conf no 11. Tall Timbers Research Station, Tallahassee, pp 419–471

Golley FB, Gentry JB (1964) Bioenergetics of the southern harvester ant, *Pogonomyrmex badius.* Ecology **45:** 217–225

Goodall DW, Perry RA (eds) (1979) Arid-land ecosystems, vol I. Int Biol Programme 16. Cambridge Univ Press, Cambridge London New York Melbourne, p 881

Goodman D (1979) Regulating reproductive effort in a changing environment. Am Nat **113:** 735–748

Gordon RD, Cartwright OL (1974) Survey of food preferences of some no. American Canthonini (Coleoptera: Scarabaeidae). Entomol News **85:** 181–185

Gordon RD, Howden HF (1973) Five new species of Mexican *Aphodius* (Coleoptera: Scarabaeidae) associated with *Thomomys umbrinus (Geomyidae).* Ann Entomol Soc Am **66:** 436–443

Goudie A, Wilkinson J (1977) The warm desert environment. Cambridge Univ Press, Cambridge London New York Melbourne, p. 88

Graetz RD, Cowan I (1979) Microclimate and evaporation. In: Goodall DW, Perry RA (eds) Arid-land ecosystems, vol I. Int Biol Programme 16. Cambridge Univ Press, Cambridge London New York Melbourne, pp 409–433

Greenaway P, MacMillen RE (1978) Salt and water balance in the terrestrial phase of the inland crab *Holthuisana (Austrothelphusa) transversa* Martens (Parathelphusoidea: Sundathelphusidae). Physiol Zool **51:** 217–229

Greenaway P, Taylor HH (1976) Aerial gas exchange in the Australian arid-zone crab *Parathelphusia transversa* Von Martens. Nature (London) **262:** 711–713

Greenslade P (1975) The role of soil fauna in arid shrubland in South Australia. In: Vaněk J (ed) Progress in soil zoology. Academia, Prague, pp 113–119

Greenslade PJM, Greenslade P (1973) Epigaeic Collembola and their activity in a semi-arid locality in Southern Australia during summer. Pedobiologia **13:** 227–235

Grenot CJ (1974) Physical and vegetational aspects of the Sahara desert. In: Brown GW Jr (ed) Desert biology, vol II. Academic Press, London New York, pp 103–164

Grigg GC (1973) Some consequences of the shape and orientation of "magnetic" termite mounds. Aust J Zool **21:** 231–237

Gunstream SE, Chew RM (1967) The ecology of *Psorophora confinnis* (Diptera: Culicidae) in southern California. II. Temperature and development. Ann Entomol Soc Am **60:** 434–439

Gut LJ, Schlising RA, Stopher CE (1977) Nectar-sugar concentrations and flower visitors in the western Great Basin. Great Basin Nat **37:** 523–529

Guthrie DM, Tindall AR (1968) The biology of the cockroach. St Martin's Press, New York, p 408

Gwynne DT (1979) Nesting biology of the spider wasps (Hymenoptera: Pompilidae) which prey on burrowing wolf spiders (Araneae: Lycosidae: *Geolycosa*) J Nat Hist **13:** 681–692

Gwynne DT, Evans HF (1975) Nesting behavior of *Larropsis chilopsidis* and *L. vegeta* (Hymenoptera: Specidae: Larrinae). Psyche **82:** 275–282

Gwynne DT, Hostetler BB (1978) Mass emergence of *Prionus emarginatus* (Say) (Coleoptera: Cerambycidae). Coleopt Bull **32:** 347–348

Gwynne DT, Watkiss J (1975) Burrow-blocking behaviour in *Geolycosa* wrightii (Araneae: Lycosidae). Anim Behav **23**: 953–956

Hadley NF (1970a) Water relations of the desert scorpion, *Hadrurus arizonensis*. J Exp Biol **53**: 547–558

Hadley NF (1970b) Habitat micrometeorology and energy exchange in two desert arthropods. Ecology **51**: 434–444

Hadley NF (1972) Desert species and adaptation. Am Sci **60**: 338–347

Hadley NF (1977) Epicuticular lipids of the desert tenebrionid beetle, *Eleodes armata:* Seasonal and acclimatory effects on composition. Insect Biochem **7**: 277–283

Hadley NF (1978) Epicuticular permeability of tenebrionid beetles: Correlations with epicuticular hydrocarbon composition. Insect Biochem **8**: 17–22

Hadley NF (1979) Wax secretion and color phases of the desert tenebrionid beetle *Cryptoglossa verracosa* (LeConte). Science **203**: 367–369

Hadley NF (1980) Cuticular lipids of adults and nymphal exuviae of the desert cicada, *Diceroprocta apache* (Homoptera, Cicadidae). Comp Biochem Physiol **65B**: 549–553

Hadley NF, Filshie BK (1979) Fine structure of the epicuticle of the desert scorpion, *Hadrurus arizonensis,* with reference to location of lipids. Tissue Cell **11**: 263–275

Hadley NF, Hill RD (1969) Oxygen consumption of the scorpion *Centruroides sculpturatus*. Comp Biochem Physiol **29**: 217–226

Hadley NF, Jackson LL (1977) Chemical composition of the epicuticular lipids of the scorpion, *Paruroctonus mesaenis*. Insect Biochem **7**: 85–89

Hadley NF, Szarck SR (1981) Productivity of desert ecosystems: Producer, consumer, and decomposer organisms. Bioscience (in press)

Hadley NF, Williams SC (1968) Surface activities of some North American scorpions in relation to feeding. Ecology **49**: 726–734

Hallmark MD, Ward CR (1972) The life history and life process studies of the water scavenger beetle, *Hydrophylus triangularis* Say. US/IBP Desert Biome Res Memo 72–49 24

Hamilton WI III (1971) Competition and thermoregulatory behavior of the Namib Desert tenebrionid beetle genus *Cardiosis*. Ecology **52**: 810–822

Hamilton WJ III (1973) Life's color code. McGraw-Hill, New York, p 238

Hamilton WJ III, Seely MK (1976) Fog basking by the Namib Desert beetle *Onymacris unguicularis*. Nature (London) **262**: 284–285

Hamilton WJ III, Buskirk RE, Buskirk WH (1976) Social organization of the Namib desert tenebrionid beetle *Onymacris rugatipennis* Can Entomol **108**: 305–316

Hammer M (1966) A few oribatid mites from Ram, Jordan. Zool Anz **177**: 272–276

Hammond PM (1975) The Steninae (Coleoptera, Staphylinidae) of South-Western Africa with special reference to the arid and semi-arid zones. Cimbebasia Ser A **4**: 1–33

Hansen SR (1978) Resource utilization and coexistence of three species of *Pogonomyrmex* ants in an Upper Sonoran Grassland Community. Oecologia **35**: 109–117

Hardy AR (1971) The North American Areodina with a description of a new genus from California. Pan Pac Entomol **47**: 235–242

Hardy AR (1973) A new species of *Phobetus* (Coleoptera: Scarabaeidae). Pan Pac Entomol **49**: 127–131

Hardy AR, Andrews FG (1974) Observations on *Megasoma* with behavioral notes on some lamellicorn beetles associated with sand dunes (Coleoptera: Scarabaeidae, Lucanidae). Pan Pac Entomol **50:** 124–128

Hare FK (1961) The causation of the arid zone. In: Stamp LD (ed) A history of land use in arid regions. UNESCO, Paris, pp 25–30

Hare FK (1977) Connections between climate and desertification. Environ Conserv **4:** 81–90

Hartman HB, Walthall WW, Bennett LP, Stewart RR (1979) Giant interneurons mediating equilibrium reception in an insect. Science **205:** 503–505

Haverty MI, Nutting WL (1975) Environmental factors affecting the geographical distribution of two ecologically equivalent termite species in Arizona. Am Midl Nat **95:** 20–27

Hawke SD, Farley RD (1973) Ecology and behavior of the desert burrowing cockroach, *Arenivega* sp. (Dictyoptera, Polyphagidae). Oecologia **11:** 263–279

Hazel JR, Prosser CL (1974) Molecular mechanism of temperature compensation in poikilotherms. Physiol Rev **54:** 620–677

Heath JE, Wilkin PJ (1970) Temperature responses of the desert cicada, *Diceroprocta apache* (Homoptera, Cicadidae). Physiol Zool **43:** 145–154

Heath JE, Wilkin PJ, Heath MS (1972) Temperature responses of the cactus dodger, *Cacama valvata* (Homoptera, Cicadidae). Physiol Zool **45:** 238–246

Heatwole H, Muir R (1979) Thermal micro-climates in the pre-Saharan steppe of Tunisia. J. Arid Environ **2:** 119–136

Hebard M (1943) The Dermaptera and orthopterous families Blattidae, Mantidae and Phasmidae of Texas. Trans Am Entomol Soc **68:** 239–311

Heeg J (1967a) Studies on Thysanura. II. Orientation reactions of *Machiloides delanyi* Wygodzinski and *Ctenolepisma longicaudata* Escherich to temperature, light and atmospheric humidity. Zool Afr **3:** 43–57

Heeg J (1967b) Studies on the Thysanura. I. The water economy of *Machiloides delanyi* Wygodzinski and *Ctenolepisma longicaudata* Escherich. Zool Afr **3:** 21–41

Heinrich B (1975) Thermoregulation and flight energetics of desert insects. In: Hadley NF (ed) Environmental physiology of desert organisms. Dowden Hutchinson & Ross Inc, Stroudsburg Penn, pp 90–105

Heinrich B (1979) Keeping a cool head: Honeybee thermoregulation. Science **205:** 1269–1271

Helfner JR (1953) How to know the grasshoppers, cockroaches and their allies. Wm C Brown Co, Dubuque Iowa, p 353

Heller J (1975) The taxonomy, distribution and faunal succession of *Buliminus* (Pulmonata: Enidae) in Israel. Zool J Linn Soc **57:** 1–57

Heller J (1979) Distribution, hybridization and variation in the Israeli landsnail *Levantina* (Pulmonata: Helicidae). Zool J Linn Soc **67:** 115–148

Henwood K (1975a) Infrared transmittance as an alternative thermal strategy in the desert beetle *Onymacris plana.* Science **189:** 993–994

Henwood K (1975b) A field-tested thermoregulation model for two diurnal Namib Desert tenebrionid beetles. Ecology **56:** 1329–1342

Herreid CF II (1977) Metabolism of land snails *(Otala lactea)* during dormancy, arousal, and activity. Comp Biochem Physiol **56A:** 211–215

Herreid CF II, Rokitka MA (1976) Environmental stimuli for arousal from dormancy in the land snail *Otala lactea* (Müller). Physiol Zool **49:** 181–190

Hetz MW, Werner FG (1979) Insects associated with roots of some rangeland Compositae in southern Arizona. Southwest Entomol **4:** 285–288

Hewitt PH, Nel JJC, Schoeman I (1971) The influence of group size on water imbibition by *Hodotermes mosambicus* alate termites. J Insect Physiol **17:** 587–800

Hickman JC (1974) Pollination by ants: A low-energy system. Science **184:** 1290–1292

Hillyard SD, Vinegar A (1972) Respiration and thermal tolerance of the phyllopod Crustacea *Triops longicaudatus* and *Thamnocephalus platyurus* inhabiting desert ephemeral ponds. Physiol Zool **45:** 189–195

Hinds WT, Rickard WH (1966) Soil temperatures near a desert steppe shrub. Northwest Sci **42:** 5–13

Hinds WT, Rickard WH (1973) Correlations between climatological fluctuations and a population of *Philolithus densicollis* (Horn) (Coleoptera: Tenebrionidae). J Anim Ecol **42:** 341–351

Hochachka PW, Somero GN (1973) Strategies of biochemical adaptation. WB Saunders Company, Philadelphia London Toronto, p 358

Hoff CC (1959) The ecology and distribution of the pseudoscorpions of North-Central New Mexico. Univ New Mexico Press, Albuquerque, p 68

Hoffman RL, Orcutt BS (1960) A synopsis of the Atopetholidae, a family of spiroboloid millipedes. Proc US Nat Mus **3:** 95–165

Holdaway FG, Gay FJ (1948) Temperature studies of the habitat of *Eutermes exitiosus* with special reference to the temperatures within the mound. Aust J Sci Res Ser B **1:** 464–493

Holdgate MW (1977) Terrestrial ecosystems in the Antarctic. Philos Trans R Soc London Ser B **279:** 5–25

Holm E, Edney EB (1973) Daily activity of Namib desert arthropods in relation to climate. Ecology **54:** 45–56

Holm E, Kirsten JF (1979) Pre-adaptation and speed mimicry among Namib Desert scarabaeids with orange elytra. J Arid Environ **2:** 263–271

Horne F (1967) Effects of physical-chemical factors on the distribution and occurrence of some southeastern Wyoming phyllopods. Ecology **48:** 472–477

Horne FR (1968) Survival and ionic regulation of *Triops longicaudatus* in various salinities. Physiol Zool **41:** 180–186

Horne FR (1971a) Accumulation of urea by a pulmonate snail during aestivation. Comp Biochem Physiol **38A:** 565–570

Horne FR (1971b) Some effects of temperature and oxygen concentration on phyllopod ecology. Ecology **52:** 343–347

Horne FR (1973) The utilization of foodstuffs and urea production by a land snail during estivation. Biol Bull **144:** 321–330

Howden HF, Hardy AR (1971) Generic placement and adult behavior of the genus *Leptohoplia* Saylor (Coleoptera: Scarabaeidae). Proc Entomol Soc Wash **73:** 337–341

Hsiao TS, Kirkland RL (1973) Demographic studies of sagebrush insects as functions of various environmental factors. US/IBP Desert Biome Res Memo **73–34:** 28

Huey RB, Pianka ER (1977) Natural selection for juvenile lizards mimicking noxious beetles. Science **195:** 201–203

Huey RB, Slatkin M (1976) Cost and benefits of lizard thermoregulation. Q Rev Biol **51:** 363–384

Hughes RD (1977) The population dynamics of the bushfly: The elucidation of population events in the field. Aust J Ecol **2**: 43–54

Hughes RD, Greenham PM, Tyndale-Briscoe M, Walker JM (1972) A synopsis of observations on the biology of the Australian bushfly (*Musca vetustissima* Walker). J Aust Entomol Soc **11**: 311–331

Hughes RD, Tyndale-Briscoe M, Walker J (1978) Effects of introduced dung beetles (Coleoptera: Scarabaeidae) on the breeding and abundance of the Australian bushfly, *Musca vetustissima* Walker (Diptera: Muscidae). Bull Entomol Res **68**: 361–372

Hull FM (1973) The bee flies of the world. Smithson Inst US Natl Mus Bull **286**: 687

Humphrey RR (1958) The desert grassland. A history of vegetational change and an analysis of causes. Univ of Arizona Press, Tucson, p 74

Hunter WR (1968) Physiological aspects of ecology in nonmarine molluscs. In: Drake ET (ed) Evolution and environment. Yale Univ Press, New Haven, pp 83–126

Hurd DD Jr, Linsley EG (1975) Some insects other than bees associated with *Larrea tridentata* in the southwestern United States. Proc Entomol Soc Wash **77**: 100–120

Hutchinson GE (1937) A contribution to the limnology of arid regions. Trans Conn Acad Arts Sci **33**: 47–132

Hutchinson GE, Pickford GE, Schuurman JFM (1932) A contribution to the hydrology of pans and other inland waters of South-Africa. Arch Hydrobiol **24**: 1–154

Jaeckel SGA Jun (1969) Die Mollusken Südamerikas. In: Fittkau EJ, Illies J, Klinge H, Schwabe GH, Sioli H (eds) Biogeography and ecology in South America, vol II. Dr Junk Publishers, The Hague, pp 794–827

Jaeger EC (1957) The North American deserts. Stanford Univ Press, Stanford Calif, p 308

James MT (1947) The flies that cause myiasis in man. US Government Printing Office, Washington DC, Misc Publ 631, p 175

Joern A (1979) Feeding patterns in grasshoppers (Orthoptera: Acrididae): Factors influencing diet specialization. Oecologia **38**: 325–347

Johnson CG (1969) Migration and dispersal of insects by flight. Methuen & Co Ltd, London, p 763

Johnson JD, Allred DM (1972) Scorpions of Utah. Great Basin Nat **32**: 154–170

Johnson KA, Whitford WG (1975) Foraging ecology and relative importance of subterranean termites in Chihuahuan desert ecosystems. Environ Entomol **4**: 66–70

Johnston JS, Heed WB (1976) Dispersal of desert-adapted Drosophila: The saguaro-breeding *D. nigrospiracula*. Am Nat **110**: 629–651

Joviet P (1965) Notes sur l'ecologie des *Timarcha* Marocaines (Col. Chrysomelidae). Soc Sci Nat Phys Maroc Bull **44**: 159–190

Kaestner A (1968) Invertebrate zoology, vol II (Translated from German by Levi HW, Levi RL) Interscience Publishers, New York London Sydney, p 479

Kaplin VG (1978) A comparative ecological and morphological description of bristletails of the family Lepismatidae (Thysanura) in the Eastern Karakum sands. Entomol Rev **56**: 72–84

Kaufman T (1966) Observations on some factors which influence aggregation by *Blaps sulcata* (Coleoptera: Tenebrionidae) in Israel. Ann Entomol Soc Am **59**: 660–664

Kay CA, Whitford WG (1975) Influence of temperature and humidity on oxygen consumption of five Chihuahuan Desert ants. Comp Biochem Physiol **52A:** 281–286

Keister M, Buck J (1964) Respiration: Some exogenous and endogenous effects on rate of respiration. In: Rockstein M (ed) The physiology of insecta, vol III. Academic Press, London New York, pp 617–658

Key KHL (1970) Orthoptera (grasshoppers, locusts, crickets). In: The insects of Australia. Melbourne Univ Press, CSIRO Melbourne, pp 323–347

Kheirallah AM (1979) The ecology of the isopod *Periscyphis granai* (Arcangeli) in the western highlands of Saudi Arabia. J Arid Environ **2:** 51–59

Kheirallah AM (1980) Aspects of the distribution and community structure of isopods in the Mediterranean coastal desert of Egypt. J Arid Environ **3:** 69–74

King WW, Hadley NF (1979) Water flux and metabolic rates of free-roaming scorpions using the doubly-labeled water technique. Physiol Zool **52:** 176–189

Kingsolver JM, Johnson CD, Swier SR, Teran AL (1977) Prosopis fruits as a resource for invertebrates. In: Simpson BB (ed) Mesquite—Its biology in two desert scrub ecosystems. US/IBP Synthesis Series No 4. Dowden Hutchinson & Ross Inc, Stroudsburg Penn, pp 108–122

Kistner DH (1975) A new species of the termitophilous tribe Skatitoxenini (Coleoptera: Staphylinidae) with notes on its interactions with its host termites (Isoptera: Termitidae). Cimbebasia Ser A **4:** 99–114

Kitchell JF, O'Neill RV, Webb D, Gallepp GW, Bartell SM, Koonce JF, Ausmus BS (1979) Consumer regulation of nutrient cycling. BioScience **29:** 28–34

Koch C (1961) Some aspects of the abundant life in the vegetationless sand of the Namib Desert dunes. J Southwest Afr Sci Soc **15:** 9–33

Koch C (1962) The Tenebrionidae of southern Africa XXXI. Comprehensive notes on the tenebrionid fauna of the Namib Desert. Ann Transvaal Mus **24:** 63–104

Köppen W (1954) Classification of climates and the world patterns. In: Trewartha GT (ed) An introduction to climate, 3rd edn. McGraw-Hill, New York, pp 225–226, 381–383

Kovda VA, Samoilova EM, Charley JL, Skujiņš JJ (1979) Soil processes in arid lands. In: Goodall DW, Perry RA (eds) Arid-land ecosystems, vol I. Int Biol Programme 16. Cambridge Univ Press, Cambridge London New York Melbourne, pp 439–470

Kozlovskaja LS, Striganova BR (1977) Food, digestion and assimilation in desert woodlice and their relations to the soil microflora. In: Lohm U, Persson T (eds) Soil organisms as components of ecosystems. Proc 6th Int Colloq Soil Zool Ecol Bull Stockholm, pp 240–245

Kozlovsky DC (1968) A critical evaluation of the trophic level concept. 1. Ecological efficiencies. Ecology **49:** 48–60

Kraus O (1966) Phylogenie, Chorologie und Systematik der Odontopygoideen (Diplopoda, Spirostreptomorpha). Abh Senckenb Naturforsh Ges **512:** 1–143

Krehoff RC (1975) Adaptive advantages of activity rhythms in five sympatric species of *Eleodes* (Coleoptera: Tenebrionidae) from central New Mexico. PhD Dissertation, Univ of New Mexico, Albuquerque, p 64

Krogh A, Weis-Fogh T (1951) The respiratory exchange of the desert locust *(Schistocerca gregaria)* before, during and after flight. J Exp Biol **28:** 344–357

Kromarek EV Sr (1969) Fire and animal behavior. In: Proc Annu Tall Timbers Fire Ecol Conf, no 9. Tall Timbers Research Station, Tallahassee, pp 161–207

Kronk AE, Riechert SE (1979) Parameters affecting the habitat choice of a desert wolf spider, *Lycosa santrita* Chamberlin and Ivie. J Arachnol 7: 155–166

Labeyrie V (1978) The significance of the environment in the control of insect fecundity. Annu Rev Entomol 23: 69–89

LaFage JP, Nutting WL (1977) Nutrient dynamics of termites. In: Brian MV (ed) Production ecology of ants and termites. IBP 13. Cambridge Univ Press, Cambridge London New York Melbourne, pp 165–232

LaFage JP, Nutting WL, Haverty MI (1973) Desert subterranean termites: A method for studying foraging behavior. Environ Entomol 2: 954–956

LaFage JP, Haverty MI, Nutting WL (1976) Environmental factors correlated with the foraging behavior of a desert subterranean termite, *Gnathamitermes perplexus* (Banks). Sociobiology 2: 155–169

Larsen TB (1979) Lepidoptera: Fam. Papilionidae, Pieridae, Danaidae, Nymphalidae, Lycaenidae. In: Fauna of Saudi Arabia, vol I. Wittmer W, Büttiker W (eds) Pro Entomologia co/Natural History Museum Ciba-Geigy Ltd, Basle, pp 324–344

Lawrence RF (1959) The sand-dune fauna of the Namib desert. South Afr J Sci 55: 233–239

Lawrence RF (1966) The Myriapoda of the Kruger National Park. Zool Afr 2: 225–262

Lawrence RF (1972) New psammophilous Solifugae, chiefly from desert regions of the Kalahari and South West Africa. Madoqua 1: 54–62

Lawrence RF (1975) The Chilopoda of South West Africa. Cimbebasia Ser A 4: 35–45

Lee KE, Wood TG (1971) Termites and soils. Academic Press, London New York, p 251

Lee RM (1961) The variation of blood volume with age in the desert locust (*Schistocerca gregaria* Forsk.). J Insect Physiol 6: 36–51

Leouffre A (1953) Phénologie des insectes du Sud-Oranais. Israel. Ha-mo'atsah Ha-le' umit Le-mehkar Ule-Fituah. Spec Publ 2: 325–331

Levin SA, Paine RT (1974) Disturbance, patch formation, and community structure. Proc Natl Acad Sci USA 71: 2744–2747

Levy G, Shulov A (1964) The Solifuga of Israel. Isr J Zool 13: 102–120

Lewis JGE (1969) The biology of *Scolopendra amazonica* in Nigerian Guinea savannah. Bull Mus Nat Hist Nat 41: 85–90

Lewis JGE (1972) The life histories and distribution of the centipedes *Rhysida nuda togoensis* and *Ethmostigmus trigonopodus* (Scolopendromorpha: Scolopendridae) in Nigeria. J Zool London 167: 399–414

Lewis JGE (1973) The taxonomy, distribution and ecology of centipedes of the genus *Asanada* (Scolopendromorpha: Scolopendridae) in Nigeria. Zool J Linn Soc 52: 97–112

Lewis T (1973) Thrips—Their biology, ecology and economic importance. Academic Press, London New York, p 349

Linsenmair KE (1972) Die Bedeutung familienspezifischer "Abzeichen" für den Femilienzusammenhalt bei der sozialen Wüstenassel *Hemilepistus reaumuri* Audouin u. Savigny (Crustacea, Isopoda, Oniscoidea). Z Tierpsychol 31: 131–162

Linsenmair KE, Linsenmair C (1971) Paarbildung und Paarzusemmenhalt bei der monogamen Wüstenassel *Hemilepistus reaumuri* (Crustacea, Isopoda, Oniscoidea). Z Tierpsychol 29: 134–155

Linsley EG (1957) Host relationships in the genus *Crossidius* (Coleoptera, Cerambycidae). J Kans Entomol Soc **30**: 81–89

Linsley EG (1958) The ecology of solitary bees. Hilgardia **27**: 543–599

Linsley EG (1978) Temporal patterns of flower visitation by solitary bees, with particular reference to the southwestern United States. J Kans Entomol Soc **51**: 531–546

Linsley EG, Eisner T, Klots AB (1961) Mimetic assemblages of sibling species of lycid beetles. Evolution **25**: 15–29

Loest RA (1979) Ammonia volatilization and absorption by terrestrial gastropods: A comparison between shelled and shell-less species. Physiol Zool **52**: 461–469

Logan RF (1968) Causes, climates, and distribution of deserts. In: Brown GW Jr (ed) Desert biology, vol I. Academic Press, London New York, pp 21–50

Loomis RF (1966) Descriptions and records of Mexican Diplopoda. Ann Entomol Soc Am **59**: 11–27

Loots GC, Ryke PAJ (1967) The ratio Oribatei: Trombidiformes with reference to organic matter content in soils. Pedobiologia **7**: 121–124

Louw GN, Hamilton WJ III (1972) Physiological and behavioral ecology of the ultrapsammophilous Namib Desert tenebrionid *Lepidochora argentogrisea*. Madoqua Ser II **1**: 87–95

Loveridge JP (1968) The control of water loss in *Locusta migratoria migratorioides* R. and F. II. Water loss through the spiracles. J Exp Biol **49**: 15–29

Loveridge JP (1973) Age and the changes in water and fat content of adult laboratory-reared *Locusta migratoria migratorioides* R. and F. Rhod J Agric Res **11**: 131–143

Loveridge JP (1974) Studies on the water relations of desert locusts. II. Water gain in the food and loss in the faeces. Trans Rhod Sci Assoc **56**: 1–30

Loveridge JP, Bursell E (1975) Studies on the water relations of adult locusts (Orthoptera, Acrididae). 1. Respiration and the production of metabolic water. Bull Entomol Res **65**: 13–20

Low WA (1979) Spatial and temporal distribution and behavior. In: Goodall DW, Perry RA (eds) Arid-land ecosystems, vol I. Int Biol Programme 16. Cambridge Univ Press, Cambridge London New York Melbourne, pp 769–795

Lowe CH (1968) Fauna of desert environments—with desert disease information. In: McGinnies WG, Goldman BJ, Paylove P (eds) Deserts of the world. Univ of Arizona Press, Tucson, pp 567–645

Lowe, CH, Heed WB, Halpern EA (1967) Supercooling of the saguaro species *Drosophila nigrospiracula* in the Sonoran Desert. Ecology **48**: 984–985

MacArthur RH (1972) Geographical ecology: Patterns in the distribution of species. Harper & Row, New York, p 269

Machin J (1967) Structural adaptation for reducing water-loss in three species of terrestrial snail. J Zool London **152**: 55–65

Machin J (1974) Osmotic gradients across snail epidermis: evidence for a water barrier. Science **183**: 759–760

Mackerras MJ (1970) Blattodea. In: The insects of Australia. Melbourne Univ Press, CSIRO Melbourne, pp 262–274

MacMillan RE, Greenaway P (1978) Adjustments of energy and water metabolism to drought in an Australian arid-zone crab. Physiol Zool **51**: 230–240

Main BY (1956) Taxonomy and biology of the genus *Isometroides keyserling* (Scorpionida). Aust J Zool **4**: 158–164

Main BY (1957) Biology of aganippine trapdoor spiders (Mygalomorphae: Ctenizidae). Aust J Zool **5**: 402–473

Mann J (1969) Cactus-feeding insects and mites. Smithson Inst US Natl Mus Bull **256**: 158

Mansingh A (1971) Physiological classification of dormancies in insects. Can Entomol **103**: 983–1009

Mares MA, Blair WF, Enders FA, Greegor D, Hulse AC, Hunt JH, Otte D, Sage RD, Tomoff CS (1977a) Strategies and community patterns of desert animals. In: Orians GH, Solbrig OT (eds) Convergent evolution in warm deserts. US/IBP Synthesis Ser 1. Dowden Hutchinson & Ross Inc, Stroudsburg Penn, pp 107–163

Mares, MA, Enders FA, Kingsolver JM, Neff JL, Simpson BB (1977b) *Prosopis* as a niche component. In: Simpson BB (ed) Mesquite—Its biology in two desert scrub ecosystems. US/IBP Synthesis Ser 4. Dowden Hutchinson & Ross Inc, Stroudsburg Penn, pp 123–149

Marks CF, Thomason IJ, Castro CE (1968) Dynamics and the permeation of nematodes by water, nematocides and other substances. Exp Parasitol **22**: 321–337

Martin MM, Martin JS (1978) Cellulose digestion in the midgut of the fungus-growing termite *Macrotermes natalensis:* The role of acquired digestive enzymes. Science **199**: 1453–1455

Mateu J, Pierre F (1974) Aridité et variation spécifique de quelques populations d'insectes du Sahara et de la zone Sahélienne. In: Recherches biologiques contemporaines. Vagner, Nancy, pp 97–105

Mathieu JM (1980) The ontogeny of blister beetles (Coleoptera, Meloidae) IV.— *Pyrota insulata* Leconte. Southwest Nat **5**: 149–152

Matthews EG (1976) Insect ecology. Univ Queensland Press, St Lucia, p 226

McClure MS (1976) Spatial distribution of pit-making ant lion larvae (Neuroptera: Myrmeleontidae): density effects. Biotropica **8**: 179–183

McCluskey ES (1965) Circadian rhythms in male ants of five diverse species. Science **150**: 1037–1039

McGinnies WG (ed) (1968) Deserts of the world—An appraisal of research into their physical and biological environment. Univ of Arizona Press, Tucson, p 788

McKinnerney M (1978) Carrion communities in the northern Chihuahuan desert. Southwest Nat **23**: 563–576

McMichael DF, Iredale T (1959) The land and freshwater Mollusca of Australia. In: Keast A, Crocker RL, Christian CS (eds) Biogeography and ecology of Australia. Den Haag: Uitgeverij Dr Junk Publishers, The Hague, pp 224–245

McNeill S, Lawton JH (1970) Annual production and respiration in animal populations. Nature (London) **225**: 472–474

McQuaid CD, Branch GM, Frost PGH (1979) Aestivation behaviour and thermal relations of the pulmonate *Theba pisana* in a semi-arid environment. J Therm Biol **4**: 47–55

McQueen DJ (1979) Interactions between the pompilid wasp *Anoplius relativus* (Fox) and the burrowing wolf spider *Geolycosa domifex* (Hancock). Can J Zool **57**: 542–550

Medvedev GS (1965) Adaptations of leg structure in desert darkling beetles. Entomol Rev **44**: 473–485

Meigs P (1953) World distribution of arid and semi-arid homoclimates. Rev Res Arid Zone Hydrol. Arid Zone Programme **1**: pp 203–209

Michener CD (1944) The distribution of the osmiine bees of the deserts of North America. Am Nat **78:** 257–266

Michener CD (1969) Comparative social behavior of bees. Annu Rev Entomol **14:** 299–342

Miller PL (1960) Respiration in the desert locust. III. Ventilation and the thoracic spiracles during flight. J Exp Biol **37:** 264–278

Miller WB (1972) *Greggilex,* a new genus of autochthonous land snails (Helmintho-glyptidae) from Baja California. Nautilus **85:** 128–135

Minch EW (1978) Daily activity patterns in the tarantula *Aphonopelma chalcodes* Chamberlin. Bull Br Arachnol Soc **4:** 231–237

Minch EW (1979) Annual activity patterns in the tarantula, *Aphonopelma chalcodes* Chamberlin. Nov Arthrop **1:** 1–33

Mispagel ME (1978) The ecology and bioenergetics of the acridid grasshopper, *Bootettix punctatus* on creosotebush, *Larrea tridentata,* in the northern Mojave desert. Ecology **59:** 779–788

Mitchell MJ (1977) Life history strategies of oribatid mites. In: Dindal DL (ed) Biology of oribatid mites. State Univ NY Coll Environ Sci Forest, Syracuse, pp 65–69

Moeur JE, Eriksen CE (1972) Metabolic responses to temperature of a desert spider, *Lycosa (Pardosa) carolinensis* (Lycosidae). Physiol Zool **45:** 290–301

Moffett DF (1975) Sodium and potassium transport across the isolated hindgut of the desert millipede, *Orthoporus ornatus* (Girard). Comp Biochem Physiol **50A:** 56–63

Mooney HA, Simpson BB, Solbrig OT (1977) Phenology, morphology, physiology. In: Simpson BB (ed) Mesquite—Its biology in two desert ecosystems. US/IBP Synthesis Ser No 4. Dowden Hutchinson & Ross Inc, Stroudsburg Penn, pp 26–43

Mordue AJ, Hill L (1970) The utilization of food by the adult female desert locust, *Schistocerca gregaria.* Entomol Exp Appl **13:** 352–358

Morton SR (1979) Diversity of desert-dwelling mammals: A comparison of Australia and North America. J Mammal **60:** 253–264

Moutia LA (1940) The search for parasites of white grubs (melolonthids) in Zanzibar, Algeria, Morocco and France. Bull Entomol Res **31:** 193–208

Mulroy TW, Rundel PW (1977) Annual plants: Adaptations to desert environments. BioScience **27:** 109–114

Muma MH (1966) Feeding behavior of North American Solpugida (Arachnida). Fla Entomol **49:** 199–216

Muma MH (1967a) Scorpions, whip scorpions and wind scorpions of Florida. Arthropods of Florida and neighboring land areas. Bull Fla Dep Agric **4:** 1–28

Muma MH (1967b) Basic behavior of North American Solpugida. Fla Entomol **50:** 115–123

Muma MH (1974) Maturity and reproductive isolation of common solpugids in North American deserts. J Arachnol **2:** 5–10

Murphy GI (1968) Pattern in life history and the environment. Am Nat **102:** 390–404

Nel JJC, Hewitt PH (1969) Effect of solar radiation on the harvester termite, *Hodotermes mossambicus.* Nature (London) **223:** 862–863

Newell IM, Tevis L Jr (1960) *Angelothrombium pandorae* N.G., N.SP. (Acari, Trombidiidae), with notes on the biology of the giant red velvet mites. Ann Entomol Soc Am **53**: 293–304

Newlands G (1978) Arachnida (except Acari). In: Werger MJA (ed) Biogeography and ecology of southern Africa, vol II. Dr. Junk Publishers, The Hague, pp 685–702

Nielsen ET (1962) Illumination at twilight. Oikos **14**: 9–21

Noirot Ch (1970) The nests of termites. In: Krishna K, Weesner FM (eds) Biology of termites, vol II. Academic Press, London New York, pp 73–125

Norris MJ (1961) Group effects on feeding in male adults of the desert locust, *Schistocerca gregaria* (Forsk.), in relation to sexual maturation. Bull Entomol Res **51**: 731–753

Norton BE, Smith LB (1975) Response to insect herbivory. US/IBP Desert Biome Res Memo **75–15**: 6

Moy-Meir I (1973) Desert ecosystems: Environment and producers. Annu Rev Ecol Syst **4**: 25–51

Noy-Meir I (1974) Desert ecosystems: Higher trophic levels. Annu Rev Ecol Syst **5**: 195–213

Noy-Meir I (1978) Structure and function of desert ecosystems. Abstr 2nd Int Congr Ecol, vol I, Jerusalem, p 265

Nunez FS, Crawford CS (1976) Digestive enzymes of the desert millipede *Orthoporus ornatus* (Girard) (Diplopoda: Spirostreptidae). Comp Biochem Physiol **55A**: 141–145

Nutting WL, Haverty MI (1976) Seasonal production of alates by five species of termites in an Arizona desert grassland. Sociobiol **2**: 145–153

Nutting WL, Haverty MI, LaFage JP (1975) Demography of termite colonies as related to various environmental factors: Population dynamics and role in the detritus cycle. US/IBP Desert Biome Res Memo **75–31**: 1–26

Omer SM, Cloudsley-Thompson JL (1968) Dry season biology of *Anopheles gambiae* Giles in the Sudan. Nature (London) **217**: 879

Orians GH, Solbrig OT (1977a) Degree of convergence of ecosystem characteristics. In: Convergent evolution in warm deserts. US/IBP Synthesis Ser 1. Dowden Hutchinson & Ross Inc, Stroudsburg Penn, pp 226–255

Orians GH, Solbrig OT (eds) (1977b) Convergent evolution in warm deserts. US/IBP Synthesis Ser 3. Dowden Hutchinson & Ross Inc, Stroudsburg Penn, p 333

Orians GH, Cates RG, Mares MA, Moldenke A, Neff J, Rhoades DF, Rosenzweig ML, Simpson BB, Schultz JC, Tomoff CS (1977) Resource utilization systems. In: Orians GH, Solbrig OT (eds) Convergent evolution in warm deserts. Dowden Hutchinson & Ross Inc, Stroudsburg Penn, pp 164–224

Otte D (1976) Species richness patterns of New World desert grasshoppers in relation to plant diversity. J Biogeogr **3**: 197–209

Otte D, Joern A (1975) Insect territoriality and its evolution: Population studies of desert grasshoppers on creosote bushes. J Anim Ecol **44**: 29–54

Otterman J (1974) Baring high-albedo soils by overgrazing: A hypothesized desertification mechanism. Science **186**: 531–533

Paarmann W (1979) A reduced number of larval instars, as an adaptation of the desert carabid beetle *Thermophilum (Anthia) sexmaculatum* F. (Coleoptera, Carabidae) to its arid environment. In: Boer den PJ, Thiele HU, Weber F (eds) Symp Rep Zool Inst Univ Cologne 1978 H Veenman and Zonen BV, Wageningen, pp 113–117

Pajunen VI (1970) Adaptation of *Arctocorisa carinata* (Sahlb.) and *Callocorixa producta* (Reut.) populations to a rock pool environment. Proc Adv Study Inst Dyn Numbers Popul, Oosterbeck, pp 148–158

Paramenter C, Folger DW (1974) Eolian biogenic detritus in deep sea sediments: A possible index of equatorial ice age aridity. Science **185**: 695–697

Paramonov SJ (1959) Zoogeographical aspects of the Australian dipterofauna. In: Keast A, Crocker RL, Christian CS (eds) Biogeography and ecology in Australia. Dr Junk Publishers, The Hague, pp 164–191

Pennak RW (1953) Fresh-water invertebrates of the United States. Ronald Press Co, New York, p 769

Penrith M-L (1973) Redescription of *Pachynotelus kuehnelti* Koch, 1962 (Coleoptera: Tenebrionidae: Cryptochilini). Cimbebasia Ser A **2**: 125–130

Penrith M-L (1974) The subtribe Dactylocalcarina (Coleoptera: Tenebrionidae: Zosphosini) with description of a new species. Cimbebasia Ser A **2**: 145–154

Penrith M-L (1975) The species of *Onymacris* Allard (Coleoptera: Tenebrionidae). Cimbebasia Ser A **4**: 47–97

Peterman RM (1973) Possible behavioral thermoregulation in *Tanatharus salinus* and *T. inyo* (Coleoptera: Anthicidae). Pan Pac Entomol **49**: 67–73

Peterson A (1953) Larvae of insects, part II, 2nd edn. Edwards Brothers Inc, Ann Arbor Mich, p 416

Petrov MP (1976) Deserts of the world. John Wiley & Sons, New York Toronto, p 447

Petrusewicz K, Macfadyen A (1970) Productivity of terrestrial animals—Principles and methods. IBP Handbook no 13. FA Davis, Philadelphia, p 190

Phipps J (1966) Ovulation and oocyte resorption in Acridoidea (Orthoptera). Proc R Entomol Soc London Ser A **41**: 78–86

Pianka ER (1969) Sympatry of desert lizards *(Ctenotus)* in western Australia. Ecology **50**: 1012–1030

Pierre F (1958) Écologie et peuplement entomologique des sables vifs du Sahara Nord. Occidental. CNRS, Paris, p 332

Pinhey E (1978) Lepidoptera. In: Werger MJA (ed) Biogeography and ecology of southern Africa, vol II. Dr Junk Publishers, The Hague, pp 763–773

Poinsot-Balaguer N (1976) Dynamique des communautes de Collemboles en milieu xerique meditaraneen. Pedobiologia **16**: 1–17

Polis GA (1979) Prey and feeding phenology of the desert sand scorpion *Paruroctonus mesaensis* (Scorpionidae: Vaejovidae). J Zool London **188**: 33–346

Polis GA (1980a) Seasonal patterns and age-specific variation in the surface activity of a population of desert scorpions in relation to environmental factors. J Anim Ecol **49**: 1–18

Polis GA (1980b) The effect of cannibalism on the demography and activity of a natural population of desert scorpions. Behav Ecol Sociobiol 7: 25–35

Polis GA, Farley RD (1979a) Characteristics and environmental determinants of natality, growth and maturity in a natural population of the desert scorpion, *Paruroctonus mesaensis* (Scorpionida: Vaejovidae). J Zool London **187**: 517–542

Polis GA, Farley RD (1979b) Behavior and ecology of mating in the cannibalistic scorpion, *Paruroctonus mesaensis* Stahnke (Scorpionida: Vaejovidae). J Arachnol 7: 33–46

Polis GA, Farley RD (1980) Population biology of a desert scorpion: Survivorship, microhabitat and the evolution of a life history strategy. Ecology **61**: 620–629

Polk KL, Ueckert DN (1973) Biology and ecology of a mesquite twig girdler, *Oncideres rhodosticta*, in West Texas. Ann Entomol Soc Am **66**: 411–417

Pomeroy DE (1969) Some aspects of the ecology of the land snail, *Helicella virgata*, in South Australia. Aust J Zool **17**: 495–514

Pomeroy DE (1978) The abundance of large termite mounds in Uganda in relation to their environment. J Appl Ecol **15**: 51–63

Powell JA, Mackie RA (1966) Biological interrelationships of moths and *Yucca whipplei*. Univ Calif Publ Entomol **42**: 1–46

Pradhan S (1957) The ecology of arid zone insects excluding locusts and grasshoppers. In: Arid zone research, vol VIII. Hum Anim Ecol. UNESCO, Paris, pp 199–240

Pressland AJ (1976) Soil moisture redistribution as affected by throughfall and stem-flow in an arid zone shrub community. Aust J Bot **24**: 641–649

Prins AJ (1978) Hymenoptera. In: Werger MJA (ed) Biogeography and ecology of southern Africa, vol II. Dr Junk Publishers, The Hague, pp 823–875

Prophet CW (1963) Physical-chemical characteristics of habitats and seasonal occurrence of some Anostraca in Oklahoma and Kansas. Ecology **44**: 798–801

Prosser CL (1973) Water; osmotic balance; hormonal regulation. In: Prosser CL (ed) Comparative animal physiology, 3rd edn. WB Saunders, Philadelphia London Toronto, pp 1–78

Pugach S, Crawford CS (1978) Seasonal changes in hemolymph amino acids, proteins, and inorganic ions of a desert millipede *Orthoporus ornatus* (Girard) (Diplopoda: Spirostreptidae) Can J Zool **56**: 1460–1465

Putshkov VG (1978) New and little-known mirid bugs (Heteroptera, Miridae) from Mongolia and Soviet Central Asia. Entomol Rev **56**: 91–100

Rafes PM (1960) The life forms of insects inhabiting the Naryn sands of the semidesert Transvolga region. Entomol Rev **38**: 19–31

Rainey RC (1967) A note on some migrations of moths and locusts. Isr J Entomol **2**: 187–189

Raitt RJ, Pimm SL (1976) Dynamics of bird communities in the Chihuahuan desert, New Mexico. Condor **78**: 427–442

Ramaswamy C (1977) The age of the present deserts over Central Asia. Curr Sci **46**: 727–733

Ranasinghe MASK (1977) Bionomics of a subterranean gall midge (Diptera: Cecido-myiidae) from *Artemesia ludoviciana*. Great Basin Nat **37**: 429–442

Raske A (1967) Morphological and behavioral mimicry among beetles of the genus *Moneilema*. Pan Pac Entomol **43**: 239–244

Raven PH, Axelrod DI (1974) Angiosperm biogeography and past continental movements. Ann Mo Bot Gard **61**: 439–673

Rehn JAG (1958) The origin and affinities of the Dermaptera and Orthoptera of western North America. In: Hubbs CL (ed) Zoogeography. Am Assoc Adv Sci, pp 255–298

Reichle DE (1977) The role of soil invertebrates in nutrient cycling. In: Lohm U, Persson T (eds) Soil organisms as components of ecosystems. Proc 6th Int Colloq Soil Zool Ecol Bull, Stockholm, pp 145–156

Reichman OJ, Prakash I, Roig V (1979) Food selection and consumption. In: Goodall DW, Perry RA (eds) Arid-land ecosystems, vol I, Int Biol Programme 16. Cambridge Univ Press, Cambridge London New York Melbourne, pp 681–716

Rentz DC (1978) Orthoptera. In: Werger MJA (ed) Biogeography and ecology of southern Africa, vol II. Dr Junk Publishers, The Hague, pp 685–702

Rhoades DF (1977) The antiherbivore chemistry of *Larrea*. In: Mabry TJ, Hunziker JH, DiFeo DR Jr (eds) Creosote bush—Biology and chemistry of *Larrea* in new world deserts. US/IBP Synthesis Ser 6. Dowden Hutchinson & Ross Inc, Stroudsburg Penn, pp 135–175

Rhoades DF, Cates RG (1976) Toward a general theory of plant anti-herbivore chemistry. In: Wallace JW, Mansell RL (eds) Biochemical interaction between plants and insects. Plenum Press, New York, pp 168–213

Richardson AMM (1975) Food, feeding rates and assimilation in the land snail *Cepaea nemoralis* L. Oecologia (Berlin) **19:** 59–70

Riddle WA (1975) Water relations and humidity-related metabolism of the desert snail *Rabdotus schiedeanus* (Pfeiffer) (Helicidae). Comp Biochem Physiol **51A:** 579–583

Riddle WA (1976) Respiratory physiology of *Paruroctonus aquilonalis*. PhD Dissertation, Univ of New Mexico, Albuquerque, p 119

Riddle WA (1977) Comparative respiratory physiology of a desert snail *Rhabdotus schiedeanus*, and a garden snail, *Helix aspersa*. Comp Biochem Physiol **56A:** 369–373

Riddle WA (1978) Respiratory physiology of the desert grassland scorpion *Paruroctonus utahensis*. J Arid Environ **1:** 243–251

Riddle WA (1979) Metabolic compensation for temperature change in the scorpion *Paruroctonus utahensis*. J Therm Biol **4:** 125–128

Riddle WA, Pugach S (1976) Cold hardiness in the scorpion, *Paruroctonus aquilonalis*. Cryobiology **13:** 248–253

Riddle WA, Crawford CS, Zeitone AM (1976) Patterns of hemolymph osmoregulation in three desert arthropods. J Comp Physiol **112:** 295–305

Riechert SE (1974) The pattern of local web distribution in a desert spider: Mechanisms and seasonal variation. J Anim Ecol **43:** 733–746

Riechert SE (1978) Energy-based territoriality in populations of the desert spider *Agelenopsis aperta* Gertsch). Symp Zool Soc London **42:** 211–222

Riechert SE, Tracy CR (1975) Thermal balance and prey availability: Bases for a model relating web-site characteristics to spider reproductive success. Ecology **56:** 265–284

Riechert SE, Reeder WG, Allen TF (1973) Patterns of spider distribution (*Agelenopsis aperta* (Gertsch)) in desert grassland and recent lava bed habitats, south-central New Mexico. J Anim Ecol **42:** 19–35

Riek EF (1970) Neuroptera (lacewings). In: The insects of Australia. Melbourne Univ Press, CSIRO Melbourne, pp 472–494

Riek EF, Michener CD, Brown WLJ, Taylor RW (1970) Hymenoptera (Wasps, bees, ants). In: The insects of Australia. Melbourne Univ Press, CISRO Melbourne, pp 867–959

Rissing SW, Wheeler J (1976) Foraging responses of *Veromessor pergandei* to changes in seed production. Pan Pac Entomol **52:** 63–72

Roer H (1975) Zur Lebensweise des Namibwüstenkäfers *Onymacris plana* Peringuey (Col., Tenebrionidae, Adesmiini) unter besonder Berüksichtigung seines Migrationsverhaltens. Bonn Zool Beitr **26:** 239–256

Roever K (1975) Family Megathymidae (the giant skippers). In: Howe WH (ed) The butterflies of North America. Doubleday & Co Inc, Garden City NJ, pp 411–422

Roffey J, Popov GB (1968) Environmental and behavioural processes in a desert locust outbreak. Nature (London) **219**: 446–450

Rogers L, Lavigne R, Miller JL (1972) Bioenergetics of the harvester ant in the shortgrass plains ecosystem. Environ Entomol **1**: 763–768

Roonwall ML (1977) Termite ecology in the Indian desert ecosystem: A review of recent work. In: Mann HS (ed) Desert eco-system and its improvement. Central Arid Zone Research Institute, Jodhpur India, CAZRI Monogr 1, pp 323–328

Roth LM, Willis ER (1961) The biotic associations of cockroaches. Smithson Misc Collect **141**: 470

Rumpp NL (1961) Three new tiger beetles of the genus *Cicindela* from southwestern United States. Bull South Calif Acad Sci **60**: 165–187

Ryckman RE (1962) Biosystematics and hosts of the *Triatoma protracta* complex in North America (Hemiptera: Reduviidae) (Rodentia: Cricetidae). Univ Calif Publ Entomol **27**: 93–240

Rzóska J (1961) Observations on tropical rainpools and general remarks on temporary waters. Hydrobiologia **17**: 265–286

Salt RW (1968) Location and quantitative aspects of ice nucleators in insects. Can J Zool **46**: 329–333

Santos PFD (1979) The role of microarthropods and nematodes in litter disappearance in a Chihuahuan desert ecosystem. PhD Dissertation, New Mexico State Univ, Las Cruces, p 91

Santos PF, DePree E, Whitford WG (1978) Spatial distribution of litter and microarthropods in a Chihuahuan desert ecosystem. J Arid Environ **1**: 41–48

Schmidt-Nielsen K, Taylor CR, Shkolnik A (1971) Problems of heat, water and food. J Exp Biol **55**: 385–398

Schmidt-Nielsen K, Taylor CR, Shkolnik A (1972) Desert snails: Problems of survival. In: Maloiy GMO (ed) Comparative physiology of desert animals. Symp Zool Soc London, pp 1–13

Schmoller RR (1970) Terrestrial desert arthropods: Fauna and ecology. Biologist **52**: 77–98

Schneider P (1971) Lebensweise und soziales Verhalten der Wüstennasel *Hemilepistus aphganicus* Borutzky 1958. Z Tierpsychol **29**: 121–133

Schneider P (1975) Beitrag zur Biologie der afghanischen Wüstenassel *Hemilepistus aphganicus* Borutzky 1958 (Isopoda, Oniscoidea). Aktivitätsverlauf, Zool Anz **195**: 155–170

Schoener TW (1974) Resource partitioning in ecological communities. Science **185**: 27–39

Schowalter TD, Whitford WG (1980) Territorial behavior of *Bootettix argentatus* Bruner (Orthoptera: Acrididae). Am Midl Nat **102**: 182–184

Schultz JC, Otte D, Enders F (1977) *Larrea* as a habitat component for desert arthropods. In: Mabry TJ, Hunziker JH, DiFeo DR Jr (eds) Creosote bush—Biology and chemistry of *Larrea* in new world deserts. US/IBP Synthesis Ser 6. Dowden Hutchinson & Ross, Stroudsburg Penn, pp 176–208

Schulze L (1974) The Tenebrionidae of southern Africa, XLIII—Description of some larvae of the Zophosini with observations on the possible origin of phylogenetic evolution of dune-living genera (Coleoptera). Ann Transvaal Mus **29**: 71–98

Schumacher A, Whitford WG (1976) Spatial and temporal variation in Chuhuahuan desert ant faunas. Southwest Nat **21**: 1–8

Schwartzbach M (1963) Climates of the past; an introduction to paleoclimatology. Van Nostrand, London-Princeton, p 328

Seely MK, Hamilton WJ III (1976) Fog catchment sand trenches constructed by tenebrionid beetles, *Lepidochora*, from the Namib Desert. Science **193**: 484–486

Seely MK, Louw GN (1980) First approximation of the effects of rainfall on the ecology and energetics of a Namib Desert dune ecosystem. J Arid Environ **3**: 25–54

Seely MK, deVos MP, Louw GN (1977) Fog imbibition, satellite fauna and unusual leaf structure in a Namib Desert dune plant *Trianthema hereroensis.* S Afr J Sci **73**: 169–172

Seymour RS, Vinegar A (1973) Thermal relations, water loss and oxygen consumption of a North American tarantula. Comp Biochem Physiol **44A**: 83–96

Shachak M (1981) Energy allocation and life history strategy of the desert isopod *Hemilepistus reaumuri.* Oecologia (Berlin) (in press)

Shachak M, Steinberger Y, Orr Y (1979) Phenology, activity and regulation of radiation load in the desert isopod, *Hemilepistus reaumuri.* Oecologia (Berlin) **40**: 133–140

Shachak M, Orr Y, Steinberger Y (1975) Field observations on the natural history of *Sphincterochila* (S.) *zonata* (Bourguignat, 1853) (= *S. boissieri* Charpentier, 1847). Argamon. Isr J Malacol **5**: 20–46

Shachak M, Chapman EA, Orr Y (1976a) Some aspects of the ecology of the desert snail *Sphincterochila boissieri* in relation to water and energy flow. Isr J Med Sci **12**: 887–891

Shachak M, Chapman EA, Steinberger Y (1976b) Feeding, energy flow and soil turnover in the desert isopod, *Hemilepistus reaumuri.* Oecologia (Berlin) **24**: 57–69

Shalem N (1949) L'influence de la rosée et des brouillards sur la repartition des escargots. J Conchyliol **89**: 95–107

Shaw J, Stobbard RH (1972) The water balance and osmoregulatory physiology of the desert locust *(Schistocerca gregaria)* and other desert and xeric arthropods. In: Maloiy GMO (ed) Comparative physiology of desert animals. Symp Zool Soc London **31**: 15–38

Shelly TE, Pearson DL (1978) Size and color discrimination of the robber fly *Efferia tricella* (Diptera: Asilidae) as a predator on tiger beetles (Coleoptera: Cicindelidae). Environ Entomol **7**: 790–793

Shinn RS, Anderson RD, Merritt M, Osborne W, MacMahon JA (1975) Curlew Valley Validation Site Report. US/IBP Desert Biome Res Memo **75–1**: 1–68

Shook RS (1978) Ecology of the wolf spider *Lycosa carolinensis* Walkenauer (Araneae: Lycosidae) in a desert community. J Arachnol **6**: 53–64

Shorthouse DJ (1971) Studies on the biology and energetics of the scorpion *Urodacus yaschenkoi* (Birula 1904). PhD Thesis, Australian National Univ, Canberra Australia, p 163

Simon D (1979) The ant-lions (Myrmeleontidae) of Israel. MSci Thesis, Tel-Aviv Univ, Tel-Aviv Israel

Simpson BB, Neff JL, Moldenke AR (1977) *Prosopis* flowers as a resource. In: Simpson BB (ed) Mesquite—Its biology in two desert ecosystems. US/IBP Synthesis Ser 4. Dowden Hutchinson & Ross Inc, Stroudsburg Penn, pp 84–107

Sims RW (1978) Megadrilacea (Oligochaeta). In: Werger MJA (ed) Biogeography and ecology of southern Africa, vol II. Dr Junk Publishers, The Hague, pp 661–676

Sivinski JM (1978) Factors affecting mating duration in the walkingstick *Diapheromera velii* (Walsh) (Phasmatodea: Heteronemiidae). MSci Thesis, Univ of New Mexico, Albuquerque, p 157

Slater JA (1976) The biology, distribution and taxonomy of some Lygaeidae of South-west Australia (Hemiptera: Heteroptera). J Aust Entomol Soc **15:** 129–151

Sleeper EL, Mispagel ME (1975) Shrub-dwelling arthropods. In: Turner FB (ed) Rock Valley validation site report. US/IBP Desert Biome Res Memo **75–2:** pp 35–42

Slobodchikoff CN (1978) Experimental studies of tenebrionid beetle predation by skunks. Behaviour **LXVI:** 313–322

Slobodchikoff CN (1979) Utilization of harvester ant debris by tenebrionid beetles. Environ Entomol **8:** 770–772

Smith RL, Langley WM (1978) Cicada stress sound: An assay of its effectiveness as a predator defense mechanism. Southwest Nat **23:** 187–195

Solbrig OT (1976) The origin and floristic affinities of the South American temperate desert and semidesert regions. In: Goodall DW (ed) Evolution of desert biota. Univ of Texas Press, Austin, pp 7–49

Solbrig OT, Orians GH (1977) The adaptive characteristics of desert plants. Am Sci **65:** 412–421

Solbrig OT, Barbour MA, Cross J, Goldstein G, Lowe CH, Morello J, Yang TW (1977) The strategies and community patterns of desert plants. In: Orians GH, Solbrig OT (eds) Convergent evolution in warm deserts. US/IBP Synthesis Ser 3. Dowden Hutchinson & Ross Inc, Stroudsburg Penn, pp 68–106

Soo Hoo CF, Fraenkel G (1966) The consumption, digestion and utilization of food plants by a polyphagous insect, *Prodenia eridania* (Cramer). J Insect Physiol **12:** 711–730

Spears BM, Ueckert DN (1976) Survival and food consumption by the desert termite *Gnathamitermes tubiformans* in relation to dietary nitrogen source and levels. Environ Entomol **5:** 1022–1025

Stahnke HL (1966) Some aspects of scorpion behavior. Bull South Calif Acad Sci **65:** 66–80

Stange LA (1970) Revision of the ant-lion tribe Brachynemurini of North America (Neuroptera: Myrmeleontidae). Univ Calif Publ Entomol **55:** 1–192

Stearns SC (1976) Life-history tactics: A review of the ideas. Q Rev Biol **51:** 3–47

Steinberger Y (1979) Some aspects of the ecology of the desert snail *Sphincterochila prophetarum*. PhD thesis, Bar-Ilan Univ, Ramat-Gan Israel, p 135

Stewart TC, Woodring JP (1973) Anatomical and physiological studies of water balance in the millipedes *Pachydesmus crassicutis* (Polydesmida) and *Orthoporus texicolens* (Spirobolida). Comp Biochem Physiol **44A:** 734–750

Størmer L (1969) Oldest known terrestrial arachnids. Science **164:** 1276–1277

Strickland M (1950) Differences in toleration of drying between species of termites *(Reticulitermes)*. Ecology **31:** 373–385

Striganova BR, Valiachmedov BV (1976) Participation of soil saprophaga in the leaf-litter decomposition in pistachio stands. Pedobiologia **16:** 219–227

Sublette JE, Sublette MS (1967) The limnology of playa lakes on the Llano Estacado, New Mexico and Texas. Southwest Nat **12:** 369–406

Sutcliffe DW (1963) The chemical composition of haemolymph in insects and some other arthropods, in relation to their phylogeny. Comp Biochem Physiol **9:** 121–135

Tasch P, Zimmerman JR (1961) Fossil and living conchostrocan distribution in Kansas-Oklahoma across a 200-million-year time gap. Science **133:** 584–586

Tauber MJ, Tauber CA (1976) Insect seasonality: Diapause maintenance, termination, and postdiapause development. Annu Rev Entomol 21: 81–107

Tauber MJ, Tauber CA (1978) Evolution of phenological strategies in insects: A comparative approach with eco-physiological and genetic considerations. In: Dingle H (ed) Evolution of insect migration and diapause. Springer, Berlin Heidelberg New York, pp 53–71

Taylor EC (1979) Seasonal distribution and abundance of fungi in two desert grassland communities. J Arid Environ 2: 295–312

Taylor F (1977) Foraging behavior in ants: experiments with two species of myrmicine ants. Behav Ecol Sociobiol 2: 147–167

Taylor F (1978) Foraging behavior of ants: Theoretical considerations. J Theor Biol 71: 541–565

Taylor F (1980) Timing in the life histories of insects. Theor Popul Biol 18: 112–124

Tevis L, Newell IM (1962) Studies on the biology and seasonal cycle of the giant red velvet mite, *Dinothrombium pandorae* (Acari, Trombidiidae). Ecology 43: 497–505

Thomas DB Jr (1979) Patterns in the abundance of some tenebrionid beetles in the Mojave desert. Environ Entomol 8: 568–574

Tiemann DL (1967) Observations on the natural history of the western banded glowworm *Zarhippus integripennis* (Le Conte) (Coleoptera: Phengodidae). Proc Calif Acad Sci 35: 235–264

Tilden JW (1962) General characteristics of the movements of *Vanessa cardui* (L.) J Res Lepid 1: 43–49

Tillbrook PJ (1967a) The terrestrial invertebrate fauna of the Maritime Antarctic. Philos Trans R Soc London Ser B 252: 261–278

Tillbrook PJ (1967b) Arthropod ecology in the Maritime Antarctic. In: Gressitt PJ (ed) Entomology of Antarctica. Antarct Res Ser 10: 331–356

Tinkham ER (1948) Faunistic and ecological studies on the Orthoptera of the Big Bend region of Trans-Pecos Texas, with especial reference to the orthopteran zones and faunae of midwestern North America. Am Midl Nat 40: 521–663

Tinkham ER (1968) Studies in Nearctic sand dune Orthoptera. Part XI. A new arenicolous species of *Stenopelmatus* from Coachella Valley with key and biological notes. Great Basin Nat 28: 124–131

Toolson EC, Hadley NF (1977) Cuticular permeability and epicuticular lipid composition in two Arizona vejovid scorpions. Physiol Zool 50: 323–330

Toolson EC, Hadley NF (1979) Seasonal effects on cuticular permeability and epicuticular lipid composition in *Centruroides sculpturatus* Ewing 1928 (Scorpiones: Buthidae). J Comp Physiol 129: 319–325

Tourtlotte GI (1974) Studies on the biology and ecology of the northern scorpion, *Paruroctonus boreus* (Girard). Great Basin Nat 34: 167–179

Troughton JH, Wells PV, Mooney HA (1974) Photosynthetic mechanisms and paleoecology from carbon isotope ratios in ancient specimens of C_4 and CAM plants. Science 185: 610–612

Tschinkel WR (1972) The sorption of water vapor by windborne plant debris in the Namib Desert. Madoqua 2: 63–68

Tschinkel WR (1975) A comparative study of the chemical defensive system of tenebrionid beetles. Defensive behavior and ancillary features. Ann Entomol Soc Am 68: 439–453

Tuculescu R, Topoff H, Wolfe S (1975) Mechanisms of pit construction in antlion larvae. Ann Entomol Soc Am **68:** 719–720

Turner FB, Medica PA, Kowalewsky BW (1976) Energy utilization by a desert lizard *(Uta stansburiana).* US/IBP Desert Biome Monogr **1:** 57

Ueckert DN, Bodine MC, Spears BM (1976) Population density and biomass of the desert termite *Gnathamitermes tubiformans* (Isoptera: Termitidae) in a short-grass prairie: relationship to temperature and moisture. Ecology **57:** 1273–1280

Upton SJ, Crawford CS, Hoffman RL (1981) A new species of thelastomatid (Nematoda: Thelastomatidae) from the desert millipede, *Orthoporus ornatus* (Diplopoda: Spirostreptidae). Proc Helminthol Soc Washington (in press)

Uvarov BP (1957) The aridity factor in the ecology of locust and grasshoppers of the Old World. In: Arid zone research, vol VIII, Hum Anim Ecol. UNESCO, Paris, pp 64–187

Uvarov BP (1977) Grasshoppers and locusts—A handbook of general acarology, vol II. Behaviour, ecology, biogeography, population dynamics. Centre for Overseas Pest Research, London, pp 613

van Bruggen AC (1978) Land molluscs. In: Werger MJA (ed) Biogeography and ecology of southern Africa, vol II. Dr Junk Publishers, The Hague, pp 887–923

Van Devender TR, Spaulding WG (1979) Development of vegetation and climate in the southwestern United States. Science **204:** 701–710

Vannier G (1978) La resistance a la desiccation chez les premiers arthropodes terrestres. Bull Soc Ecophysiol **3:** 13–42

Van Valen L (1976) Energy and evolution. Evol Theory **1:** 179–229

van Zinderen Bakker EM Sr (1978) Quaternary vegetation changes in southern Africa. In: Werger MJA (ed) Biogeography and ecology of southern Africa, vol I. Dr Junk Publishers, The Hague: pp 131–143

Verhoeff KW (1935) Zur Biologie der Spirostreptiden. Zool Anz **109:** 288–292

Vollmer AT, MacMahon JA (1974) Comparative water relations of five species of spiders from different habitats. Comp Biochem Physiol **47A:** 753–765

Wainwright CM (1978a) The floral biology and pollination ecology of two desert lupines. Bull Torrey Bot Club **105:** 24–38

Wainwright CM (1978b) Hymenopteran territoriality and its influences on the pollination ecology of *Lupinus arizonicus.* Southwest Nat **23:** 605–616

Waldbauer GP (1968) The consumption and utilization of food by insects. In: Beament JWL, Treherne JE, Wigglesworth VB (eds) Advances in insect physiology, vol V. Academic Press, London New York, pp 229–298

Walker LJ, Crawford CS (1980) Integumental ultrastructure of the desert millipede, *Orthoporus ornatus* (Girard) (Diplopoda: Spirostreptidae). Int J Insect Morphol Embryol **9:** 231–249

Wallwork JA (1972) Distribution patterns and population dynamics of the microarthropods of a desert soil in southern California. J Anim Ecol **41:** 291–310

Wallwork JA (1976) The distribution and diversity of soil fauna. Academic Press, London New York, p 355

Wallwork JA (1980) Desert soil microarthropods an 'r'-selected system. In: Dindal DL (ed) Soil biology as related to land use practices. Proc 7th Int Colloq Soil Zool. Office of Pesticide and Toxic Substances EPA, Washington, DC, pp 759–767

Walton ML (1963) Length of life in west American land snails. Nautilus **76:** 127–131

Warburg MR (1965a) On the water economy of some Australian land-snails. Proc Malacol Soc London **36**: 297–305

Warburg MR (1956b) The microclimate in the habitats of two isopod species in southern Arizona. Am Midl Nat **73**: 363–375

Warburg MR (1965c) The evolutionary significance of the ecological niche. Oikos **16**: 205–213

Warburg MR (1968) Behavioral adaptations of desert isopods. Am Zool **8**: 545–559

Warburg MR (1972) On the physiological ecology of the Israeli Clausiliidae, a relic group of land snails. Trans Conn Acad Arts Sci **44**: 379–394

Warburg MR, Rankevich D, Chasanmus K (1978) Isopod species diversity and community structure in mesic and xeric habitats of the Mediterranean region. J Arid Environ **1**: 157–163

Warburg MR, Goldenberg S, Ben-Horin A (1980) Scorpion species diversity and distribution within the Mediterranean and arid regions of northern Israel. J Arid Environ **3**: 205–213

Wasbauer MS (1973) The male brachycistidine wasps of the Nevada Test Site (Hymenoptera: Tiphiidae). Great Basin Nat **33**: 109–112

Watson JAL, Gay FJ (1970) The role of grass-eating termites in the degradation of a mulga ecosystem. Search **1**: 43

Watson JAL, Hewitt PH, Nel JJC (1971) The water-sacs of *Hodotermes mossambicus*. J Insect Physiol **17**: 1705–1709

Watson JAL, Lendon C, Low BS (1973) Termites in Mulga lands. Trop Grassl **7**: 121–126

Watts JG (1965) *Chirothrips falsus* on black gramma grass. Las Cruces: NMS Agric Exp Stn Bull 499: 20

Weir JS (1973) Air flow, evaporation and mineral accumulation in mounds of *Macrotermes subhyalinus* (Rambur). J Anim Ecol **42**: 509–520

Weis-Fogh (1964) Biology and physics of locust flight VIII. Lift and metabolic rate of flying locusts. J Exp Biol **41**: 257–271

Weis-Fogh T (1967) Respiration and tracheal ventilation in locusts and other flying insects. J Exp Biol **47**: 561–587

Wells PV (1974) Post-glacial origin of the present Chihuahuan desert less than 11,500 years ago. In: Wauer RH, Riskind DH (eds) Transactions of the symposium on the biological resources of the Chihuahuan Desert Region—United States and Mexico. US Natl Park Service, pp 67–83

Werner FG, Enns WR, Noller ML (1966) The meloidae of Arizona. Ariz Agric Exp Stn Tech Bull **175**: 95

West NE, Skujiņš J (1978) Nitrogen in desert ecosystems. US/IBP Synthesis Ser 9. Dowden Hutchinson & Ross Inc, Stroudsburg Penn, p 307

Weygoldt P (1969) The biology of pseudoscorpions. Harvard Univ Press, Cambridge Mass, p 145

Weygoldt P (1971) Notes on the life history and reproductive biology of the giant whip scorpion, *Mastigoproctus giganteus* (Lucas) (Uropygi, Thelyphonidae) from Florida. J Zool London **164**: 137–147

Wheeler WM (1930) Demons of the dust. W Norton & Co, New York, p 378

White J, Strehl CE (1978) Xylem feeding by periodical cicada nymphs on tree roots. Ecol Entomol **3**: 323–327

White L (1969) Effects of wildfire on several desert grassland shrub species. J Range Manage **22**: 284–285

White MJD, Webb GC (1968) Origin and evolution of parthenogenetic reproduction in the grasshopper *Moraba virgo* (Eumasticidae: Morabinae). Aust J Zool **16:** 647–671

White MJD, Cheyney J, Key KHL (1963) A parthenogenetic species of grasshopper with complex structural heterozygosity (Orthoptera: Acridoidea). Aust J Zool **11:** 1–19

White TCR (1978) The importance of a relative shortage of food in animal ecology. Oecologia **33:** 71–86

Whitford WG (1975) Jornada Validation Site Report. US/IBP Desert Biome Res Memo **75–4:** 1–104

Whitford WG (1976) Temporal fluctuations in density and diversity of desert rodent populations. J Mammal **57:** 351–369

Whitford WG (1978a) Structure and seasonal activity of Chihuahua desert ant communities. Insectes Soc **25:** 79–88

Whitford WG (1978b) Foraging in seed-harvesting ants *Pogonomyrmex* spp. Ecology **59:** 185–189

Whitford WG, Creusere FM (1977) Seasonal and yearly fluctuations in Chihuahuan desert lizard communities. Herpetologica **33:** 54–65

Whitford WG, Ettershank G (1975) Factors affecting foraging in Chihuahuan desert harvester ants. Environ Entomol **4:** 689–696

Whitford WG, Kay CA, Schumacher AM (1975) Water loss in Chihuahuan Desert ants. Physiol Zool **48:** 390–397

Whitford WG, Johnson P, Ramirez J (1976) Comparative ecology of the harvester ants *Pogonomyrmex barbatus* (F. Smith) and *Pogonomyrmex rugosus* (Emery). Insectes Soc **23:** 117–132

Whitham TG (1977) Coevolution of foraging in *Bombus* and nectar dispensing in *Chilopsis:* A last dreg theory. Science **197:** 593–596

Whyte RO (1976) Bioclimatic and taxonomic consequences of tectonic movement and orogeny. Ann Arid Zone **15:** 247–269

Wickstrom CE, Castenholz RW (1973) Thermophylic ostracod: Aquatic metazoan with the highest known temperature tolerance. Science **181:** 1063–1064

Wiens JA (1976) Population responses to patchy environments. Annu Rev Ecol Syst **7:** 81–120

Wieser W (1978) Consumer strategies of terrestrial gastropods and isopods. Oecologia (Berlin) **36:** 191–201

Wieser W, Schweizer G (1972) Der Gehalt an Ammoniak und freien Aminosauren, sowie die Eigenschaften einer Glutaminase bei *Porcellio scaber* (Isopoda). J Comp Physiol **81:** 73–88

Williams SC (1966) Burrowing activities of the scorpion *Anuroctonus phaeodactylus* (Wood) (Scorpionida: Vejovidae). Proc Calif Acad Sci **34:** 419–428

Williams SC (1969) Birth activities of some North American scorpions. Proc Calif Acad Sci **37:** 1–24

Williams SC (1970) Coexistence of desert scorpions by differential habitat preference. Pan Pac Entomol **46:** 254–267

Williams SC (1980) Scorpions of Baja California, Mexico, and adjacent islands. Occas Pap Calif Acad Sci **35:** 1–127

Wilson EO (1971) The insect societies. Belknap Press, Cambridge, p 548

Wise DH (1981) A removal experiment with darkling beetles: Lack of evidence for interspecific competition. Ecology **62:** 727–738

Wood TG (1970) Micro-arthropods from soils of the arid zone in Southern Australia. Search 1: 75–76

Wood TG (1971) The distribution and abundance of *Folsomides deserticola* (Collembola: Isotomidae) and other micro-arthropods in arid and semi-arid soils in Southern Australia, with a note on nematode populations. Pedobiologia 11: 446–468

Wooten RC Jr, Crawford CS (1974) Respiratory metabolism of the desert millipede *Orthoporus ornatus* (Girard) (Diplopoda). Oecologia (Berlin) 17: 179–186

Wooten RC Jr, Crawford CS (1975) Food, ingestion rates, and assimilation in the desert millipede *Orthoporus ornatus* (Girard) (Diplopoda). Oecologia (Berlin) 20: 231–236

Wooten RC Jr, Crawford CS, Riddle WA (1975) Behavioural thermoregulation of *Orthoporus ornatus* (Diplopoda: Spirostreptidae) in three desert habitats. Zool J Linn Soc 57: 59–74

Wygodzinski P (1972) A review of the silverfish (Lepismatidae, Thysanura) of the United States and Caribbean area. Am Mus Nov No 2481:25

Yom-Tov Y (1970) The effect of predation on population densities of some desert snails. Ecology 51: 905–911

Yom-Tov Y (1971a) The biology of two desert snails *Trochoidea (Xerocrassa) seetzeni* and *Sphincterochila boissieri*. Isr J Zool 20: 231–248

Yom-Tov Y (1971b) Body temperature and light reflectance in two desert snails. Proc Malacol Soc London 39: 319–325

Yom-Tov Y (1972) Field experiments on the effect of population density and slope direction on the reproduction of the desert snail *Trichoidea (Xerocrassa) seetzeni*. J Anim Ecol 41: 17–22

Yom-Tov Y, Galun M (1971) Note on feeding habits of the desert snails *Sphincterochila boissieri* Charpentier and *Trochoidea (Xerocrassa) seetzeni* (Charpentier). Veliger 14: 86–89

York JC, Dick-Peddie WA (1969) Vegetation changes in southern New Mexico during the past hundred years. In: McGinnies WG, Goldman BJ (eds) Arid lands in perspective. Univ of Arizona Press, Tucson, pp 157–166

Young SR (1979a) Respiratory metabolism of *Alaskozetes antarcticus*. J Insect Physiol 25: 361–369

Young SR (1979b) Effect of temperature change on an antarctic mite. J Comp Physiol 131: 341–346

Youthed GJ, Moran VC (1969a) The solar-day activity rhythm of myrmeleontid larvae. J Insect Physiol 15: 1103–1116

Youthed GJ, Moran VC (1969b) Pit construction by myrmeleontid larvae. J Insect Physiol 15: 867–875

Zachariassen KE, Hammel HT (1976a) Freeze-tolerance in adult tenebrionid beetles. Norw J Zool 24: 349–352

Zachariassen KE, Hammel HT (1976b) Nucleating agents in the haemolymph of insects tolerant to freezing. Nature (London) 262: 285–287

Index

Note: Numerals in **boldface** type refer to pages on which information can be found in illustrations; numerals in *italic* type refer to pages on which information can be found in tables.

H. Remmert

Ecology

A Textbook

Translated from the German by
M. A. Biederman-Thorson

1980. 189 figures, 12 tables. VIII, 289 pages
ISBN 3-540-10059-8

Contents: Ecology: the Basic Concept. – Autecology. – Population Ecology. – Ecosystems. – Outlook. – References. – General Books on Subjects Related to Ecology. – Subject Index.

"The literature is not exactly poor in attempts to describe ecological relationships in textbook form. What makes Remmert's book stand out from the rest is the author's dynamic perspective, his simple, flowing style, and, in many instances, the interpretations themselves... Appropriately enough, the coevolution of the various members of an ecosystem is given special emphasis. This point usually receives inadequate attention in comparable textbooks. The author tackles generally accepted or postulated trends, discusses them, reformulates them, and, wherever possible, authenticates and explains them with individual analyses and case studies..."
translated from: *Helgoländer wissenschaftliche Meeresuntersuchungen*

Springer-Verlag
Berlin
Heidelberg
New York

E. B. Edney

Water Balance in Land Arthropods

1977. 109 figures, 36 tables. XII, 282 pages
(Zoophysiology and Ecology, Volume 9)
ISBN 3-540-08084-8

"...Dr. Edney has provided a wealth of organized information
on prior work and ideas for needed research, all of which
make the book a bargain. The volume should prove useful,
not only to those who work in arthropod water relations
(it is a must for them), but also to those of us interested
in invertebrate and general ecology, entomology, comparative physiology, and biophysics."

AWRA Water Resources Bull

"...The virtue of the work is that it reviews most comprehen-
sively, and it reports accurately in clear and simple style, the
extensive literature on cuticular permeability..."

Nature

H.-U. Thiele

Carboid Beetles in Their Environments

**A Study on Habitat Selection by Adaptations in Physiology
and Behaviour**

Translated from the German by J. Wieser
1977. 152 figures, 58 tables. XVII, 369 pages
(Zoophysiology and Ecology, Volume 10)
ISBN 3-540-08306-5

"...Because the book is comparative both in method and interpretation, it is a contribution to systematics as well as to
ecology ...a fine synthesis of current knowledge of homeo-
static aspects of ecological relationships of carabids, and it is
a fitting tribute to the man to whom it is dedicated:
Carl H. Lindroth, who was instrumental in formulating the
approaches and techniques that are commonly used in ecological research on these fine beetles. The material is well
organized and the text is easily readable, thanks to the
clarity of thought and expression of the author and to the
skill of an able translator."

Science

Springer-Verlag
Berlin
Heidelberg
New York